First published in 2014 by Voyageur Press, an imprint of
Quarto Publishing Group USA Inc., 400 First Avenue North, Suite 400,
Minneapolis, MN 55401 USA

Voyageur Press titles are also available at discounts in bulk quantity for
industrial or sales-promotional use. For details write to Special Sales
Manager at Quarto Publishing Group USA Inc., 400 First Avenue North,
Suite 400, Minneapolis, MN 55401 USA.

To find out more about our books, visit us online at www.VoyageurPress.com.

ISBN: 978-0-7603-4538-2

Library of Congress Cataloging-in-Publication Data

Beechum, Drew.
   Experimental homebrewing : mad science in the pursuit of great beer / by
Drew Beechum and Denny Conn.
      pages cm
    ISBN 978-0-7603-4538-2 (paperback)
 1. Beer. 2. Beer--Flavor and odor. 3. Brewing. I. Conn, Denny. II. Title.
 TP577.B363 2014
 641.2'3--dc23

                          2014014497

Printed in China
10 9 8 7 6 5 4 3

Acquisitions Editor: Thom O'Hearn
Project Manager: Elizabeth Noll
Design Manager: James Kegley
Cover Designer: Nick Zdon
Layout Designer: Karl Laun
Layout: Diana Boger

Photo credits:

Eric Gaddy: frontis and pages, 1, 12, 13, 17,
25, 27, 28, 29, 31, 32, 39, 42, 45, 51, 52, 57,
62, 64, 65, 72, 74, 78, 86, 87, 88, 89, 95, 96,
98, 100, 110, 115, 121, 128, 156, 169, 173,
175, 178, 179 (bottom), 180, 182, 185, 187,
189, 191, 207

Diane Griffin: Pages 20, 54, 61, 66, 67, 237
(right)

Charlie Essers: Page 237 (left)

Shutterstock.com: Front cover: (scientist)/
Everett Collection, pages 6 Creativa, 10
Sergey Peterman, 23 Sergey Peterman, 40 A.
L. Spangler, 48 isak55, 69 Carrie Dow, 90
Pavol Kmeto, 93 DigiCake, 104 MaxyM, 131
PSD photography, 137 grekoff, 143 Natali
Zakharova, 148 Kuttelvaserova Stuchelova,
152 Adam Gryko, 160 discpicture, 162 Mircea
Bezergheanu, 165 stockcreations, 171
sai0112, 176 Shaiith, 179 (top) Shaiith, 184
Anna Hoychuk, 209 isak55

iStockphoto.com: Pages 81 InCommunicado;
192, 196, 222, 234 JJRD

MAD SCIENCE IN THE PURSUIT OF GREAT BEER

EXPERIMENTAL HOMEBREWING

BY DREW BEECHUM AND DENNY CONN

Voyageur
Press

CONTENTS

Italics indicate a recipe

INTRODUCTION

CLOSE YOUR EYES FOR A MOMENT and picture the classic mad scientist's lab: bubbling beakers, electricity arcing through the air, thunder crashing on a dark and stormy night. A wild-eyed, white-frocked man is at work bringing his newest creation to life—he zips around the lab with the excitement of discovery.

Now open your eyes. Do you get this feeling when you brew? It's okay. We aren't sizing you up for a padded cell. We feel the same way. In fact, we're obsessive when it comes to unlocking the secrets of beer and stumbling upon the next great discovery. New flavors! New sensations! One day, they'll see our true genius! We'll show them!

Ahem . . . sorry about that. It's hard not to get carried away when you get us going about homebrewing. If you're just beginning to brew or haven't yet begun, oh are you in for a treat. Some of the stuff we talk about will seem bewildering, but don't worry. There are great beginners' books out there to help you master the basics (see page 236). In this book, we've tried to create a companion to those books, a book that will help you on your way from ordinary brewer to accomplished mad scientist.

For those of you who brew but go into a cold, sweaty panic when you hear the word *science*, don't worry. You won't find us breaking out anything more complicated than what was available to the average brewery of pre-Prohibition times. The idea is to try new stuff, decide if it makes beer that you like, and go from there. Really, we're all about getting a chance to play and learn in the brewhouse.

ABOUT OUR PROCESS

When we first sat down and debated what this book was going to look like, we spent a lot of time talking about our brew day processes. In other words, how should we look at Denny's techniques for brewing a world-famous bourbon vanilla porter or Drew's constant twists and turns on a familiar style, like saison?

As we sat and pondered our successful beers, we realized the weird and wacky side of things only worked due to some reasoned experimentation. We can talk endlessly about the strange ideas we have, but the success with a recipe always comes back to the trial and error. It comes back to the experiment.

Merriam-Webster defines an experiment as "an operation or procedure carried out under controlled conditions in order to discover an unknown effect or law, to test or establish a hypothesis, or to illustrate a known law." For scientists, an experiment is an attempt to answer a question. This is where the vaunted scientific method, oft-misunderstood cornerstone of the modern world, comes into play. The method consists of a series of steps that the experimenter must follow for it to be an official experiment:

Question: What is the question you're seeking to answer?

Hypothesis: What do you think the answer is? You must be able to prove your hypothesis true or false.

Prediction: How will you know that your hypothesis is right or wrong?

Test: This is your experiment.

Review and analysis: Look at your results and see whether your hypothesis is true or false based on your data.

Now let's apply the scientific method to brewing. Perhaps we want to find out if late-hop-only (hop-bursted) beers exhibit the same bitterness as traditionally hopped beers:

Question: Do late-hop-only beers exhibit the same bitterness as traditionally hopped beers?

Hypothesis: Beers with only late additions will have a noticeably less bitter flavor than beers bittered to the same calculated international bittering units (IBUs) with a start-of-boil bittering charge.

Prediction: The less bitter beer will be discernible in a taste test focused on evaluating bitterness.

Test: Brew two beers from one mash. One boil kettle will get a standard 60-minute addition with enough alpha acid units (AAUs) to create 30 IBUs. The second boil kettle will get a late-hop-only charge at 5 minutes with enough AAUs to create 30 IBUs.

Review and analysis: Does a blind triangle tasting confirm the hypothesis? How many judges got it correct? What were their comments?

This may seem pretty straightforward, but the details can sink any experiment. For instance, if we change the word *flavor* in the hypothesis to *level*, then it calls into question the prediction. What does level mean? A quantified IBU? Great! But that would require fancy equipment to measure. On the other hand, *flavor* allows us to use a taste test. And in the end, isn't that what you care about?

In the professional world, scientists spend countless hours designing and redesigning their experiments to make sure that what they're testing is what they think they're testing. It takes weeks of careful strategizing for scientists to make sure they've got the right plan in place. On the other hand, the experimentation that we'll be doing is going to be simple kitchen science—without the rigorous controls and designs that are required if you're releasing, say, a cancer treatment. It's somewhat scientific, but it's not Science with a capital *S*. It's about the beer.

WHAT WE'LL DISCOVER

While humans have been making beer for at least seven thousand years, science and brewing weren't properly introduced to each other until the late 1700s, after the invention of the thermometer and saccharometer. It wasn't until Louis Pasteur that people figured out why beer spoiled, or that yeast was responsible for wort becoming beer.

These days, a number of big breweries, such as Carlsberg and Anheuser-Busch, have large brewing laboratories focused both on quality control and on making discoveries: new strains of lager yeast, mashing profiles, maximizing efficiency, minimizing oxidation, extending shelf life, and so on. With scientists on staff at breweries, what's left for us amateurs noodling in our kitchens, garages, and basements? Turns out there's plenty that we need to do, for one not-so-obvious reason: our needs and concerns as homebrewers are not the same as those of the pros. We also have more freedom than the commercial brewers we know and love. Experimenting with even seven barrels of beer—a small amount by most brewery standards—will translate to a loss of $2,000 or more if the batch goes sideways. If you mess up a batch, you're probably out $40 at the most.

Do you get different hop aromas from hops steeped at different temperatures? Can you change your flavor and aroma characters by pitching different amounts of yeast? What are the impacts of different mash tuns? What's the best way to add vanilla or chocolate to a beer? These are all questions that we care about, but that won't necessarily be covered by the research funds of large brewers. These questions are exciting, so we'll do our best to answer some of them and provide jumping-off points to experiment with others.

KEEPING THE EXPERIMENT ALIVE

Experimental brewing can be about individual exploration, understanding how processes work, harnessing a new ingredient, or figuring out how to save some time, but it's also about helping other brewers by passing along what you've learned. One of the most fun and gratifying parts of being a homebrewer is the camaraderie with other homebrewers. Giving back and helping out by sharing the knowledge you gain through experimentation can be as rewarding as popping the cap or tapping the keg of your latest beer. Pay it forward, and your hobby will become even more fulfilling than that third pint of doppelbock.

To that end we've setup www.ExperimentalBrew.com, which will serve as the home for everyone's data. That's right, this is your chance to contribute—start performing your own experiments in Chapter 10 and join us. Share your results with the homebrewing community at large and be an IGOR (independent group of researchers)!

Cheers,
Drew Beechum and Denny Conn

CHAPTER 1

THE BASICS

BEFORE YOU START RUNNING AROUND

all wild-eyed, we need to discuss our basics. Everyone brews a little differently. In this chapter, we'll outline the all-important standards that apply to all the recipes in this book. Also, since we've brewed hundreds and hundreds of batches, we'll share our recommendations for all-grain, extract, and even brew-in-a-bag brew days. (Right down to the music playing while we brew.)

What follows is just a brewing précis, not a complete in-depth tutorial of homebrewing. (For that, we encourage you to check out *The Everything Homebrewing Book* by Drew Beechum or John Palmer's *How to Brew*.) Fortunately for humanity, beer happens. There's very little that you can do to completely mess up. Malted barley *wants* to become beer. As long as you get your beer started, it will get itself the rest of the way. Will it be the perfect little gem that you have in your head? Maybe not, but it will be beer!

GETTING STARTED

BASIC ASSUMPTIONS

In this book, we want to give you techniques that will help you decide for yourself what ingredients and processes work for you and how you want to brew. But for our recipes, we have to start with some basic assumptions. Here are the ones we're going to use as a baseline:

- Recipes are written for all grain brewing. If you want to brew with extract, we recommend substituting dry malt extract (DME) for the base malt (use an online calculator for adjustments based on what you're using and the recipe).
- Most recipes assume a 5.5-gallon batch at 75 percent efficiency. If your batch size or efficiency are different, be sure to adjust grain amounts accordingly.
- Unless the recipe states otherwise, it assumes you'll be mashing with a ratio of 1.25 quarts of water per pound of grain, batch sparging, and performing a full boil for 60 minutes.
- Even though we specify whole or pellet hops, feel free to use whichever you have that are good quality.
- Pellet hops are assumed to get 10 percent better utilization than whole hops. Therefore, use 10 percent fewer hops when substituting pellet hops for whole. If you're subbing whole for pellets, use 10 percent more.
- Recipes assume the IBU contributed from first wort hopping is counted as a 20-minute hop addition.
- For the best utilization of hops, wait until the hot break subsides, then add bittering hops and start your timing.
- All hop IBU calculations in this book are done using the Tinseth formula.
- If the alpha acid of the hops you have is different from what we listed, use the alpha acid units (AAU) method to substitute: multiply the alpha acid (AA) of the hops by the amount used. For example: 1 ounce of 5 percent AA hops gives you 5 AAU (1 x 5 = 5). If the hops you have are 4 percent, then you need 1.25 ounces (1.25 x 4 = 5). Use this substitution for any hops that will contribute to bitterness (up to the 15-minute addition). After 15-minutes, you can simply substitute ounce for ounce for similar flavor and aroma contributions.
- Yeast options are changing rapidly for today's brewer, but a lot of our recipes are built around familiar strains that we've used from Wyeast (WY) and White Labs (WLP) yeast companies. These will be specified with the company's yeast number and name, such as "WY1056 American Ale." Feel free to play around and substitute your favorite similar yeast in the recipes, keeping in mind that a different yeast can dramatically alter a recipe.
- Unless otherwise noted in the experiments, we insist on good yeast health. That means make a starter, rehydrate dry yeast, or use a yeast slurry from a previous batch. Treat your yeast right to get great beer!

- Many of the experiments in Chapter 10 call for a batch of our California Magnum Blonde (page 27). Feel free to substitute the base malt in the recipe or use a recipe of your choosing as long as the beer itself stays simple.
- Read through the experiments carefully before you begin. Some of the techniques and experiments in this book may require equipment not in your normal brew-day arsenal.

THE EXPERIMENTAL BREWING MINIMALIST GUIDE TO ALL-GRAIN BREWING

Some brewers like fancy gear and shiny stainless steel. But sometimes in all that gear lust, brewers overlook the fact that they're making beer . . . the equipment is just a tool. If you're the type who enjoys building equipment as much as using it, more power to you! We won't tell you you're wrong. However, it's important to realize that you can make great-tasting, award-winning beers without all that stuff. Both of us use minimal equipment compared to some home brewers. Don't let the lack of fancy gear keep you from brewing and experimenting.

Starting on page 16, we'll go into more detail about our individual brew days. However, all the work of brewing is encapsulated in the few steps that follow.

You Will Need

- Mash tun
- Pot for heating water (at least 6 gallons for a 5-gallon batch)
- Pot for boiling wort (can be the same as the one for heating water—at least 8 gallons for a 5-gallon batch)
- Thermometer
- Spoon
- Heat source (propane or natural gas burner or stove)
- Wort chiller
- Sanitizer
- Fermenter
- Assorted airlocks and tubing
- Your ingredients, including yeast

Instructions

1. Crush your barley and other grain if it's not already crushed. Crush it enough to crack the kernels without shredding the husk. Crush till you're scared!
2. For most beers, mash your grain in 1.25 quarts of 164°F water per pound for 60

minutes. (The temperature will drop to about 152°F once you mix the water with the grain.) 1.25 quarts per pound doesn't have to be an exact figure. Feel free to round up to an even number.

3. Recirculate some of the liquid through the grain bed until it runs clear, then run off the liquid into your kettle.

4. After you run off your mash, measure how much wort you have in your kettle. Subtract that from the amount you want to boil. (You'll usually need to boil around 6–7 gallons for a 5-gallon batch. It will depend on your own equipment, and you'll have to determine the exact amount through experience.) The answer you get is how much sparge water to use. Sparge by infusing your grain with that amount of 180°F water. Recirculate and run off like you did for the mash. Go ahead and heat up a little more than you think you'll use. Extra hot water always comes in handy on brew day.

5. Boil the combined runnings in your kettle for 60 minutes, adding hops according to the recipe. (Note that some recipes call for adding first wort hops, which would be added in step 3.)

6. Chill the wort and transfer it to a cleaned and sanitized fermenter. Pitch your yeast and aerate.

7. Ferment and condition for 2 to 3 weeks. For most yeast strains, keep the temperature in the mid-60'sF.

8. Rack to a keg or bottling bucket and package. (Keep your bottles at room temperature for a couple of weeks to let them carbonate.) Drink your beer!

THE EXPERIMENTAL BREWING SUPREMELY MINIMALIST GUIDE TO EXTRACT BREWING (FULL BOIL AND LATE ADDITION), AKA THE ONLY WAY TO GO

Traditional extract recipes have advised brewers to bring their water to a boil, turn off the heat, stir in the extract until dissolved, and bring to a full boil for 60 minutes. This advice is modeled on what all-grain brewers do. Just as we shouldn't expect professional brewing techniques to apply to homebrewing, we shouldn't expect that things all-grain brewers do make sense when using extract.

That's why we recommend that you add a small portion (⅓) of the extract when your water comes to a boil. This helps change the water's chemistry for hop utilization. Then when the boil is almost done (10 minutes left), add the remaining extract so that it will dissolve and become sanitized. Why? The extract you're adding has already been boiled and concentrated once. There's no sense in boiling it again, caramelizing the sugars, darkening your beer, increasing your wort gravity, and messing up your hop utilization just because that's how all-grain brewers do it.

And for all the all-grain folks out there, don't look down your nose at extract brewing. Know why your extract beers sucked? It's because you were a new brewer who didn't know what you were doing. For experimentation, extract batches can even be preferable when you want to save time or have increased control over the mashed fermentables.

You Will Need

- Pot for heating water and boiling (at least 8 gallons for a 5-gallon batch)
- Measuring cup or pitcher with volume marks
- Large bowl
- Colander or strainer

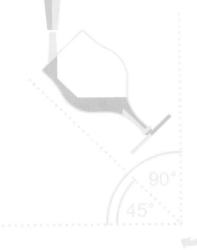

- Cheesecloth
- Thermometer
- Spoon
- Heat source (propane or natural gas burner or stove)
- Wort chiller or ice bath
- Sanitizer
- Fermenter
- Assorted airlocks and tubing
- Your ingredients, including yeast

Instructions

1. Heat 3 quarts of water to 170°F. Pour the water over your steeping grains in a large bowl, making sure the grains are fully submerged, and steep for 30 minutes.
2. Pour the grains and water through a colander lined with cheesecloth into your boil kettle.
3. Rinse the grains with another 3 quarts of 170°F water, letting the water pass through into your boil kettle.
4. Top off the kettle with filtered water until it is filled with 6 gallons. Bring the liquid to a boil.
5. Take your pot off the heat and add ⅓ of your extract. Stir to dissolve.
6. Bring the liquid back to a boil for 60 minutes, adding hops as you go. When you have 10 minutes left, add the remaining extract. Again, take the pot off the heat and stir to dissolve.
7. Chill the wort and transfer to a cleaned and sanitized fermenter. Pitch your yeast and aerate.
8. Ferment and condition for 2 to 3 weeks. For most yeast strains, keep the temperature in the mid-60°sF.
9. Rack to a keg or bottling bucket and package. (Keep your bottles at room temperature for a couple of weeks to let them carbonate.) Drink your beer!

SMALL BATCH BREWING (ONE GALLON B.I.A.B.)

You will undoubtedly find there are times you want to do an experiment to see what happens, and you don't want 5 gallons of beer gone wrong if you happen to make the wrong assumptions. Or maybe you want to compare two techniques with side-by-side mashes, but you don't have the space or equipment to conduct two mashes for 5 gallons each of finished beer.

While 5-gallon batches have long been the most popular size amongst homebrewers, there's been a bit of a sea change lately. It turns out that even the equipment for a 5-gallon batch can be a bit cumbersome if you're living in a shared apartment with someone who doesn't want the whole space dominated by brewing gear. (Why beer equipment isn't considered a valid decoration option, we'll never understand!) Thanks to suppliers like Brooklyn Brew Shop, 1-gallon brewing has grown in popularity and now serves as a gentle introduction to brewing for folks tight on space, time, and money. Of course, it's also great for experimentation!

Drew: Seriously, if you had told me a few years ago that a number of brewers were going to be homebrewing in 1-gallon batches, I would have thought you crazy. It takes close to the same amount of time as a 5-gallon batch, and who wouldn't want to make fifty bottles of beer instead of ten? But recent history has shown that for a lot of brewers, 1 gallon is a great way to start!

Working all grain at the 1-gallon batch size is similar in some ways to extract brewing: use a small pot, run the grains into the liquid, strain, rinse, and go. That means this is the perfect situation for using the brew in a bag (BIAB) method. While it can be cumbersome for larger batches, BIAB is perfect when you want to brew multiple 1-gallon batches for side-by-side experiments. Not only that, but since you probably started brewing by steeping grains in a bag, you already know how to do it!

You Will Need

- 3- to 5-gallon stockpot
- 1 nylon or fabric grain sack
- 1 thermometer
- 1 stainless-steel spoon
- Colander that fits across your pot
- 1-gallon glass jug
- Your ingredients, including yeast

Instructions

1. Transfer the grains you want to mash into the bag.
2. Place the bag into 2 gallons of 162°F hot water, open the bag, and mix the grains to ensure even wetting. Hold it at your mash temperature for the desired amount of time. (Normally that would be 60 minutes, but this a great way to experiment with the length of the mash. How easy is that? You can even have a beer while you wait!) Just as with extract, you can hold your temperature in a pot on your stove, in the oven, or in a small cooler.
3. After your mash time is up, remove the bag from the water, place it in a strainer across your pot or cooler, and allow it to drain. Once you've collected approximately 1.5 gallons of wort, you're ready to go.
4. Treat this like any other beer during the boil, but remember to make sure you've compensated with enough wort to deal with the boil-off. Your boil-off rate is not dependent on the amount of liquid, but on the size of the pot and the vigor of your stove.
5. Unless you have a pint-size chiller (and making one would be easy), you can cool your wort by immersing the pot in a sink full of cold water and ice. Stir the wort occasionally with a sanitized spoon and wait for the temperature to drop below 70°F. Transfer to your fermenter and pitch and ferment as normal.

Note: Just because you're dealing with a smaller batch doesn't mean that you can be footloose with your sanitation practices. Actually, working in a smaller volume with new or repurposed gear makes sanitation even more important. Any small growth will quickly overwhelm the flavor of your wee batch.

A BREW DAY WITH THE EXPERIMENTALISTS

Though we live 884 miles apart and didn't influence each other's brewing habits in the formative stages, we both settled on remarkably similar processes. A word of warning: neither of us is a huge automation gearhead. We'll talk about some of the stuff that we've been playing with starting on page 53, but for the most part, both of us are old-fashioned, hands-on brewers. We're just process and recipe geeks. Also, keep in mind that what follows is just the way that we usually brew. It's not the only way to brew. We'll even cover other techniques throughout the book—some that we use and some that our IGORs (independent group of reseachers) use.

PREPARATION

Good brew days start a few nights ahead with the creation of a yeast starter. You can make wort for starters as needed using a standard formula of 0.75 ounces of dry malt extract per 1 cup of water—about 2–3 quarts is a good size for most beers. Cool and empty the wort into a 1-gallon glass jug and set it onto a stir plate for 48–72 hours. The starters then go into the fridge for 1–3 days so that the yeast drops out and the spent wort can be easily poured off.

Drew: To save time, I make wort for starters months in advance and pressure-can it in Mason jars. I keep it on the shelf until I need it, then pop the lid off and proceed as usual. (As a bonus, the pressure cooker becomes a focal point for my nosy neighbors, who are convinced I'm making moonshine or cooking meth.) See page 79 for a how-to.

There are a few other things you may or may not want to do the night before you brew. Making sure your gear is accessible and ready to go is always a good idea. You can weigh out and mill your grains. You can filter or use Campden tablets to purify your water. You can fill your hot liquor tank as well. (See page 159 for more on filtering and treating your water.)

MASHING

On the morning of brew day, things start with the water. If you didn't filter it or otherwise treat it the night before, now is the time to do so. Fill up your hot liquor tank and heat the water to 12°F–14°F higher than your target mash temperature. At some point during this whole process, make sure to get comfortable. Turn on some music, light some incense for the brew gods, and so on.

Denny: For me, the mash tun is usually a blue 48-quart cooler with a stainless-steel braid from a toilet supply line inside it and an inexpensive nylon valve and a piece of tubing on the outside. You can learn how to build it on page 60.

I will sometimes use a 70- or 152-quart cooler mash tun for large, high-gravity batches. My soundtrack is anything but the Grateful Dead. (Surprising, I know!)

Drew: For me, the mash tun varies. If it's a standard-strength brew, it gets mashed in a 72-quart blue cooler. If it's a bigger beer or a bigger batch, I use a massive 150-quart cooler that doubles as a hot tub. I also use a braid, but it's a big and beefy thing made of military-grade shielded communication cables found in a scrap yard. Oh . . . and I usually play something bluesy or maybe some Jimmy Buffet.

SPARGING

After the grain sits in hot water for 60–90 minutes, it's time to draw off the first batch of wort. Start with the valve just barely cracked and run the wort into a pitcher, a pan, or whatever container works for you. When the wort looks fairly free of pieces of grain, direct the runoff to your kettle and gently pour what you've collected in your pitcher back over the top of the mash. When all the wort has been run off from your mash tun, pour the sparge water into the tun all at once, stir well, and then *vorlauf*. (That's running wort into a pitcher and pouring it back into the tun.) Again, once the wort is free of grain pieces, direct the runoff to your boil kettle. And yes, that's really all there is to it.

This method is called batch sparging, and it is a radical departure from more traditional methods used in brewing. It's simpler, and it's easy to use at homebrewer volumes. Look at traditional fly sparging. You fiddle with flow rates in and out of the mash tun. You aim to keep the rinse water just above the level of the grain bed until that magic moment when you've added the precise amount of water to perfectly reach your needed kettle volume. You need to keep track of the pH or specific gravity of your runnings to be sure you don't get an astringent beer. Any extra water added to the mash tun results in waste or overdiluted wort that must be boiled longer to reach your targets.

Drew: This point, I think, reflects a truth about homebrewing. Not everything that professional brewers do is appropriate or necessary at our volumes. Similarly, the resounding cry for many homebrewers turned pro is that it is nothing like homebrewing. In other words, put down your "but that's not how the pros do it!" argument. Realize that there are many valuable lessons that the homebrewer can take away from the pros, but dogmatic adherence to processes so far outscaled from our needs can be foolhardy.

Denny: Wow, did he say "outscaled?" Whatever . . . Drew is exactly right. Of course there is basic science that affects both homebrewing and commercial brewing, but the vast difference in scale means that the science is sometimes applied differently or may not be applicable at all in one case or the other. Revel in the beauty of being a homebrewer, free from the constraints that commercial brewers labor under. You are free, like a butterfly, like a wild cat, like a beautiful soul floating on the wind . . . okay, too much? Just remember that you don't have customers to please or a board of directors for whom you need to show a profit. Be a homebrewer! And always keep this mantra in mind: Make the best beer possible with the least effort possible while having the best time possible.

Drew: You're making fun of me for *outscaled* and then you become Denny Conn, Beat poet? Dig it, cat!

BOIL

Once the sparge is complete, it's time for the boil. The precise means of the boil are not important, but both of us run open-flame boilers outside to prevent kitchen mishaps. Remember your fire safety, folks, and keep a fire extinguisher on hand. If you run an electric brewery, then keep everything grounded and on GFCI circuits.

Both of us do a quick gravity check after the boil starts to determine if we need to adjust hopping rates or boil length to reduce volume or increase gravity. Run a solid boil for 30–90 minutes, depending on your needs. You want some turmoil in the boil, but gushing geysers of wort are a little much. Not only do you run a burn risk, but a boil's purpose, in part, is to cause the conglomeration of malt proteins into easily removed hot break strands. An overly aggressive boil will form these strands and then break them down!

Drew: I use another mondo braid in my boil kettle and thus avoid having to worry about hot break infiltrating the kettle. Instead, a quick, vigorous whirlpool collects the trub in the center of the kettle, and settling for 20 minutes allows plenty of last-minute "I forgot to clean my fermenter" panic and yields clear wort.

Denny: I use a piece of curved copper tubing for the pickup in the kettle and don't worry too much about getting hot break in the fermenter. I'm also whirlpool challenged and have never gotten a whirlpool to work. I just run the wort into the fermenter and get on with the cleaning part.

Drew: To chill, I use a two-step chilling rig that runs the wort through a counterflow chiller with tap water cooling before running into an immersion coil sitting in a bucket of ice water.

Denny: On the other hand, I use an immersion chiller with a pump for recirculation. I'm fortunate that the water in my well is a constant 50°F–55°F, so there's almost never a need for the ice water that Drew needs to use in the southern California climate. The point, regardless of the method, is to rapidly chill and hit a preferred fermentation temperature—say, 65°F. I like to chill to a few degrees below my intended fermentation temperature and let the heat created by fermentation bring it up to fermentation temperature.

Drew: Once the wort cools, it goes into 10-gallon stainless-steel kegs. Then I add about a minute of burbling oxygen from a little portable tank through a sintered stone.

Denny: I use buckets for fermentation and a wine degasser that attaches to a drill to whip air into my wort. I start the fermentation using a blow-off tube, just in case the fermentation gets more vigorous than I expected. After a week or so, I remove the tubing and replace it with an airlock.

From there it's all fermentation all the time. This is where the biggest lesson of homebrewing is learned: patience. The beer is gonna do what it's gonna do. All you can do is set up the conditions. But if you do that well, you will be rewarded with high-quality beer in a week or two. If the recipe you use contains a timetable for the beer, look at it as a guideline, not a rule. Learn to commune with your beer and follow its lead. Don't be afraid to open the fermenter and take a gravity reading, but don't go crazy doing that, either.

We hope you can see that there's more than one way to brew at home. Learn what works best for you and what makes your brew day the most enjoyable. How do you do that? Experiment!

DREW AND DENNY'S MOST IMPORTANT TIPS

DREW'S TIPS

- **Sanitation and cleaning:** There are times when as a brewer you may feel like a janitor. Get used to it. Keeping your fermentation gear clean and making it sanitary is so important that it cannot be overstressed. Bad sanitation will yield bad beer—maybe not all the time, but often enough to make you sad.
- **Fermentation control:** With everything clean and sanitary, you're free to run wild but, with a few exceptions, you'll need to worry about the temperatures you're running at. The difference

between beers fermented at proper temperature as opposed to fermented 5°F warmer is astonishing.

- **Yeast:** Last in the chain but not least is healthy and happy yeast. For this, a starter or a slug of yeast from a previous batch is absolutely necessary. Some of the world's best brewers preach the gospel of cell counts and perfect pitches, but that's a repeatability refinement, not a necessity. I follow a rule of thumb of 1 quart for every 5 gallons of beer below a gravity of 1.070.
- **A note on what's not in my list:** recipe design, mash control, water chemistry, and so on. All of those factors are important for making and remaking your target beer, but beer will still happen without them. And yeah, I'm not huge on repeatability measures; I want more interesting things!

DENNY'S TIPS

Drew made some good points (maybe he really can brew good beer!) that I'll briefly echo before I get to my own list:

- The guy who introduced me to brewing told me 90 percent of brewing is cleaning. I've never measured the exact percentage, but if you don't want to do the work of cleaning, your beer will tell people that you didn't do it!
- Fermentation temperature control is one of the biggest things you can do to make truly great beer. If you don't control the fermentation temp, all the delicious ingredients, all the effort you put into designing your equipment, and all the time you spend brewing will be wasted. That doesn't necessarily mean you need a dedicated fridge or freezer. I've used the Cheap 'n' Easy tub of water method (page 65) for hundreds of batches, and it works great.
- Pitching the proper amount of healthy yeast is overlooked too often, especially by new brewers. As the old saying goes: Brewers make wort, yeast makes beer. If you want great beer, you need happy yeast.

Now, here are a few other things:

- **Take good notes.** Whether things go great or not so great with the beer, it's important to know and recall what happened so you can do it again—or not! Even if you make recipes digitally, on brew day there's nothing like a good old spiral notebook and pencil. Take notes on how close you were to hitting temperatures and volumes, what the pH is, and how things look and smell as you brew. When you finally taste it, write down your impressions of the flavor, aroma, and body so that you'll have a record of how your experiments turned out.
- **Don't freak out.** Inevitably, something won't go as you planned. Deal with it! Think things through, remember the basics, and figure out how to move on from the screwup. We'll cover some techniques later to help you correct mistakes. Remember, malted barley wants to become beer.
- **Have fun when you brew.** It's not life or death; it's beer! Plan your equipment, your schedule, and your techniques so that you have the most enjoyable day you can possibly have when you brew. Whether you're brewing a small extract batch on the stove or a megabatch on a new stainless rig, make certain that you're gonna end up standing there on brew day thinking to yourself, "Damn, this has got to be the greatest hobby in the world!" And that's before you even crack open a beer from a previous batch!

CHAPTER 2

RECIPE DESIGN

WHILE WE MIGHT talk often about crazy ingredients or off-the-wall techniques, our beers are not actually crazy stacks of flavors and aromas. We've brewed enough to know that more should never be confused with better. In fact, we love nothing more than stripping away the needless artifice and creating recipes with only the bare essentials. Only once that's done can you really brew like a nutter and expect any chance of pulling it off. Join us in this chapter as we get simple before we get complex, as we learn the rules that we will soon break.

A LESSON IN UNSIMPLICITY WITH DREW

A perfect example of what not to do can be found in one of my early recipes. The year was 2003, and I had discovered a debate over an emerging style: The Double or Imperial IPA. What was this odd creature? Was it even a thing? Hoary old veterans insisted that this big, hoppy beer was nothing more than an American Barleywine going by a street name. Others disagreed, and it was an awesome debate—complete with gnashing of teeth, rending of clothes, brother versus brother, and so on. So I did what any reasonable person would do and grabbed my standard IPA recipe of the time and embiggened it. Because this was to be a special beer, I went even bigger and badder. "More stuff! More stuff is good!" I thought at the time. Without further ado, I present to you my Double Trouble Double IPA on page 25.

At this point, I had been brewing for four years and followed some well-tread rules. I used some wheat malt for head retention. I used no more than a pound of crystal malt per 5-gallon batch. I even followed my own rule of shooting for balanced IBU additions. (Each of the hop addition slots are calculated to add roughly the same IBUs in order to give an even hop character.

Yet the ingredients clearly showed my inexperience: six malts and seven varieties of hops in eight additions. It was heading for the flavor that we call "brown." Yes, brown is a color. But in the world of beer flavor, brown means an overly busy, overly complicated flavor. It is the gustatory version of smashing your hands onto a piano keyboard and hitting as many notes as possible. There may be a lot going on, but because it's not harmonious, it's not impressive. It washes over the palate and leaves you with a feeling of "meh."

When you look at the Double Trouble recipe, it seems a fairly typical homebrew. Maybe it suffers from extra exuberance, but what's a little enthusiasm amongst friends? The downside is this beer wasn't what we expect a DIPA to be. In my defense, not many DIPAs back then met today's mark. But this beer felt like white noise on the tongue, with so many different sensations buzzing that your brain couldn't concentrate on anything.

So how do you correct for this? How do you avoid the dangers of overcomplication? The answer is, of course, that less is more.

BREWING SMaSH-STYLE WITH DREW

Overcomplicating a recipe is a modern problem. Go back and look at some historical recipes. You'll see one or two sets of ingredients at the most for the mash. Hops are almost always a single variety, based on what the brewer could procure. In fact, some brewers' notes read "1 bushel of fine hops," because they knew what they were getting or didn't have a choice! Homebrewers were in a very similar situation until the 1990s. Reading back through old club archives, we can see that when a new malt was announced for sale, it was big news!

The folks over at www.homebrewtalk.com coined the term SMaSH to describe a return to first principles that had been floating around for years. It's an acronym that stands for "Single Malt and Single Hop." SMaSH offers a clarifying beacon of simplicity in the midst of chaos. You get your choice of any malt and any hop, but only a single variety! No cheating!

DOUBLE TROUBLE DIPA

Just because this poor beer is being held up as an example of what not to do, don't assume it sucks. It's just a tasty beer that lacks focus and is needlessly complicated, like its creator.

For 5.5 gallons at 1.087, 99.9 IBUs, 10.2 SRM, 9.7% ABV

GRAIN BILL

7.5 lbs	Domestic 2 Row Ale Malt
7.5 lbs	Maris Otter Pale Malt
12.0 oz	Crystal 55°L Malt
12.0 oz	Munich Malt
8.0 oz	Wheat Malt
4.0 oz	Biscuit Malt

MASH SCHEDULE

Rest	152°F	60 minutes

HOPS

0.5 oz	Cascade	Whole	8.1% AA	First wort hop
0.5 oz	Simcoe	Pellet	13.7% AA	First wort hop
0.75 oz	Centennial	Pellet	9.1% AA	60 minutes
0.25 oz	Chinook	Pellet	10.8% AA	45 minutes
1.0 oz	Crystal	Pellet	4.0% AA	30 minutes
0.5 oz	Cascade	Whole	8.1% AA	30 minutes
0.5 oz	Warrior	Pellet	15.6% AA	15 minutes
0.5 oz	Amarillo	Pellet	8.9% AA	5 minutes
1.5 oz	Cascade	Whole	8.1% AA	0 minutes
0.5 oz	Simcoe	Pellet	13.7% AA	0 minutes
1.5 oz	Cascade	Whole	8.1% AA	Dry hop

OTHER INGREDIENTS

½ tablet Whirlfloc	10 minutes

YEAST

WLP001 California Ale or WY1056 American Ale

ADDITIONAL INSTRUCTIONS

Ferment in primary for 2 weeks. Rack to a secondary or keg and add the dry hop. Age on the dry hop for 2 weeks at 50°F for a more subtle flavor.

VARIANT

You can extract more aroma and push the hop character by adding multiple doses of dry hop for shorter periods. For instance, double the dose of Cascade (3.0 ounces total) and add it in 1-ounce increments for 5 days each.

For the malt, you'll need to choose one that can self-convert. (You can calculate conversion safety by looking at our lessons about diastatic power and Litner ratings on page 44.) Some safe choices for SMaSH malts include:

- Pale Ale Malt
- Pilsner Malt
- Domestic 2 Row Malt
- Domestic 6 Row Malt
- Mild Malt
- Munich Malt
- Wheat Malt
- Oat Malt

For hops, your primary concern is not overloading the kettle with vegetation that makes your beer taste like lawn clippings. If you have a fondness for grass or dandelion wine, then never mind. Otherwise, you'll want to stick with moderately high alpha hops for any beer with a serious IBU level. A solid rule of thumb is to start reaching for hops with alpha acid levels above 7 percent when your SMaSH beer begins to exceed 25 IBUs. An exception to this rule (because a rule needs exceptions) is if you're making a beer with only traditional bittering additions, like a classic English Barleywine. See the Queen's Diamonds Barleywine, page 29, for an example of this.

What about sugars and other flavor additions? Do spices violate SMaSH? Fruit? Can you use multiple yeast strains? A SMaSH purist will take the Teutonic route and deny these items their place in a true example of the technique. To that, we simply stick out our tongues, since this technique is extraordinarily useful for gaining information about the flavors of a particular ingredient—whether it be the malt, the hop, the yeast, or any other addition. The single-minded focus means nothing gets in the way of your attempts to be sensorially savvy.

That said, the primary focus of American homebrewers using SMaSH has been discovering the flavors and aromas of hops. SMaSH, when viewed from this hoppy approach, has great exploratory value; however, the resulting beer is often lackluster. This is because most of the world's hoppy beer styles do require a little bit more than pale malt and a hop.

Are All SMaSH Beers Just Meh?

Denny: A well-known commercial brewer from a large, highly respected brewery once said something to the effect of, "SMaSH is a great way to learn about ingredients, but it makes a lousy recipe." I have yet to try a SMaSH beer that I thought was really a great (or just not boring) beer.

Drew: That's not true, Denny. I'm sure you've had a great SMaSH Pilsner! The truth is, there are a few classic styles that naturally fall into a SMaSH-like pattern: think barleywines, dunkels, tripels, and more.

Denny: When you're right, you're right! I have had some great German Pilsners that were one malt and one hop. For my own, I prefer a little more hop complexity, but it would be foolish of me to overlook some truly great beers that are made that way. I guess I should modify my statement to include most SMaSH beers, but certainly not all of them.

Drew: That's right, save your angry e-mails. Not all SMaSH beers are lackluster—just the vast, vast majority of them!

CALIFORNIA MAGNUM BLONDE

If you want the simplest, cleanest, and most interesting beer you can hand to a non–craft beer drinker (you know what we mean), this is it. Needless to say, it's an easy drinker.

For 5.5 gallons at 1.050, 45 IBUs, 3.4 SRM, 5.0% ABV, 90-minute boil

GRAIN BILL

10.25 lbs	Great Western California Select Pale Malt

MASH SCHEDULE

Rest	154°F	60 minutes

HOPS

0.75 oz	Magnum	Pellet	11.6% AA	60 minutes
0.75 oz	Magnum	Pellet	11.6% AA	20 minutes
0.75 oz	Magnum	Pellet	11.6% AA	0 minutes

OTHER INGREDIENTS

½ tablet Whirlfloc	10 minutes

YEAST

WLP001 California Ale, WY1056 American Ale, or Safale US-05

NOTES

Ferment in primary for 1–2 weeks.

VARIANT

Want a more sessionable beer? Drop the grain to 8 pounds and the hops to 0.6 ounces per addition, and you'll have a California Magnum Pale Mild.

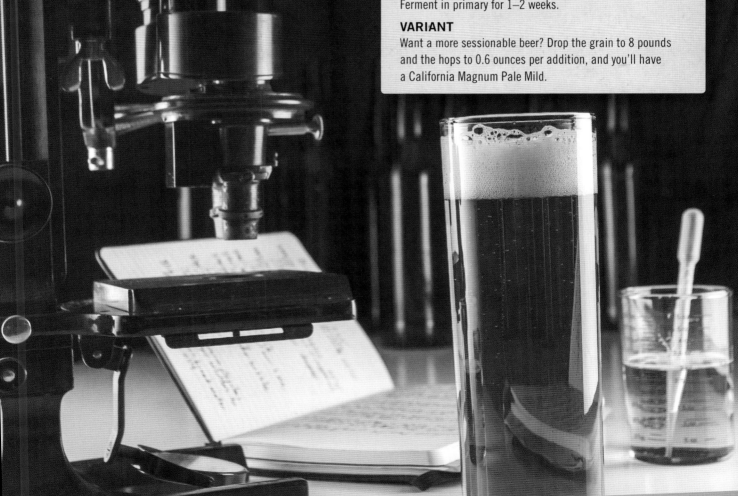

SMaSH THE PILS

No doubt about it, the classic Bohemian Pilsener is the official inspiration of most of the world's beer. It's amazing that it has only been around since the 1850s. This is a SMaSH pils, which hews closely to classic specs.

For 5.5 gallons at 1.050, 45 IBUs, 3.4 SRM,
5.0% ABV, 90-minute boil

GRAIN BILL

10.25 lbs   Weyermann or BestPilz Pilsner Malt

MASH SCHEDULE

- Rest at 124°F for 20 minutes.
- Decoction 1: Pull ⅓ of the mash as a thick pull (mostly grain with very little water) and heat to 154°F. Hold for 20 minutes, then bring it to a boil while continuously stirring.
- Return the boiled grain mixture to main mash. The combined temperature should now be 148°F–150°F.
- Decoction 2: Pull ⅓ of the mash as a thin pull (grain and liquid in equal parts) and bring it to boil stirring often.
- Return the mixture to the main mash. The combined temperature should be 165°F.

HOPS

2.25 oz	Saaz	Pellet	4.5% AA	60 minutes
1.00 oz	Saaz	Pellet	4.5% AA	0 minutes

OTHER INGREDIENTS

½ tablet Whirlfloc   10 minutes

YEAST

WY2278 Czech Pilsner Lager or WLP800 Pilsner Lager

NOTES

- Ferment in primary for 2 weeks at 48°F–50°F.
- Raise the beer over 2 days to 65°F and allow to rest there for 1 day.
- Drop the temperature to 50°F and slowly reduce the temperature, 1 degree per day until at 32°F.
- Rack the beer to secondary (if desired) and hold for an additional 2 weeks before kegging.

THE QUEEN'S DIAMONDS
BARLEYWINE

This recipe is inspired by the British habit of making special beers for big national occasions, such as the Queen's Diamond Jubilee.

For 5.5 gallons at 1.117, 62 IBUs, 8.2 SRM, 12.5% ABV, 120-minute boil

GRAIN BILL
25.0 lbs Maris Otter Malt

MASH SCHEDULE
Rest   150°F   60 minutes

HOPS
| 1.5 oz | Target | Pellet | 11.0% AA | 90 minutes |
| 0.5 oz | Target | Pellet | 11.0% AA | 5 minutes |

OTHER INGREDIENTS
½ tablet Whirlfloc   10 minutes

YEAST
WLP007 Dry English Ale

NOTES
Give this beer plenty of yeast. In fact, make another beer first (one under 1.060) and use the yeast cake from that in here. Put this away for storage after a long ferment (2–3 months, plus 2–3 months in package, minimum).

VARIANT
This would be a killer beer for a little bit of oak aging. Just grab some oak cubes (2 ounces) and age them in your favorite spirit (say, whiskey) for a few weeks or longer. Add to the beer during the secondary aging phase and rack off the cubes when your samples indicate that you have enough oak character.

BREWING ON THE ONES WITH DREW

The discipline of SMaSH appeals to the ascetic in all of us. But is there a way to expand the borders of the SMaSH world without losing the clarity granted by the rules? Remember that the appeal in SMaSH is the restriction. There's a natural push-pull that adds extra contemplation along the artificial barrier. Coincidentally, most commercial breweries operate under a similar rule of restriction.

As homebrewers we tend to not think twice about buying another couple of grains for a recipe. Our worst supply problem is often not getting all of the exact malts a recipe specifies. "Oh god, they don't have both Crystal 45°L and Crystal 55°L! Now my clone of the Pan Galactic Gargle Blaster will never taste right!" The professional, on the other hand, has a limited amount of storage space available in the brewery. There's not a lot of extra room to keep a little of this or that around. Instead, most breweries standardize their recipes around a few ingredients that they can buy and use in bulk. That means most of those great craft beers you enjoy are made from a very limited palette of ingredients.

In the same vein, you may fret over the precise addition of ¼ pound of malt to a 5-gallon batch. In a small craft brewery (7 barrels), that tiny addition equates to just under 11 pounds. Do you think a brewer operating with 50- and 55-pound sacks is going to carefully weigh out 11 pounds and store the rest? More than likely, you're going to see a brewer running a full or half sack of all but the most intense malts. (This observation comes in handy when you're thinking about cloning a beer!)

So, maybe a better path of learning is to follow a rule of forced scarcity. The idea of Brewing on the Ones is purposeful restriction. Instead of free rein in your recipe design, limit yourself to one choice per category. One base malt, one specialty malt, one adjunct, one hop, and maybe one surprise ingredient.

It's simple: don't run wild, and you'll be surprised at how happy you are with the results. This may stem from a psychological phenomenon called the paradox of choice. The term comes from Barry Schwartz's 2004 book *The Paradox of Choice*, in which he argues and presents data that show consumers derive more satisfaction when their choices are limited. An oft-cited example: diners presented with a choice of steak or lobster were less satisfied with their steak dinners than diners just given a steak dinner.

Brewing on the Ones forces you into a reduced choice mode (aka just the steak dinner). The artificial scarcity makes you slow down and carefully consider each ingredient. It also makes you stop and think about your techniques. For instance, if you want a deeper malt flavor in a Scottish ale, you could take the first gallon of runnings and reduce it to a near syrup in order to achieve a more complex malt flavor from simple ingredients.

Before we move on, it should be clear that the Brewing on the Ones philosophy is not the only way you should brew, and we're certainly not saying that if you don't brew this way, then you're a horrible person and the universe should swallow you whole. It's about remembering that there is complexity in the simple and that your recipes are generally going to be better when they are simpler. Consider easing off the gas pedal even if you can mash it to the floor. Restraint can get you around a corner faster than all-out speed.

SINGULAR QUAD

The much-vaunted Westvleteren 12 has been an object of desire for a good many brewers and beer lovers. Rumors abound that the recipe for the beer is blindingly simple. The fermentables are supposedly just Pilsner malt and Belgian candi syrup, a byproduct of the sugar making process that wasn't available to US brewers until recently. Now several folks import the stuff from Belgium, and some are even making it here in the States, so take this as an opportunity to explore their different properties.

For 5.5 gallons at 1.096, 32 IBUs, 3.8 SRM, 9.3% ABV, 90-minute boil

GRAIN BILL
19 lbs   Dingeman Pilsner Malt
1.5 lbs   Belgian candi syrup (D2 or D-180)

MASH SCHEDULE
Rest   151°F   60 minutes

HOPS
0.75 oz   Magnum   Pellet   11.6% AA   60 minutes

YEAST
WLP530 Abbey Ale or WY3787 Trappist High Gravity

NOTES
Add the syrup late to the boil, with 10–15 minutes remaining. It will allow for better hop utilization. Alternately you can add the syrup to the ferment as opposed to the boil. You'll need a large amount of yeast, so consider making a starter beer. (In fact, try the variant below.) And for the love of all that's holy, pitch and start this beer in the low 60°sF and let it rise to fermentation in the higher 60°sF. A beer with this much oomph is asking for fusel alcohols and headaches if you let it ferment hotter.

VARIANT
The Singular Half: Cut all the ingredients in half and ferment away for a not-quite Single or Double. The yeast can be used to ferment the Quad.

BOSWELL'S OAT BEER

Samuel Johnson defined oats as "a grain, which in England is generally given to horses, but in Scotland appears to support the people." His biographer, James Boswell, was a Scotsman—and he supposedly took great umbrage at this in his biography of Johnson. In memory of the irascible Scot, how about an oat wine? Note: this is still a Ones beer, since it has but one base, one specialty malt, and one sugar.

For 5.5 gallons at 1.084, 32 IBUs, 3.8 SRM, 9.3% ABV, 90-minute boil

GRAIN BILL
14.0 lbs Golden Promise Malt
2.5 lbs   Thomas Fawcett Oat Malt
1.0 lbs   Dark British Brown Sugar

MASH SCHEDULE
Rest   152°F   60 minutes

HOPS
1.5 oz   Target   Pellet   11% AA   60 minutes

YEAST
WY1728 Scottish Ale or WLP028 Edinburgh Ale

NOTES
- With all the extra sugar, the ferment cool rule (low 60s) definitely applies! Otherwise, it's as simple as ferment, age for a month or two, and serve.
- Expect it to be a little cloudy from the addition of the oat malt.

VARIANT
Substitute a Belgian yeast strain for the Scottish strain above, and you'll end up with a beer close to a lost Dutch style of beer called Haarlem Bokbier. (The actual Haarlem beer uses more oats. If you want that experience, drop the Golden Promise to 8.5 pounds and up the oat malt to 8.5 pounds while getting rid of the sugar.)

DOUBLE TROUBLE SIMPLIFIED

For 5.5 gallons at 1.087, 99.9 IBUs, 10.2 SRM, 9.7% ABV

GRAIN BILL
8.0 lbs   Domestic 2 Row Pale Malt
8.0 lbs   Maris Otter Pale Malt
2.0 lbs   Munich Malt

MASH SCHEDULE
Rest   152°F   60 minutes

HOPS

1.5 oz	Warrior	Pellet	15.6% AA	60 minutes
0.5 oz	Chinook	Pellet	13% AA	60 minutes
0.5 oz	Centennial	Pellet	10% AA	0 minutes
0.5 oz	Simcoe	Pellet	13% AA	0 minutes
0.5 oz	Centennial	Pellet	10% AA	Dry hop
0.5 oz	Simcoe	Pellet	13% AA	Dry hop

OTHER INGREDIENTS
½ tablet Whirlfloc   10 minutes

YEAST
WLP001 California Ale or WY1056 American Ale

NOTES
- Ferment in the primary for 2 weeks.
- Rack to a secondary or keg and add the dry hop.
- Age on the dry hop for 2 weeks at 50°F for a more subtle flavor.

TYING IT ALL TOGETHER WITH DREW

Let's revisit the Double Trouble recipe after looking at it through the lens of the Ones philosophy. You'll notice pretty quickly that the recipe breaks from the original in some distinct ways, and there's now a care behind the ingredient choices that wasn't in the original recipe.

The combination of base malts boosts the body of the relatively thin 2-Row with the more luscious Maris Otter. While I wish I could claim it was my invention, it turns out that some professional brewers do this exact same thing to replicate the fabled White Malt of the original IPA days. (Thanks to Mitch Steele of Stone Brewing and author of *IPA*.) The Munich malt is there to provide some malt complexity without the sweetness of crystal malts.

On the hop side of the kettle, we're looking at four varieties of hops. The Warrior provides most of the bitterness, but since it's a low-cohumulone hop, it needs a little something to kick the drinker in the teeth. That's the role of Chinook, which in moderation provides a pleasant raspy bitterness. Centennial and Simcoe both offer the big, bright citrus flavors that I was trying to coax out of multiple hop varieties in the original example.

In the end, the beer turned into a crisp, clean, and bitter citrus bomb of a Double IPA. Even better, it doesn't end up muddled and confused on the palate. All it took was a little focus and a willingness to stop grabbing every little thing off the shelf.

THE RECIPE ROAD MAP WITH DENNY

There are two ways Drew and I approach recipe formulation. One way is what we call the Hey, Hold My Beer and Watch This method. In this method, you combine ingredients without a lot of thought or concern about hitting a predetermined outcome. The object of this method is to learn about the interactions of the various ingredients and techniques you use. You may learn that you've understood the interactions perfectly and made great guesses. Or you may learn that everything you thought you knew is wrong and you now have 5 gallons of toilet cleaner. Every homebrewer has had this experience. It's still valuable in its own disgusting way!

The other way to approach recipe formulation is what we call the Road Map approach. Imagine that you're about to take a car trip to somewhere you've never been. Your bags are packed. Your car is gassed up and ready to go. You hop in and start driving. Pretty soon, you realize you have no idea where you are or how to get to where you're going. You need a road map. A beer recipe is like a road map for brewing, and it greatly increases the chances that your finished beer will be what you intend. Even better, the thought process behind designing a recipe can help ensure that the combination of ingredients you use produces an outstanding beer. But just as there are multiple routes to a destination, and some are better than others, there are multiple routes to producing a beer. With some thought and planning, you'll find the best way to get to your beer destination.

TASTE IMAGINATION

Before you can figure out how to get to your destination, you have to know where you're going. That's where taste imagination comes in. By mentally tasting the beer you want to drink, you create a target for your recipe.

Start by imagining what you want the finished beer to taste like. Is it balanced toward hops or malt? Is it light-colored or dark? Are the flavors subtle or extreme, straightforward or complex and layered? Have you had a commercial or homebrewed beer that has some of the characteristics of the beer you want to create? You want to sit back, close your eyes, and taste the beer in your mind.

As an example, here's the kind of thought process I went through when I was formulating the recipe for my Bourbon Vanilla Imperial Porter: It's almost time to make a Christmas beer. I know I want it to be something out of the ordinary. Christmas beers are usually on the big side, both in gravity and flavor. Since it's winter, I probably want to go with a darker style—something along the lines of a robust porter. Maybe even bigger than a robust porter: an imperial porter. A big, rich porter with some chocolate notes to it. I'll try some Munich and crystal malts to add some maltiness and sweetness, which will enhance and balance the chocolate flavors from the malt. How about barrel aging it? Nope, by the time I brew some test batches and settle on a recipe, I won't have time for that. In addition, I'm not a big fan of heavily oaked beers. What kind of properties do I like from barrel aging? Well, oak can impart some nice vanilla flavors, so maybe I'll add vanilla. And I'd probably enjoy some of the bourbon flavors from the barrel, too, so how about adding some bourbon to it? But I want a balance of flavors, so I want to be sure the vanilla and bourbon integrate into the beer, not overpower it.

At this point, it's helpful to get outside your head when you're thinking about the characteristics of the beer you're developing. Taste commercial examples of beers that have ingredients or attributes of the beer you want to brew. Ask the knowledgeable local brewers in your homebrew club questions about similar beers. Another great resource is online beer discussion groups. (See page 236.) Post a recipe draft and discuss your ideas with other brewers around the world!

Books can also help a lot in formulating your own recipe. By comparing recipes in several books, you can look for ingredients they have in common or ingredients that don't seem to make sense. Analyze the reason for using each ingredient. Compare recipes between books.

Also, the Beer Judge Certification Program (BJCP) has categorized beers into various styles. Chances are, what you have in mind falls into or near a BJCP category. Look through the BJCP Style Guidelines and get a good idea of the flavor, aroma, and body characteristics of a style, as well as the ingredients typically used to brew that style. (For more on styles and the BJCP, see page 194.) Compare those notes to what your taste imagination is telling you.

JUST BREW IT

It shouldn't come as a surprise that your taste imagination can only get you started. The best recipes are ones that have been brewed many times, with variable after variable adjusted until the recipe is fine-tuned to perfection.

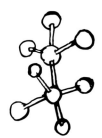

For the beer just described, I consulted some recipe books and looked at various approaches to robust porter before I wrote down the basic recipe and started the process of refining it. It took about four test batches of the base porter before I'd come up with something I thought would work in combination with the other flavors I wanted to use. One of the most important things to work out was the hopping. With the rich chocolate flavors I wanted to have, I needed to make sure the hops would keep things in balance but not be overpowering. I also kept in mind that adding the vanilla would increase the perception of sweetness in the beer. I had decided early in the recipe design that using Magnum and East Kent Goldings hops would be a good place to start. Magnum has a smooth bittering quality that wouldn't jump out from the other flavors, and Goldings are often described as having a candylike flavor to them. I felt as if those qualities would really support the other flavors in the beer. Knowing that I wanted the beer to be in the mid-80s for a starting gravity, I started with an assumption that the bitterness should be around 50 IBU.

When I tasted the first test batch brewed to that spec, it was a great porter, but I could tell that it was too bitter for what I had in mind. I added a couple more pounds of Munich malt and cut the IBUs back to the low 20s. That version was too sweet, even before the vanilla was added. I dropped a pound of Munich and upped the IBUs to the low 30s. That batch was just what I was looking for. Then I brewed exactly the same recipe again to be sure that it was repeatable before dialing in the right amounts of vanilla and bourbon.

A lot of brewers hate repeatedly brewing similar recipes and continually want to move on and brew something new, and there's nothing wrong with that. However, unless you happen to get lucky enough to come up with your perfect recipe on the first try, rebrewing while making only one change at a time is the surest way to home in on the best version of your recipe. In fact, I'm not ashamed to admit that some of my recipes went through more than a dozen test batches before I had the AHA! moment that told me I'd achieved what I had in mind. Even when my first draft is close to perfect, I consider what would happen by adding more or less of an ingredient, swapping one ingredient for another, or changing my mash temperature.

Before we move on, I should mention that it's always a good idea to keep some of the previous batch, so you can compare ingredient or process changes. Admittedly, the older batch will have undergone some changes that will somewhat alter the flavor, but if you took good notes when you first tasted that batch, you should be able to account for any flavor differences. Take careful notes when you taste the test batches, so you'll have a good idea of where you want to go with the next batch. Make sure to evaluate the samples objectively, so your preconceptions don't influence your perceptions. (See page 194 for more on evaluating your beer.)

The result of all this thinking, imagining, and repeated brewing is a beer you can sit down with and say, "I truly made this and I made it good!" Not just the production of the beer, but the concept from which it sprang. You can drink a beer while you're sitting on your deck and know that you conceived it for the express purpose of drinking it there. When someone compliments you on the beer, you can have the satisfaction of knowing that you're represented in every sip of the beer you so carefully crafted!

CHRIS COLBY ON RECIPE DESIGN

Chris Colby is the former editor of *Brew Your Own* magazine. He currently runs the Beer and Wine Journal website (beerandwinejournal.com), along with James Spencer of Basic Brewing Radio.

We asked Chris to describe the process he goes through in designing a recipe. Here are some excerpts from his answer.

TWEAK AN ESTABLISHED RECIPE

For many brewers, their first experience formulating a recipe is making an adjustment to an existing recipe. A brewer may have made a pale ale, for instance, and later repeated the recipe but added more hops. Tweaking an existing recipe is a good way to start down the road to writing your own recipes because a little more or less of any basic beer ingredient isn't going to ruin a beer. Making a beer a little stronger or weaker, adding more or less hops, or adding more or less of one of the specialty malts will make the beer different. However, in the vast majority of cases, you can't really screw up. A beer recipe meant to produce a certain style of beer may no longer do so after tweaking, but the odds that the ingredients clash in a way that makes the beer unpleasant is slim—especially if you're basing the tweak on a personal preference and adjusting the amount of ingredients already present in the recipe.

The strengths of this method are that you start with an existing recipe (hopefully reflecting the knowledge of an experienced brewer), and you put your own stamp on it. In addition, unless you add some new ingredient that's terribly inappropriate, the success rate using this method is high.

COMPILING AN AVERAGE OR CONSENSUS RECIPE

Sometimes you want to try something that is new to you and need a recipe. In this instance, one approach would be to assemble an average or consensus recipe. The idea would be to examine several recipes for the type of beer you want to brew and make a recipe based on the collective ideas in those recipes.

This method also allows you to make use of the knowledge of other brewers, but there are a couple potential drawbacks. If you find three or four recipes that are very similar, you may believe that is the correct way to brew that particular beer. However, it's also possible that those recipes are simply variants of one another, not independently formulated.

A BEERY VISION

What if you have an idea for a beer that isn't an established beer style or a copy of another beer? What if you have a vision of a beer in your mind and want to assemble a recipe for it? In this case, you'll need to have brewed long enough to be familiar with many of the malts, hops, and yeast strains available to homebrewers. You'll also need to know things like what happens when you mash or ferment beers at the high or low end of the normal ranges. Essentially, you'll have to have some grasp of what different ingredients add and how different processes affect beer flavor.

In this case, I would start by asking what the basic idea of the beer is, and build around that. If you are envisioning a malty beer, start with the grain bill and focus on what malts are going to be front and center. Is it going to be a pale or amber beer with some Munich malt or aromatic malt flavor? Is it going to be a dark beer with some caramel notes?

If you're thinking of a hoppy beer, start with the hops. Do you want the beer to be bitter, with relatively low amounts of flavor and aroma? Do you want the bitterness restrained, with tons of hop flavor and aroma? Or do you want it to be both highly bitter and highly aromatic? And what character do you want the hops to have?

If you're thinking of a beer with strong character from the yeast—such as a Belgian-inspired beer or something with an aroma similar to hefeweizen—you might even start by selecting a yeast strain and the fermentation conditions first.

Once you've figured out the centerpiece of your beer, add the remaining ingredients (and procedures), with an eye toward how they work with the main element of the beer. When it comes to malts, think not only of the flavor they add, but their effect on body. When it comes to hops, consider that the IBUs don't tell the whole story. Hop character is influenced by the malt character, body, and carbonation of the beer. Consider every element of the beer, including the level and method of carbonation.

In order to approach beer recipe formulation in this manner, you'll need some experience brewing and tasting beer. However, keep in mind that it's hard to make a beer that is terrible unless you're trying to. I've had plenty of beers turn out differently than I thought they would, but—with a few exceptions—they were mostly decent. Sometimes they were even close to my imagined idea and good.

One trap when formulating recipes is the idea that adding a bit of this and a bit of that adds complexity. (You see the same thing when guys make up spice rubs for their grilling and use every spice in the rack.) I would argue that each ingredient should have a purpose in the beer that you clearly understand, or remove it from the recipe. One brewer's complex is another's muddled. For every ingredient you add, you're taking some focus away from the other main ingredients. Some very outstanding beers are made from very simple recipes; fresh ingredients and a skilled brewer can make good beer out of pale malt and some hops. Of course, some beers do have a lot of different ingredients, and this doesn't necessarily make them bad. I think that some big, dark beers can benefit from a variety of specialty malts. However, don't fall into the trap of thinking more is always better.

ZEN AND THE ART OF HOMEBREW RECIPE FORMULATION

When it comes to Zen, here's as close as I can get. When you formulate the recipe, try to think of the ingredients as you actually experience them. Don't be swayed by the names or descriptions of the ingredients; think about how they actually taste or smell to you. For example, you'll sometimes hear that biscuit malt adds a biscuitlike flavor to your beer. However, biscuit malt doesn't taste like biscuits; it tastes like biscuit malt. There are similarities—enough to name and describe the malt that way—but there are also differences. The same thing goes for hop descriptions. Some folks say Amarillo hops smell like grapefruit, but that's really saying that they smell like hops, with sufficient grapefruitlike notes that we'll describe them that way so you know how they differ from other varieties of hops. (In a triangle test among a grapefruit, Amarillo hops, and any other variety of hops, you'd pick the grapefuit as the outlier.) So when you think of caramel malt, chocolate malt, coffee malt, biscuit malt, and so on, think of the malts shorn of their names and descriptors. Imagine the flavors and aromas in your mind, and base your recipe decisions on that . . . uh, grasshopper. Or something. I must now go investigate this ancient question: what is the sound of one hand lifting a beer to my lips?

Trompe le Schnoz

In the art world, trompe l'oeil is a style of painting intended to deceive your eyes. It creates oceanscapes on walls and angels holding the dome of heaven on flat ceilings. Or maybe you've seen pieces of sidewalk art where the ground looks cracked open, revealing a fantastic world below.

Obviously, we're not playing much with visuals in beer making, but we do have the whole palette of taste and aroma to play with. Instead of deceiving the eyes, we can deceive the nose and mouth. So how do we give a taste and aroma impression of something without using the thing? How do you make an apple pie beer that smells and tastes like apple pie, but without actually using apple pie?

We can achieve this goal by remembering our organoleptic chemistry. Hundreds of compounds create the taste sensations we know and love, but they're repeated in different ingredients. We know that the essential oil eugenol, aka clove oil, is found over and over again in different spices. If you wanted to make apple pie beer without actually adding apples, you could plan for a ferment with a fruity yeast. Those esters we describe as fruity are the same esters that the fruit imparts!

Why fool your nose? Because it's fun. It is akin to modern chefs playing with deconstruction to deliver familiar experiences in unexpected ways. The novel presentation shocks the system out of complacency. However, in the case of many beers, deconstruction techniques can help us deliver truer versions of an experience than if we used the actual ingredient. While we've known a few people to throw apple pies in a brew, the results weren't resoundingly apple pie—like. Instead, a fruity yeast for the apple, a toasted malt for the crust, and cinnamon for the zing does a better job.

We call this attempt to fool the nose and mouth trompe le schnoz—*a term coined by* Beer Advocate *forumite Chris Nelson. It sounds so much better than the more correct* trompe l'organoleptic system.

WHITE STOUT

Here's a great example of trompe le schnoz brewing that plays not only with the sense of smell but also with historical word meanings. Today, the word *stout* conjures images of Guinness or similar tall pints of frothy, inky black goodness. But in times past, the word really just meant a beer was strong. In other words, it's similar to *Imperial* today. So, historically speaking, a white stout is no big deal. But by today's standards, you want to replicate the flavors of the roasted malts used to inkify a modern stout. The two major tones you derive from those grains are roasted coffee and dark bitter chocolate. Why not just use those then?

You can make tinctures of both of those substances (page 77 and page 79), but here it's important to realize we're taking a different tack. We want some of those harder coffee flavors to hit the palate. For the chocolate, it's cocoa powder in the boil or a tincture made with no vanilla, and let it ride a little longer (1–2 days) to extract more tannic bitterness.

For 5.5 Gallons at 1.086, 30 IBUs, 7.3 SRM, 8.1% ABV

GRAIN BILL

14 lbs	Maris Otter Malt
1 lbs	Flaked Oats
1 lbs	Flaked Barley
8.0 oz	Crystal 40°L Malt

MASH SCHEDULE

Rest	154°F	60 minutes

HOPS

1.0 oz	Magnum	Pellet	14% AA	60 minutes
1.0 oz	Crystal	Pellet	3.5% AA	10 minutes

YEAST

WY 1318 London Ale III

OTHER INGREDIENTS

3.0 oz	Defatted cacao extract (see page 179)
1 pint	Cold brewed coffee extract (1 cup ground coffee soaked overnight in 3 cups water)
1 lbs	Lactose

ADDITIONAL INSTRUCTIONS

Add the defatted cacao extract, coffee, and lactose at packaging.

3

SPLITTING BATCHES

ONE OF THE MOST COMMON PROBLEMS

for veteran homebrewers is the insatiable demand that exists for our beer. Between festivals, parties, club functions, and work functions, it feels like we're always on call for producing lots of different beers in a hurry. Of course, you also have to make beer for yourself, and what fun is that without experimenting from time to time? So to make the most of your limited time and resources, we must find creative ways to split batches! We like to think of it as The Brewing Tree.

In physics, there's a notion called the multiverse, which states that the universe we live in is but one of many universes. A possible driving force splitting the universe is the many different choices that we make. Each roll of the die, each different decision that we make creates a multitude of universes. While we may not be creating anything as profound as a new universe, we can create different beers by following different branches of exploration. For the most part, you'll probably only follow one or two branches that diverge on any one batch. But for the truly ambitious, you can try as many as you'd like!

MASHING

Splitting at the mashing stage gives you the most flexibility, but it also requires more equipment. You'll need to have at least two boil kettles and maybe additional other vessels in order to deal with the extra grain and fluids you're generating.

In a pinch, if you only have the one boil rig, hold your additional wort to the side in food-grade containers (buckets, pots, and so on). Then bring each batch of wort to a boil as fast as you're able, to prevent the naturally occurring *Lactobacillus* from taking hold!

PARTI-GYLE

This is the granddaddy of all the split mash techniques. Until the turn of the twentieth century, this was how beer was brewed. One mash created multiple beers. Before the inventions of the thermometer and the hydrometer, brewers knew that they could draw a certain volume of wort to make a strong beer, another volume to produce a slightly weaker beer, and then finally one last draw to get a table-strength beer. Many breweries also mixed these batches to create their different offerings. For example, to this day Fuller's line of beers—Chiswick Bitter, London Pride, and Fuller's ESB—involves mixing between the three "coppers" that they pull in order to create the final blend. (If you batch-sparge and calculate your water additions correctly, you're already running multiple gyles; you're just blending them together!)

Here's the primary rule you need to keep in mind. For an evenly split batch (for example, 5.5 gallons of beer one and 5.5 gallons of beer two), you can reliably predict that two-thirds of the total sugar will go to the first part and the remaining third will go to the second half. In other words, if you mash 20 pounds of pale malt, that should yield at 70 percent efficiency about 504 gravity points from the mash. Collected entirely in an 11-gallon batch, that would be a gravity of 1.046 (504/11). But if you collect the first 6 gallons for your 5.5 gallons of beer, it should contain 338 gravity points for a starting gravity of 1.061 (338/5.5). The second 5.5 gallons will contain 166 points or a gravity of 1.030. In other words:

$$\text{Gravity Points}_{\text{Total}} = \text{Pounds}_{\text{Malt}} \times 36 \times \text{Efficiency}$$

$$\text{Gravity Points}_{\text{Kettle One}} = \frac{\text{Gravity Points}_{\text{Total}} \times 0.67}{(\text{Volume}_{\text{Total}} \times 0.5)}$$

$$\text{Gravity Points}_{\text{Kettle Two}} = \frac{\text{Gravity Points}_{\text{Total}} \times 0.33}{(\text{Volume}_{\text{Total}} \times 0.5)}$$

Example for an 11-gallon batch with 20 pounds of malt on a 70 percent efficiency system:

$$\text{Gravity Points}_{\text{Total}} = 20 \times 36 \times 0.7 = 504 \text{ points}$$

$$\text{Gravity Points}_{\text{Kettle One}} = \frac{504 \times 0.67}{(11 \times 0.5)} = \frac{338}{5.5} = 61 \text{ (aka 1.061)}$$

$$\text{Gravity Points}_{\text{Kettle One}} = \frac{504 \times 0.33}{(11 \times 0.5)} = \frac{166}{5.5} = 30 \text{ (aka 1.030)}$$

The math may seem confusing at first, but it works. If your gravity falls a little short, add some sugar or extract. It's all good! For those of you who are about to object: yes, the math is simplified for the rule of thumb. To be more accurate, your Total Gravity Points should be calculated by factoring in the differing gravity contributions of your malts instead of assuming a flat contribution of 36 points per pound.

Note: If you want the ultimate set of calculations for parti-gyle brewing, do a search for the terms *Randy Mosher parti-gyle*. The first result should be Randy's *Brewing Techniques* article, "Parti-Gyle Brewing," with full calculations.

CAPPING

Think back to the days when you used to steep grains and then rinse them for your extract brews. Remember, you just couldn't throw any grain in there; some grains had to be mashed, since they need their starches converted to sugars. Here's the rule: if it's a base grain, flaked, or an adjunct, it needs to be mashed. If it's a crystal or roasted malt, steeping is okay. The same is true of carapils malts and Melanoidin malt.

This technique is a return, in part, to those early days. As you mash, grind up a second addition of grain. Draw your first runnings into one kettle. After you collect your desired first beer, stop the outflow and then add your second addition of grain.

What can this get you? Think about mashing a DIPA and then capping the mash with ½ pound of Carafa II Dehusked Malt. When you collect your second batch of runnings, you'll miraculously have a Black IPA waiting for you. Worried about your gravity being too low in your second batch? Just blend in some of your first runnings to pick up the second beer.

Also, it's not uncommon for the second beer of a parti-gyle to be a bit on the thin side. So even if you're making two different-strength variants of the same beer, there's a good argument to be made for capping the mash with some crystal or carapils malt before doing the second runoff. Since those malts don't need to be mashed, it doesn't slow down the process much, and it adds the body the second runnings beer needs.

SIDE MASH

Let's say that you want to cap a mash to make an oatmeal stout. On its face, it seems to have the same flaw as most extract-based oatmeal stouts: steeping will extract the fattiness desired from oats but carries with it a load of starch just ready for spoilage bacteria to chew on. Flaked oats, oatmeal, and malted oats all need to be mashed before they can be used. Unless you want your first beer to be an oat beer as well, you'll need to mash those oats separately before you use them.

That's right, it's as simple as a little minimash on the side. Your main concern for a side mash is to make sure you have enough diastatic power (aka enzymes) to convert your specialty grain starches into sugars. The calculation is easy: for each grain, multiply its Litner rating (a measure of enzymes) by the weight. Add those values together and divide by the weight. If the resulting value is above 30, you're golden. If not, add some more base malt, such as a 2- or 6-row.

$$Power_{Grain} = Litner_{Grain} \times Weight_{Grain}$$
$$Power_{Mash} = (Power_{Grain1} + \ldots Power_{GrainN}) / (Weight_{Grain1} + \ldots Weight_{GrainN})$$

$$Power_{Mash} >= 30 = GO!$$
$$Power_{Mash} < 30 = Add\ more\ Base\ Malt$$

Once you know you have the appropriate diastatic power, the rest of the mash is fairly straightforward. You could go whole hog and build a minimash tun, but how about using this as an easy opportunity to explore the brew in a bag (BIAB) method? (See page 15.) Most of your side mashes should be 5 or fewer pounds, which is small enough to fit in a traditional nylon grain sack readily available at the homebrew shop. Just mash in a pot with your grain contained in the bag, drain, and add the side mash to the desired portion of beer.

HALF SOUR MASH

If you've ever forgotten to clean your mash tun, you know that as little as a day later, the resulting warm mass of grain can smell like something straight out of a zombie movie. But there's a magical point—around twelve to eighteen hours—at which the wort drawn from a leftover mash is naturally soured by the *Lactobacillus* that is everywhere on a malt husk.

If you are looking to get into sour beers, you can create a normal-strength beer from the first runnings and leave a second mash overnight (combined with the sparge water). Drain and boil the next day for a light, tart brew.

BOILING AND CHILLING

Even once you hit the boil kettle(s), you have a lot of flexibility. Maybe not as much as if you started in the mash, but from this point out, your splitting techniques become a little simpler to execute. And for the most part, your different split beers are more easily repeatable. (For example, imagine you brew a parti-gyle beer, and you're fond of only half of the beer. How do you brew it without remaking both halves?) Beers split at the boil or beyond require little additional tinkering to recreate. Just scale up your next batch based on the small batch you preferred.

One important note before you begin: If you're running two separate boils, make sure you stagger the starts of your boils to allow you time to chill the first beer before chilling the second. If it takes you 20 minutes to chill, kick off the second batch's boil about 20 minutes after the first one. This allows you to chill the first beer completely and be ready to go on the second, instead of allowing the second beer to steep at a near-boil for longer than you intended.

TWO POTS

This is one of the simplest and easiest splits that you can do. Take two pots and boil half the wort in each. This allows you to hop one beer one way and another completely differently. You can explore flavors and techniques with far less work and far more consistency thanks to an identical starting point before the boil. In order to reduce possible variables, you should keep your boils equal in terms of volume, gravity, boil vigor, pot shape, and so on.

Note: To ensure an equal gravity, the easiest thing to do is collect all the wort in one giant pot and stir it to avoid stratified layers of density. Once this is done, measure your wort and split it. Don't have a big enough pot? Grab a couple of buckets or pots and carefully scoop and stir the wort back and forth. Check the gravity. After a few back-and-forths, you should reach equilibrium.

WATERED-DOWN HIGH-GRAVITY BREWING

Just because you create a 1.070 wort, that doesn't mean that you have to ferment a 1.070 wort! All you need is dechlorinated water, a spare kettle, and a little math.

Let's say you've made a 1.080 DIPA wort and want to also boil a portion as a 1.050 pale ale wort. You know you want to create 5 gallons of pale ale. So . . .

$$\text{Points}_{\text{Target}} = \text{Gravity}_{\text{Target}} \times \text{Volume}_{\text{Target}}$$
$$\text{Volume}_{\text{Addition}} = \text{Points}_{\text{Target}} / \text{Gravity}_{\text{Original}}$$

In our example we see:
    50 × 5 = 250 pts
    250 / 80 = 3.125
    You need just over 3 gallons of DIPA wort to have 5 gallons at 1.050.

Don't forget, when you're diluting preboil, to add enough extra water to account for your boil-off. If you boil off a gallon during an hour of boiling your pale ale above, make sure you add 1 extra gallon in addition to the 1.875 gallons you've added to reduce the target gravity to 1.050.

However, nobody says you have to dilute at the beginning of the boil. You can also use water after the boil to dilute a portion of beer. It's a great way to extend the amount of beer you're producing without needing larger pots and mash tuns. Just think about a four-person brew day where you want everyone to go home with beer, but you can only make 10-gallon batches. If you make your beer twice as strong and dilute with freshly boiled and chilled water in the fermenters, you can take 10 gallons of 1.080 wort and produce 20 gallons of 1.040 beer. Or (stick with us here) you can take those same 10 gallons and produce 5 gallons of 1.080 beer and 10 gallons of 1.040 beer! Not only did you produce more beer, but you produced two beers out of one mash. It's a brew day miracle!

SPLIT CHILLING AND ADDITIONS

Let's say that you don't care to futz early in the boil. Maybe you don't have the extra pots and pans necessary to pull off two near-simultaneous boils. Well, that's what the end of the boil is for!

The obvious trick for the end of the boil is to take advantage of the leftover heat in the pot and dissolve some goodies, such as hop oils. You know in your beery adventures the radical impact a jolt of late hops can make. A last-minute splash of Citra makes the beer tropical and fruity, while a dose of Columbus makes the beer dank and dark.

To make a clear difference in your two beers, just follow this practice. Kill the boil and whirlpool your beer as normal. Chill half the beer either by flowing half the batch through a counterflow chiller or by transferring half the batch to another kettle, where you can cool it with an immersion chiller. Shut off the flow, add 1 to 2 ounces of your hop, and start another whirlpool by stirring hard. Let the hops sit for at least 10 minutes before resuming chilling. Run that beer into a second fermentation vessel.

The last-minute hopping technique is going to be a little different with an immersion chiller rig, but as with all experimentation, there's a way. Run half your wort while it's still hot to another pot or heatproof container before starting this process. Chill the original pot while adding hops to the second pot (or hop both with different hops).

Don't stop at just hops! While you're thinking last-minute splits, you can boost gravities and change colors as well. Think of this as boil capping. You can add sugar and preboiled malt extracts (like cold-steeped Carafa malt). For example, you can make a Belgian Dubbel–inspired ale and then hit the second half with a dark Belgian candi syrup to boost the gravity and darken the color to make a Quadruple.

Note: We wouldn't recommend adding fruit here because of haze and loss of fruit character during the ferment. However, if you want to go for it ('cause who says we're right), you'll want to let the boil kettle heat drop to around 170°F so that you can pasteurize the fruit with less chance of activating the fruit's pectin and turning your beer into hazy, fruity snot.

FERMENTING

Remember the old saying "Brewers make wort, yeast makes beer"? It's true, and that means fermentation is one of the key times that we can affect beer's flavor. For all these techniques, you just split wort across different fermentation vessels. And just as in splitting a batch at the boil, if you discover one of the portions that you made is delicious and another isn't, you can easily replicate what you liked without ever rebrewing what you didn't like.

SPLIT YEASTS

Fermenting the same beer with wildly different yeasts is probably the first idea that occurs for a split batch fermentation. All you need to do is make two yeast starters and pitch them in the respective carboys. Just remember that for some yeasts you may need to hit different temperature ranges for the ferment.

What if you don't want two radically different beers? It turns out that pitching two different strains can also be the best way to appreciate the subtle differences between similar strains—or the same strain produced by different companies. Is there any difference between WLP001, WY1056, and Safale US-05? All are purported to be the same strain, or at least have the same origin. The only way you'll ever know to your own satisfaction is to carry out this experiment.

If you're feeling ambitious, you can go large and brew a really mondo batch. Enlist the help of your homebrew club or partner up with a commercial brewery to pitch a dozen different saison yeasts to find the differences between the strains or discover the secret of avoiding the dreaded saison stall. (Spoiler alert: Use a vigorous starter and skip the airlock. The combination of backpressure and carbon dioxide (CO_2) toxicity seems to force Dupont and similar strains—namely WLP565 Belgian Saison and WY3724 Belgian Saison—to go dormant.)

DIFFERENT TEMPERATURES

Instead of varying the yeast strains, why not vary the fermentation temperature? You could even be radical and swing for the fences with two samples at 35°F and 105°F. (Fun fact: It turns out that you can actually find experiments like these extreme temperature swings from the major lager breweries, which constantly seek newer, better ways to get their beers market-ready in a hurry.)

Back in the world of sane temperatures, let's look at an example. For Bavarian Hefeweizen strains, the usual argument is ferment cooler (62°F–63°F) to favor clove, ferment warmer to favor banana (67°F–68°F). Does it work? Or what happens when a lager strain is fermented a bit warmer (58°F)? These experiments are so easy to do, there's no reason not to try.

Remember to keep your fermentation temps consistent, within a few degrees. Yeast generally produce better results in a steady, warmer environment than in a fluctuating, cooler one. Don't believe us? Try it for yourself by setting one beer to ferment in a warmer fridge (69°F) and the other in an ice bath that drops to 60°F but rises to 68°F.

DRY HOPS

Just like the hops at the end of the boil, you can swing a beer's character by the addition of hops, lack of hops, or different types of hops added during the fermentation. Again, this is pretty simple and can yield some surprising results.

To use this technique at its most basic, simply choose one variety of hops per fermenter and dose with 1–2 ounces after primary fermentation has subsided or you've transferred to secondary. The choice to use a hop bag or not is up to you. Bags are convenient but may reduce the utilization.

Hops experimentation can be not only about variety, but also about schedule. There's a fair amount of debate over what is a proper dry hop schedule. Traditionally, the rule has been 1 ounce per 5 gallons for 2 weeks at fermentation temperature and then rack. However, others insist that you can leave the dry hops in the keg for 6 months and as long as it's cold, the beer tastes great. (We've both done that.) Still others have aggressive schedules along the lines of 5 days on a few ounces of hops at serving temperature, rack and hop again with a few more ounces for another 5 days. The goal is always to extract valuable aromatic oils with minimal extraction of the less desirable chlorophyll and grassy flavors that can show up with extended hopping.

If you have fermenters larger than your single share of wort (for example, 10-gallon cornies fermenting 8 gallons apiece intended for 5-gallon kegs), you can wait until kegging to dry hop as well. Monitor the progress of the hop flavor and rack the beer to a new keg if you begin to detect any excessive grassy flavors. For the love of all that's beery, if you dry hop in a keg, make sure to bag the hops or attach a filter to the keg dip tube. The Internet is full of horror stories of hop particles—including pellet particles—getting stuck in dip tubes and causing poor pouring and beer geysers.

SUGAR FEED

Until a few years ago, the master plan for every high-gravity homebrew revolved around getting every last molecule of sugar that you intended to ferment into the boil kettle. Thanks to a better understanding of yeast mechanics, recent procedures for big, strong sugar-infused beers, like a Belgian Tripel, evolved to include an additional step of sugar feeding during fermentation.

The theory goes: High starting gravities induce a fair amount of osmotic pressure on the yeast cell walls. This can damage or kill a number of the yeast cells introduced by the brewer, leading to increased stress responses from the survivors, including fusel alcohols, phenols, higher than normal finishing gravities, and so on. Instead of hitting the yeast with all that stress up front, start them in a lower-gravity wort (your recipe without the sugar) and then add the sugar in the form of a syrup a few days into primary fermentation. By that point, the yeast are at an increased population with maximum viability. Since the yeast are in consumption mode, there's less risk of off-flavors from stressed yeast.

Remember our candi syrup example from the end of the boil (page 47)? There's no reason you can't do the same thing here. Take your sugar source and, if it's not already a syrup, dissolve it in water by boiling it for at least 10 minutes. We recommend about half the volume of water to dissolve the sugar (for example, 2 cups of water for 4 cups of sugar). Pop open your target fermenter, pour in the liquid sugar, and swirl. Don't worry about superchilling the sugar syrup. Since it will be such a small portion of the wort, it won't really move the temperature of the whole batch. Just let it cool, covered, for 20 minutes or so, and that's enough.

If you're using unopened commercial prepackaged syrup such as maple, corn, Belgian candi syrup, and so on, there's no need to boil. Just take care to sanitize the outside of the package before opening it and add it to the fermenter. You never know what's settled on the surface of the bag, bottle, or pouch.

FLAVOR ADDITIONS

Up to this point, everything we've done has been fairly Reinheitsgebot-friendly. (If you care about such a thing—we don't.) But now, let's say you had done nothing else to split your beer. Following the primary fermentation, your options are wide open. This is where you can add any number of flavors.

We'll cover more about the ingredients in Chapter 7, but keep this in mind as you're making your beer. If you can figure out how to add new flavors to smaller portion of your batches, you never have to commit yourself to 5 gallons of Pomegranate White Chocolate Chile Brown. Instead, by cleverly splitting your batch into parts, you can safely explore almost suicidally complex combinations of flavors. (And if you make the aforementioned pomegranate beer expecting it to be good, we'll expect you to surrender your IGOR card.)

GOING WILD

In Stephen H. Buhner's interesting and assumption-challenging *Sacred and Herbal Healing Beers*, there is an interesting dismissal of modern fermentation practices that he summarizes as a "need for Teutonic authoritarian . . . controls." Even if you don't necessarily agree with his hypothesis (we don't), he is accurate in his description of the strict control modern brewers try to exercise.

However, folks seem to be loosening up and trying to embrace the wild side of brewing. Of course, they're doing it with carefully isolated and nurtured laboratory cultures of things like *Brettanomyces (Brett)*, *Lactobacillus*, or *Pediococcus*. After all, control is hard to let go of completely.

If you want to have a little fun without betting your whole batch on crazy critters, this is the perfect way to do it. You can treat your new cultures as you would a yeast strain and pitch separately. However, it's worth noting that *Brettanomyces* becomes muted in terms of all the crazy wild characters you're hoping to find when it's used as your main fermentation strain. For more intensity, pitch a normal yeast strain instead. Then, when the primary ferment begins to slow, add the *Brett* and a little food. Take your pick: about a quart of wort, a pound of sugar, or a few pounds of fruit should suffice. This will ensure that your culture addition has something to snack on while getting down to its funky business.

For the daring and really paleo-minded, you can try capturing cultures right from the sky. Remember, humans made beer for years without proper lab equipment or an understanding of microbiology. Brewers inspired by the example of Belgium's lambic producers leave their fermenter tops open to the air and let what floats in, float in. This usually leads to less-than-ideal results, so we recommend cheating a bit. Create your own wild culture by exposing a small portion of your wort in a Mason jar or suitable smaller vessel. If the resulting culture produces an interesting result, you can then pitch the culture into a larger vessel of beer to make your full batch wild. If the culture doesn't do well? It's easy enough to try again! Note: Our limited trials have shown that exposing wort to the air seems to work better in rural areas. How does a brewery in the middle of Brussels get away with it? Their culture seems to be stored largely in their oak barrels.

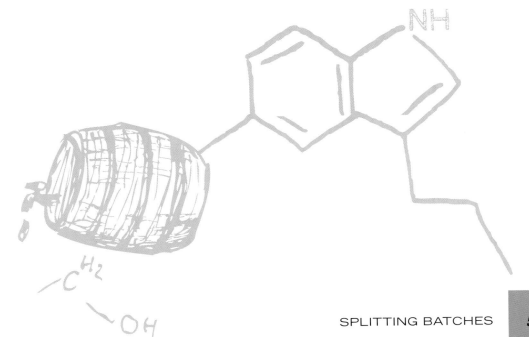

CHAPTER 4

EQUIPMENT NERDERY

AS YOU READ THROUGH THIS BOOK and look at the techniques, recipes, and experiments, you might find yourself thinking that you'd love to try some of this stuff . . . if only you had the equipment. You need gear! But isn't new equipment expensive, hard to find, or hard to build? Don't some homebrewers derive as much enjoyment in fabricating their brew gear as they do in the brewing itself?

While some brewers certainly go deep into the equipment engineering, we're not part of that group. We have little patience and would rather spend our time brewing some beer! So we often make do with simple hacks and store-bought items we can repurpose. Then, when we build equipment, it's gotta be the cheap 'n' easy way (with the emphasis on both *cheap* and *easy*)! But that doesn't mean what you find in this chapter will break down fast. While projects such as the mash tun on page 60 may look like beginner's stuff, it's served Denny well for over 15 years—500-plus batches and counting. If we can do it, *you* can do it!

OUR BASIC BUILD-OUT

Almost all brewers go through the same cycle. When you started brewing, the gear requirements were simple: a big pot, a bottle capper, and some easy-to-break sugar-measuring thingy. Over time, you became more serious. The gear accumulated. What started as a few things in the corner of the closet had grown to a substantial collection taking over the garage. Then came the purge.

At some point or another, most of us make it through that cycle and return to a point of equilibrium. We don't go back to the early days, but neither do we need a million gadgets and gizmos. On the following pages you'll find the stuff we feel makes perfect sense for the experimental brewer, from kettles and kegs to socket wrenches and spray bottles.

CORE BREWING EQUIPMENT

If you talk to four carpenters, each might have a different favorite drill or nail gun. But chances are, they all show up to the job site with a similar truck full of equipment. In brewing, we all have our own preferences as well. Here's what our garages look like.

Denny

Planning the Brew
- 1 laptop computer running ProMash brewing software (also used to access websites for yeast pitching calculations)

Yeast Management
- 1 stir plate (with stir bar)
- 1-gallon glass jug

Brew Day
- 3 cooler mash tuns (48-quart, 70-quart, and 152-quart—selection based on batch size)
- 1 banjo-style propane burner
- 1 7-gallon propane tank (lasts longer than a 5-gallon)
- 2 converted keg kettles (legally obtained) with curved copper pickup—selection based on batch size
- 1 50-foot ⅜-inch copper immersion chiller
- 1 March 809 HS Pump (with 815 Impeller upgrade) and high-temperature tubing
- 1 old desktop computer running ProMash brewing software
- Spiral notebook for recording recipe and taking notes

Fermenting and Packaging

- 10 7-gallon high-density polyethylene buckets
- Assorted bucket lids, blow-off tubes, airlocks
- 2 10-gallon kegs for 8.5-gallon batches
- 23 corny kegs (used for aging and dry hopping as well as serving)

Note: I've got an indoor-outdoor carpet on the garage floor and a center floor drain. A stainless-steel worktable functions as my brew stand.

Drew

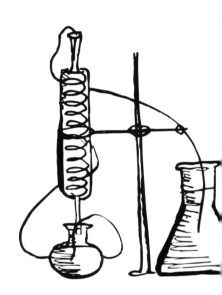

Planning the Brew

- Multiple cloud-connected computers running BeerSmith and ProMash

Yeast Management

- 1 Stir plate (with stir bar)
- 1-gallon glass jug

Brew Day

- 2 cooler mash tuns (72-quart and 150-quart for different-size mashes)
- Cheap turkey fryer burner
- 2 5-gallon propane tanks
- 1 26-gallon kettle
- 1 convoluted counterflow chiller and 1 copper immersion chiller
- 1 pump with ½-inch ball valve

Fermenting and Packaging

- 1 minifridge (for fermentation)
- 1 20–cubic foot chest freezer (for serving and storing kegs)
- 2 10-gallon kegs (for primary fermentation)
- 25 5-gallon kegs

Note: Notice any similarities with Denny's list? All of it is fairly basic stuff. Well, okay, we do have a lot of kegs! But we're simple brewers at heart.

THE BREWING TOOLBOX

Over a thousand years ago, some poor seafaring Viking lost his tools overboard, where they remained until the 1930s. When they were recovered, they provided a solid glimpse of old-school technology. But do you know why we recovered such a complete set of tools? The Viking had them organized in a massive toolbox! A toolbox doesn't need to be anything fancy, but we recommend you go the way of the Vikings and invest in at least a lightweight box that holds and organizes these basic bits.

- **Aluminum foil:** It may seem strange at first, but foil is a homebrewer's best friend. Easily sanitized and moldable, it makes a perfect temporary seal for carboys, fermenters, and flasks. It can also be used to make cheap splash panels and windshields for your burners. Always, always keep foil on hand to cover things you've sanitized. Denny: I consider foil, plastic wrap, and paper towels to be sanitary right off the roll, and this assumption has never let me down. Sanitize if you feel you must.

- **Blue painter's tape or white electrical tape:** Everything gets a slap of tape with names and dates. If it's not labeled, how the heck do you remember what it is and when you made it?
- **Spring clamps:** Hoses have a tendency to flop around in the brewery. A few cheap metal spring clamps will hold your hoses in place without pinching them. Just feed the hose through the gap left after popping the clamp onto your kettle.
- **Grease pencil or durable marker:** You need something to write with in your brewery. If it has water-resistant properties, it will save you a headache down the road.
- **Lighter:** If you're going to be cooking things with flame, get a lighter (preferably two) of the long stick variety and stash it here for emergency ignition.
- **Multitool:** A Leatherman, Swiss army knife, or similar multitool has so many uses around the brewery that once you get one, you'll wonder how you ever got along without it.
- **Nut driver:** If, like most brewers, you use worm clamps on your hoses, invest in a nut driver to save you time, frustration, and cut fingers from a sliding screwdriver.
- **Pipe cutter:** This little gizmo slides over a piece of pipe and creates a clean cut when you twist the pipe in the cutter's mechanical jaws. You'll want one of these to make quick, easy work of tubing when you start dealing with all the little pieces of pipe (copper or steel) that show up in the brewery—the mash tun, a pickup pipe in the kettle, that extra chiller you want to build, a hop back, and so on.
- **Rubber bands:** Trust us: when you need something gently held in place, you'll want to use a rubber band as cheap insurance. Remember, when securing a fermentation cover, not to aggressively double up the band unless you want your covering to explode.
- **Scales (large and small):** You need a scale with a max capacity that will handle your largest grain needs. You also need a scale to measure grams and fractional ounces for weighing out hops and chemicals. Chances are, you will not find an inexpensive scale that does both well.
- **Crescent and box wrenches:** A few sizes of box wrenches come in really handy when working around the brewery for anything repetitive. Two sizes of crescents will work for small jobs in tight spaces, such as removing a keg post or compression fitting.

Note: You may already have a bunch of these tools, but we recommend that you double up and create a brewery-exclusive toolbox. This will prevent you from discovering that you took your wrenches inside to work on the plumbing, right when you need them outside on the brew deck!

STORAGE

The toolbox holds all the tool-y stuff, but unless you prefer the wild junkman look of a hoarder, we highly recommend that you figure out how to store everything else. Even if not for neatness' sake, being organized in the brewery and having everything stored properly allows you to plan and brew better.

- **Gamma lids:** If you start holding a lot of grain at your house and want to discourage a rodent infestation while keeping your malt fresh, invest in some storage gadgets with airtight lids. Gamma lids are excellent, screw-on, airtight lids. The lids that fit 5-gallon buckets are ideal. Two 5-gallon buckets will hold 50 pounds of grain and keep it fresh for a long, long time.
- **Mason jars (ideally wide-mouth):** Mason jars are a must for all those extracts, tinctures, and cube-soaking experiments (see page 75), not to mention yeast. Really, name something you need to

store for a little while . . . you can probably put it in the nonreactive glass walls of a Mason jar. Along with a pressure cooker, a Mason jar is one of the only sterile environments a homebrewer can reliably create. Note that plastic lids are highly recommended to prevent rusting during long-term storage.

- **Pegboard:** Both of us have old garages with rafters and plenty of room for nails—this type of setup is the perfect way to store all the long, annoying pieces of gear such as hoses and racking canes. However, if you don't have rafters full of random old nails, we suggest a pegboard.

- **Plastic bins:** These days whole stores are devoted to the art of the bin. Where some brewers prefer the simplicity of buying one giant tub and chucking all their gear in there, why not use multiple bins? Each 20-quart bin gets a purpose and a label (for example, cleaning supplies, oxygen/yeast gear, or roasted malts). Even when bins are stacked on the shelves, finding things is a breeze, and the bins aren't big enough to become a jumbled mess or annoyingly heavy. If you feel like storing air-sensitive items, invest in bins with gaskets. Also, keep a number of smaller containers on hand for things like worm clamps, screws, water salts, and so on. You can also find bin units that have individual drawers in them, of course.

- **Vacuum sealer:** If you want to keep your on-hand ingredients—especially hops—at their freshest, get a high-quality vacuum sealer and bags. Good bags are the key to effective vacuum sealing! True, they're not cheap. But you can use them for food, too. You can even keep malt safe from infestation by vacuum-sealing specialty malts in recipe-size quantities and stashing the bags in a couple of gasketed bins.

CLEANING AND SANITATION

Homebrewing is a hobby that requires meticulous cleaning. If you happen to be a slob, don't despair. It takes only a few simple tools—and some vigilance—to keep your brewery spick-and-span. Remember that cleaning is much easier when the mess is fresh. Tackling your gunky bottles, carboys, and pots immediately saves you time and effort. Don't put it off. (Unless you can seal the carboy or keg completely, in which case you have a little bit of time.)

- **Brushes:** Every homebrew kit comes with at least one bottlebrush and sometimes a carboy brush, too. In addition to those, invest in a few smaller brushes (such as toothbrushes) to clean all the annoying little parts. A stout scrubbing brush to clean up the big messes can also be quite handy. Replace your brushes regularly. They're your guarantee of a clean surface; think of brushes as cheap insurance. A *new, clean* toilet brush works great for cleaning corny kegs.

- **Chemicals:** Another important facet of cleaning is to work smart with your chemicals. The Five Star lineup of products is a pretty easy way to go. PBW (Powdered

Brewery Wash) works like a charm and rinses away easily. However, OxiClean works just as well, as do other sodium percarbonate-based cleaners. An overnight soak in either of those solutions will drop almost any mess to the ground. However, if you're dealing with that hellish stubborn brownish stain of beerstone (calcium oxalate), don't use a base cleaner! Go the opposite way and use an acidic solution. Soaking a beerstoned surface in a dilute solution of vinegar and warm water will allow you to wipe the gunk off with a sponge. It beats the pants off scrubbing and scrubbing and barely making a dent! Bar Keeper's Friend is the cleaner of choice for stainless steel, and it does a great job of removing beerstone as well—albeit with a bit more scrubbing than an acid cleaner needs.

- **Sponges:** No surprise here: sponges are damn handy. Make sure to have fresh nonscouring sponges for your plastic gear. And keep a separate supply of sponges for the brewhouse! You don't want to leave the residue of your bacon-filled breakfast all over your brew pots. Speaking of pots, feel free to break out the scouring pads for them—as long as they contain no soap. Oh, and never use an abrasive scouring pad on aluminum pots. Use a nonmetallic scrubby pad instead.

- **Spray bottle:** Pick up a few of these for spraying every last surface with sanitizer. For instance, did you know it's a good idea to sanitize your keg connections every time you connect them? What a pain that would be without a spray bottle!

- **Pump:** Most brewers think of a pump as a piece of brew-day gear that becomes necessary only when you're moving around large amounts of hot wort and water. Think that way, and you miss one of the best uses for a pump: cleaning. Pump cleaner and sanitizer through your chiller or through your kegs. Take a submersible pump and attach the output to a polyvinyl chloride (PVC) pipe closed with a cap that has a few holes drilled into it. Put the pump into a bucket, fill with cleaner or sanitizer, and you have a perfect cleaning rig for carboys and kegs. Just slide one over the pipe and watch it go!

TEMPERATURE CHECKS

It's said that the man with one thermometer is certain of his temperature, while the man with two will never know for sure. The classic thermometers of the past—the red alcohol floating thermometer and the bimetal dial thermometer—are reliable until the paper slips or the dial moves. For our purposes, a good digital thermometer is a dependable one . . . but you'll still want to check it against a reference thermometer to be certain.

- **Infrared thermometer:** This is one of the most fun toys a brewer can have, although it is by no means a must-have from a functional standpoint. You can use it for the mash, the boil, or even for tasting tests. Temperature affects aroma and flavor, after all. It's so high-tech that it's like having a laser blaster. But keep in mind that it reads only surface temperature! If you use it to take the temperature of your mash, you won't know what the temperature is below the surface.

- **Instant-read thermometer:** The Thermapen is the high-end pick of chefs everywhere, but if you look around, you can find cheaper thermometers that perform similarly from Taylor or CDN. Never doubt the value of a good temperature gauge. Also, watch the Thermapen website (www. thermoworks.com) for sales.

- **Probed thermometer:** Many homebrewers have adopted the culinary probe thermometer as their measuring device of choice. The only problem is, most of the cheap ones you find for the kitchen suffer a fatal flaw: the probes aren't watertight and will die when exposed to liquids. Look for a fully encased waterproof probe thermometer like Taylor's Digital Panel Mount Thermometer, which survives well in a brewery and is relatively inexpensive as well. **Denny: My preference for most temperature measurement during brewing is an old bimetal dial thermometer with a long probe. I've used the same one for more than fifteen years, and it's going strong. In addition, it's submersible, so I can attach it to my immersion chiller to keep an eye on the temperature, and I don't have to worry if it falls over in the cooling wort. The caveat is that you also need to have a certified lab thermometer to calibrate the dial thermometer!**

TOOLS FOR SCIENCE

It's time! What follows is the gear we use that truly makes us feel like mad scientists. Even here you'll notice it's not a lot of stuff—just what we need. **Drew: Though one of these days when I strike it rich, I'll get a gas chromatograph, and a centrifuge, and a. . . .**

- **Chlorine testing:** It's important to make sure your water is free of chlorine and chlorophenols.
- **Graduated jars:** Erlenmeyer flasks may get all the mad-science love, but graduated jars are great for most brewing science tasks, including the all-important measuring of beer samples. As for the flasks: we don't trust them. People are enamored with the boil-it and chill-it aspect of the flasks, but they overflow easily at a boil, and most brands shatter fairly easily as well. It's much easier and cheaper to use a growler or jar for your yeast culturing needs.
- **Microscope with hemacytometer:** Counting yeast cells is a totally geeked-out way of ensuring that you're pitching an adequate amount of yeast. The hemacytometer is a must if you plan on counting since it provides the frame within which you count, however with just a microscope you can see if your yeast is healthy. You can also use a microscope to see if you have bacteria or mutant cells (cue sci-fi movie diabolical laugh) in your beer or yeast. A basic student-issue illuminated 400x microscope will get the job done. You can buy one, and some cheap hemacytometers, online.
- **pH meters and papers:** Water chemistry is real science with weird equations and hard mathematics to calculate impacts. It helps to know your pH for most of the calculations. Remember that pH meters require maintenance and proper storage to stay viable, but papers just need to stay somewhere dry and cool. But beware of cheap pH papers! They're notoriously hard to read, which leads to inaccurate readings. Plastic pH papers (an oxymoron if there ever was one) such as the ColorpHast brand work much better.
- **Pressure cooker or canner:** This is the poor man's autoclave. You can use it to sterilize jars, media, and so on. It also allows you to safely create shelf-stable starter wort on the cheap. (See page 80.) If you decide to explore the wild and woolly world of yeast ranching, you'll need one of these. We suggest a canner in the 20-quart range to ease your brewing needs.
- **Refractometer:** To buy one and rely on it or not to—that is the question. Even the two of us can't agree! **Drew: I swear by my refractometer as an easy-to-use gravity measuring device. In my testing, the calculations you find online or in your favorite brewing software come close enough to the comparison hydrometer readings. Denny: I really want to be able to use and trust a refractometer . . . really, I do! But I've got two of them, and neither one will agree with my hydrometer, no matter how many times I calibrate them. So, rather than buy a third one and hope for the best, I've returned to using a hydrometer. The one I use has a thermometer built into it as well as a temperature correction chart. So, with one instrument I can get a temperature-corrected gravity reading.**

And by using the Quick Hydrometer Reading technique described on page 64, I can get a reading almost as quickly as Drew does using a refractometer.

CHEAP 'N' EASY MASH TUN

For some of the experiments in this book, it can be useful to do two mashes at the same time. But that doesn't mean you need to spend a lot of money on a second mash tun. The Cheap'n' Easy Mash Tun performs like a champ, costs under $60 to build (in the 70-quart size, which allows you to brew 10 gallon batches up to 1.100 OG), and can be built in about half an hour. One thing to keep in mind is that this design is intended for batch sparging. You can use it for fly sparging, but the design will probably yield lower efficiency if you fly sparge, due to the single straight drain configuration. On the other hand, batch sparging is a good thing as far as we're concerned.

You Will Need

- **Cooler with a removable drain valve:** Although 5- or 10-gallon round coolers are what brewers have traditionally used for mash tuns, a rectangular cooler will give you more volume for your money and will be easier to use due to the large opening. In addition, since you will be batch-sparging, the usual concerns about shallow grain bed depth are not an issue. For size, try to find one between 48 and 70 quarts. With a 48-quart, you'll be able to mash enough grain for a 5-gallon batch at an OG of 1.100, although the cooler will be so full it will be difficult to stir. With a 70-quart, you'll be able to double that, and easily mash enough grain for a 10-gallon batch at a 1.100 OG.
- **Faucet supply line with a stainless-steel braid covering (12–20 inches):** This is the heart of the system. It lets you drain out the wort while holding back the grain. Make sure the one you buy is actually stainless steel. Some plastic braids look just like stainless, but they won't work the way you need them to work in a mash tun. If you can find it, Lasco brand (part number 10-0121 or 10-0321) works well.
- **Minikeg bung:** A minikeg is just what it sounds like: a small keg for beer. The bung is a small round rubber piece that fits into the keg after you fill it. The bung allows you insert a tap. However, we're gonna repurpose it for our mash tun. Bungs are available at homebrew supply stores or online.
- **About 6 feet of ⅜-inch ID x ½-inch OD vinyl tubing:** This is what we'll use to drain the wort from the mash tun.
- **⅜-inch inline nylon ball valve:** This will be the gateway to the wort. It's available at your local homebrew shop or online.
- **3 stainless-steel hose clamps:** Buy a size that will fit around the ⅜-inch tubing.
- **Silicone adhesive sealer:** You may need this for sealing the valve into the mash tun if it doesn't fit perfectly on its own.
- **Basic tools:** You'll need a hacksaw, hatchet, or other tool to cut the stainless-steel braid, pliers, a screwdriver, and a hammer.

Instructions

1. Remove the spigot from the cooler. Usually, there's a nut holding the spigot on the inside of the cooler. Unscrew that and the spigot should pop right out.

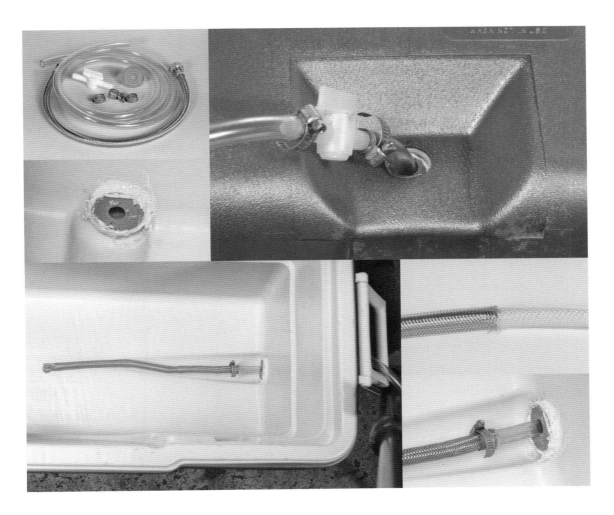

2. Remove the plastic insert from the hole in the minikeg bung, and insert the bung into the spigot hole from the inside of the cooler. The beveled edge of the bung goes in first, and the flange of the bung should end up flush with the cooler wall. It may fit snugly with a push, or you may need to use your silicone sealer to hold it in place. If you seal it in place, wait 24 hours for the sealer to set before continuing.

3. Cut off a 6-inch piece of the vinyl tubing and, from the inside of the cooler, insert it into the hole in the minikeg bung. Let a couple of inches of tubing protrude from each side of the cooler.

4. Cut the threaded fittings off the water supply line. Pull the tubing out from the braid, leaving a hollow length of hose braid. To make it easier to remove the inner tubing, push each end of the braid toward the center. That will expand the braid. Flatten the last inch or so of one end of the braid. Fold it over on itself three times to seal the end. Squeeze the fold with a pair of pliers or smack it with a hammer to crimp it closed.

5. Slip a hose clamp over the open end of the braid, and slip the braid over the end of the vinyl tubing *inside* the cooler. Tighten the clamp until snug, but don't squeeze the tubing shut!

6. Insert one end of the valve into the tubing on the outside of the cooler and secure it with a hose clamp. Slip another hose clamp over the end of the long piece of tubing, connect the

Cutting the Propane Cord

There are a few things to consider when you're thinking about using natural gas for your brewery instead of propane. The first should be which professional am I going to hire to do the plumbing work? Seriously, unless you spend your days plumbing or fixing furnaces, leave the hard work of safely delivering extraordinarily flammable gas to the professionals!

Drew: This advice comes from Kent Fletcher, Brewgyver of the Maltose Falcons. He's also my close friend, and the one who makes mechanical reality of my really dumb ideas! Kent is an actual expert at this stuff, but unless you hire him he won't be able to help with your particular situation. Find a gas plumbing professional to affirm the lay of your land. (More of this discussion can also be found at www.ExperimentalBrew.com). Ok, take it away Kent!

For natural gas, there's a lot to think about even before you get a quote. Here are the three primary concerns:

1. Location: How far is your brewery from your gas meter? The farther you travel from your meter, the more impractical it will be to plumb gas to your brewery. This is because gas, like a liquid, builds up resistance as it travels through your pipes. Since you can't change the incoming gas pressure, you have to change the width of the pipe to lower resistance. Practically speaking you'll generally want ¾" or 1" gas piping to move any sizable distance from the gas meter when you're running two simultaneous burners. A contractor or plumber should be able to plan out your run and get you set on permits to allow a safe installation.

2. Burner Size: How many BTUs are you going to be pumping out of your burners at the same time? The more heat you want running at any time, the more gas you'll need, which also plays into your piping.

3. Burner Type: While it's tempting to try and salvage your propane designed burners for this operation, please don't try a home conversion. Either buy a propane to natural gas conversion kit for the burner (if it exists) or buy a new burner designed for natural gas. Go to your local restaurant supply store and you can find inexpensive wok style burners for remarkably cheap, and they'll provide more than enough power for most homebrew setups (in some cases, they'll supply too much!). Remember bigger is not always better unless you like violently splashing wort on brew day!

tubing to the output side of the valve, and secure it with the hose clamp. Make sure the output tubing is long enough to reach the bottom of your kettle. You want to transfer the wort gently, not let it splash into the kettle. That's it! You've built your Cheap 'n' Easy Mash Tun! Now, let's brew some beer.

Drew: If you want your boil kettle to deliver fairly clean wort to the fermenter, you can get a head start by creating a braid for your kettle pickup. I've got a ridiculous 26-gallon boil kettle (I know, I know) and a ridiculously large braid that goes around the outside and filters everything. It is awesome!

Denny: If you try this, remember the emphasis on *ridiculously large* braid! I haven't had much success using the same faucet/toilet supply braid for the kettle that I use for a mash tun.

CHILLING TIPS AND TRICKS

It's no secret that consistently reaching a low pitch temperature is important. A number of variations exist, but most fall into one of two camps: immersion chiller or counterflow (coil or plate) chiller.

You'll see adherents of both faiths online arguing that theirs is the one true path of righteous cooling. The immersion chiller guys gain a point in their favor with the technique of recirculating ice water for the final part of the chilling, which isn't nearly as effective in a counterflow. However, counterflow chillers (CFCs) have one big advantage over immersion chillers (ICs): they're batch size–independent. No matter how big your batch of beer is (within reason), you can use the same CFC to cool your wort. More volume simply means a little more time. Once you've invested the money in your counterflow, you're set for your life as a homebrewer. The few techniques that follow offer some ideas for making sure your chilling is as fast as possible, no matter which chiller you use. (One technique even uses both!)

ICE BATH CHILLING

The temperature of your cooling water affects your ability to chill the wort. Think of it this way: you'll never be able to get colder than your water—it's an impossibility enforced by the laws of thermodynamics. So it's no surprise that the number one problem brewers face when cooling their beer is the lack of truly cold water. Sure, if you live in the great white north, your water temps are beautifully cold for most of the year. But for many of us, that's hardly the case.

To beat this, professional brewers use cold-water tanks to chill water for cooling. (The water is typically redirected to the HLT for the next batch of beer.) This option is impractical at a homebrew level, but with a submersible pump and some ice, you can replicate the effect.

Start by hooking your immersion chiller to your water supply and running as usual until you're in the slow part of the chill—typically when your wort is below 120°F and the thermal gradient is reduced. At this point, stop the water flow and hook your chiller into the output of a submersible pump buried in an ice-water bath. Pump the ice water into the chiller and take the output back into the ice bath. In no time, your beer will be very chilly.

WHIRLPOOL CHILLING

One problem with immersion chillers is the thermal jacket. As the chiller runs, it naturally cools the beer next to the piping. This cool wort insulates the rest of the wort from the cooling effect, impacting efficiency. In order to defeat this effect, you need to get the wort moving. The simplest way is to shake the coil periodically. It breaks up the thermal jacket surrounding the coil, restoring a steeper thermal gradient and speeding up heat transfer. But why move the coil when you can move the wort?

Take a cue from the professional breweries that employ a whirlpool step in their brewing: they pump wort from the bottom of the kettle back to the top and feed it parallel to, but under, the wort's surface. The flow quickly imparts a spin to the wort, which causes hot break material and hop matter to settle in the middle of the kettle and away from the draw port. For homebrewers using an immersion cooler, it also has the effect of breaking up the thermal jacket and increasing cooling automatically.

Quick Hydrometer Reading

Speaking of ice bath chilling, chances are you have a metal cocktail shaker in the liquor cabinet that rarely gets used. Bring it on out to your next brew day. Collect boiling wort using a Pyrex measuring cup (8 ounces is generally what it takes for my hydrometer flask), and pour it into the metal cocktail shaker. Then put the cocktail shaker into a large bowl of ice water and swirl it around for about a minute. In that amount of time, the small sample cools from boiling to 60°F. It's much faster than using a freezer. As a bonus, you can likely stick a thermometer into the shaker through a strainer hole in the top of the shaker so you can keep an eye on the temperature as it cools. (This strategy is valuable because you can actually cool the sample too much using this method!)

To do this yourself, just hook up a pump to a spigot on your boil kettle and feed the flow back into the top. Keep it gentle—you're not trying to beat the wort into a froth. If you want something permanent, you can sweat a copper pipe to your immersion chiller, but it's just as effective to use a spring clamp to affix the pump hose to the edge of your kettle before pumping begins.

COMBINATION CHILLING

Here's where we're going to go off the beaten path and use both an immersion and counterflow chiller. Whether you just won a new chiller in a raffle or decided you wanted to go counterflow, don't throw out that old immersion chiller just yet. In the heat of summer, you can use a combo cooling system to beat the dog days. With some extra ice, you can cool to pitching temperature in about 15 minutes.

The basic idea is thus: a CFC is very efficient at removing the bulk of your wort's heat over a short distance. It is, however, limited by your cooling water's temperature. You could use an ice bath to power your CFC, but the overall efficiency is lower than an immersion chiller because of the volume of water moved through a CFC. So modify things slightly. Pump wort from your boil kettle into the CFC. The CFC removes most of the heat and drops the wort to around 80°F. Then, instead of dropping the 80°F wort into a fermenter, let it flow into a spare IC that has had the interior of the coil sanitized and is sitting in an ice bath. Once the wort moves through the ice bath, it flows into the fermenter at a chilly 60°F–64°F. A small submersible pump sits in the ice bath to keep the water moving.

CHEAP 'N' EASY FERMENTATION TEMPERATURE CONTROL

Controlling the temperature of your fermenting beer is one of the most important things you can do to improve your beer quality. But not everyone has the space or money to use a temperature-controlled refrigerator or freezer. Use this method for results that approach those of a more complicated rig for a fraction of the cost and space. Depending on the weather conditions where you live, you can even use it to ferment lagers in the winter.

You Will Need

- A large plastic tub or muck bucket (the 1¾–bushel size is a good place to start)
- Either ice packs and frozen water bottles or an aquarium heater pump (depending on if you want the water bath to cool or warm your fermenting beer)

Instructions

1. Put your fermenter into the muck bucket and fill the bucket with water until it's about ½ to ¾ of the way up your fermenter.
2. If the weather is hot, add ice packs or frozen water bottles as needed to maintain your fermentation temperature. If the weather is cold, use an aquarium heater in the water in the muck bucket. Depending on your weather conditions, it can help to put the aquarium heater on a timer so that it only comes on at the coldest times of the day.

That's it! Remember, all that water in the bucket acts as a thermal buffer, reducing temperature swings. That's what helps maintain a fairly constant temperature. If you happen to live in the desert in Arizona, we can't guarantee you'll be able to ferment lagers with this. However, you will be able to keep your ale fermentations at a correct, stable temperature by changing out ice packs or frozen water bottles a couple times a day.

Drew: If you're really worried about losing temperature in your tub, wrap the bucket in a big thick blanket. I use an old sleeping bag, and it works like a charm.

PACKAGING AND SERVING WITH STYLE

SPUNDING VALVE

A strange but handy little gadget for brewers is an assembly called a spunding valve. It sounds dirty, but it's not really. A spunding valve is basically an adjustable pressure relief valve.

How is this useful to a brewer? You can ferment under pressure, for one. You can also pressure rack carbonated beer with less foam by holding high pressure in the receiving keg. You can even naturally carbonate by setting the relief valve to your carbonation pressure as you approach the end of fermentations!

You will need

- Adjustable pressure relief valve with ¼-inch fitting
- Pressure gauge with ¼-inch fitting
- ¼-inch NPT to barb fitting
- Brass ¼-inch NPT Y block
- Gas-side quick disconnect (with barb)
- 1-inch reinforced vinyl hose for gas
- Teflon tape
- 2 worm drive hose clamps

Instructions

- Wrap the relief valve, pressure gauge, and barb connections with teflon tape. Screw each into the Y block and tighten with a wrench.
- Slide the gas hose over the barb fitting and tighten a worm clamp over it. Insert the disconnect's barb fitting into the hose and fit with a clamp.
- Hook this onto a keg and use the gauge to monitor the pressure. All told, you can turn $25 worth of parts into a nifty valve arrangement in a few minutes with some teflon tape and a wrench.

DRAFT HOPBACK

Randall the Enamel Animal (or just Randall) is an organoleptic hop transducer module first unveiled by Dogfish Head Brewery at the Lupulin Slam in 2002. In 2010 it became available to the public, and in December of 2012 the design was revised to include a second chamber to reduce foaming. Although the original idea was to fill the chamber with hops, which makes it a draft hopback, it didn't take long for people to figure out that you could put fruits, vegetables, coffee, cookies, and bacon into the Randall to infuse those flavors into your beer. Want to reinforce or complement the fruit flavors of the hops in the beer? Add in some fruit! Wish you'd made a coffee stout instead of a plain one? Add some coffee beans! Here's how to build your own single-chamber Randall.

You Will Need

- 1 10-inch whole house water filter: You're looking for the kind with a screw-on lid that accepts a cartridge. The ones with ¼-inch NPT-threaded inputs and outputs are easiest to use. Also, the ones with clear housing make for the best presentation.

- 2 ¼-inch MPT to ¼-inch male flare fittings for quick disconnects: Many filter housings have ¾-inch FPT threads. If the filter housing has threads other than ¼-inch NPT threads, you will need reducers to fit the flares. Alternatively, you can use Kynar barbed fittings (McMaster-Carr #53055K213).
- 1 1-inch-long piece of ½-inch ID x ¾-inch OD PVC hose
- 1 ½-inch OD stainless-steel tubing: You can use McMaster-Carr #8989K7 cut to fit the length of the canister interior (about 10 inches).
- 1 keg line to flare (input connector)
- 1 serving line or beverage line for faucet hookup

Optional Parts for Split Service: One Keg, Two Beers

- 1 keg line (no flare)
- 1 Y barb connector
- 1 beverage line to flare
- 1 beverage line to tap or faucet

Instructions

1. Clean the filter in soapy water to remove all the packaging gunk.
2. Screw flare connectors (and optional reducers) into the input and output of the filter.
3. Plug the PVC hose into the port on the underside of the top lid. It will act as the gasket for your stainless tube.
4. Place stainless tube into the PVC hose gasket. The fit should be secure.
5. Screw the filter housing together. If your stainless is cut to the right length, it should fit snugly into the bottom port. If not, trim the tube and repeat.
6. Remove the stainless-steel tube and drill approximately 20 ¹⁄₁₆-inch holes in the bottom two-thirds of the tube.
7. Deburr the tube. Voilà, you have a draft hopback!

Usage Instructions

1. Check the placement of the PVC gasket in the lid.
2. Place the stainless-steel tube, holes down, into the well on the bottom of the housing.
3. Stuff about 2 ounces of fresh whole hops or the ingredient of your choice around the stainless rod. Enjoy the aroma!
4. Push the tube into its gasket and screw down the housing lid.
5. Securely attach the serving line to the output side of the housing.
6. Securely attach the keg line to the input side. It's important to get this right, or the beer will always pour foamy.
7. Attach the draft hopback to your keg.

8. Open the pressure relief on the filter housing and allow beer to slowly fill the chamber.

9. Once it's filled, close the housing, let it sit for a couple of minutes, and then let the beer flow!

If you'd like to be able to compare regular beer with draft-hopped, attach the input line from the keg to a Y connector. One output of the Y should go straight to a serving line or faucet. The other output gets connected to the draft hopback. Now it's possible to try a beer two separate ways from one keg!

LET'S TALK ABOUT BEER GLASSES

As the saying goes, the chalice from the palace has the brew that is true . . . or is it the vessel with the pestle? Regardless of palace intrigue, if you're reading this book, we hope we don't have to educate you on the value of drinking beer from a glass and not from the bottle.

But let's talk glassware and the rise of the marketing aspects. We've been inundated in the last thirty years with the talk of special glassware properties and a need for precisely the right glass for our brew. Much of this has risen from the habits of Belgian brewers with their specially logoed glasses that are used for service. But if you look around now, you'll see special glasses being produced by big companies such as Riedel for breweries, such as Boston Beer (Sam Adams), or for styles, such as the IPA glass. How much of this has a real organoleptic impact and how much is marketing?

Whatever the answer, there's a reason to have a few different glasses. The primary thing you need out of a glass is how far it lets your nose in and how much it concentrates the aromas. For instance, the standard straight-sided pint glass flows up and out, allowing aroma compounds and CO_2 to rapidly offgas. A Belgian chalice offers a wide and shallow dispersal, leading to a cloud effect above the glass. On the other hand, a brandy snifter and Belgian tulip glass curl back in, trapping the aromas and offering a heady hit of sensation when you take a sip.

Here's what we think you need in minimalist beer glass cabinet:

- **Straight-sided pint glass or British nonic pint:** This glass is just the ticket for all your malty and hoppy beer needs. This style is no-nonsense, but it doesn't concentrate your aromas at all. Nonic pints are a little wider to accommodate a full British Imperial Pint.
- **Belgian chalice glass:** This gives you wide access to the aroma. Think of it as a shallower glass for stronger beers to breathe.
- **Weizen glass:** You need one of these tall monsters to deal with the voluminous head of a proper wheat beer.
- **Snifter or tulip glass:** This is for the beers where you want to trap the aromas, such as big Belgian beers, eisbocks, barleywines, or a Triple IPAs. Be careful, as some of the big snifters will hold a dangerous amount of your strong brews.
- **Your favorite glass:** No judging . . . we all have a few nonstandard favorites!

Beer-Clean Glasses

Everyone knows that beer is best served from a clean glass. The whole reason pilsner became the world's dominant beer form was thanks to the fascinating show of bubbles, white foam, and golden gleam visible through inexpensive modern manufactured vessels. So, you've got this, right? A little soap, a little scrub, and you're done! Not really. It turns out that the optimum beer experience is incredibly sensitive to all sorts of debris, including soap. Your dishwasher isn't the answer either;

dishwashers don't do an adequate job cleaning the residue, and any rinse aid you use will cleave foam like nobody's business.

The answer is fairly straightforward: get a glass scrubber. Ever watch how bar staff clean their glasses? They scrub the glasses in a sink filled with a detergent and a scrubber. Then it's just a rinse and a dunk in a sanitizing solution before leaving the glasses to dry. Despite most folks using the terms interchangably, soap is not detergent, and detergents are not soaps. They both encourage the combination of fat and water, allowing you to carry away fatty residues. However, soaps are created by saponification of fats with a base (such as lye). On the other hand, detergents get their power from being chemical surfactants. Essentially, they make water wetter and increase penetration of the stained surface. They also tend to rinse cleaner, which is why you see detergents used for applications like dishwashers and clothes washing machines.

You can easily replicate the beer cleanliness of a three-basin sink with a cheap sink scrubber brush. The two-brush assembly attaches with suction cups to the sink floor and allows you to quickly scrub glasss. Dunk a glass in some PBW or OxiClean solution, scrub it, rinse it with hot water, and check it out. You should see no streaks, leftover yeast, mineral buildup, or other impurities. At this point the glass is ready to go, but if you want to sanitize it, hit it with a spray of Star San. And that, boys and girls, is the secret to beer-clean glasses.

For the cheap 'n' easy solution, try a salt scrub. Coat the inside of a damp beer glass with salt, wipe it around thoroughly with a paper towel, then rinse it well, unless you like salty beer! The first time you try this, you won't believe how it improves the foam stand of your beer.

THE DIGITAL REVOLUTION

If you're technically obsessed, you're no doubt aware that brewing is ripe for automation. With some parts and know-how, you can really step up your temperature control and brew repeatability. Be careful, though! Some brewers head down this path and get so lost that we never see them brew anymore.

FROM RIMS TO HERMS

When we first started brewing, a recirculating infusion mash system (RIMS) setup was the hot ticket for home brewery automation. The idea, credited to Rodney Morris, is to pump your mash liquor directly across a heating element that is energized to different levels to hit a set rest temperature and maintain it. It requires a big electric heating element along with a few temperature probes and a controller of some variety. A proportional-integral-derivative (PID) controller, which uses fancypants math to help slowly steer a detected value (mash temperature) to a controlled value (target rest temperature), was the tool of choice for this effort. Here's the math:

$$MV(t) = (K_p \times e(t)) + (K_i \int_o^t e(t)dt) + (K_d \times \frac{d}{dt} \times e(t))$$

The first set of parens is the effect of the proportional control. The second parens is the integral control, and the third is the derivative control. Clear as mud now? All you really need to know is that with a PID, you tune the K values and the system does the rest of the math and calculates the amount of change needed in the system. Kinda spiffy.

PIDs are old-school and require a certain amount of tinkering to dial in. And electrical knowledge is needed to pull a RIMS together. So people have started to drift toward an easier, plumbing-based solution for mash automation: the heat-exchanged recirculating mash system (HERMS).

A HERMS consists of a copper immersion coil submerged in your hot liquor tank (HLT). During the mash, you pump wort out of your mash tun and into the coil. The wort flows through the coil and back to the top of the mash tun. During its trip through the coil, it sucks heat from the pot. The result is a gentle heating of the mash liquor that avoids any risk of scorching.

While you can use a PID for a HERMS, it's overkill. What you do need is a controller with a thermometer probe. The probe stays in the mash, and when the temperature falls below the set breakpoint, it energizes a socket connected to a pump. The pump feeds the wort through the kettle, raising the heat. The other thing you need to worry about is the temperature of the HLT. The hotter the HLT, the more heat it contains, and the faster your mash will heat up, but the hotter HLT will also allow you to overshoot your target temp before the probe detects it.

NEW CONTROLLERS, NEW USES

Just a few years ago, sensors were made only for the really big guys. But now, most of us have witnessed the rise (or return) of a maker culture. For these folks, a workshop involves not only drills and lathes, but also electronics. A few of these groups have created smart gizmos for those of us in the homebrew world who never took any circuit design classes (or whose circuit design classes were obliterated over the course of many years and pints).

One invention of note is a kit microcontroller board from Italy called the Arduino. The Italian design community who put together the open-source board can be found at www.arduino.cc. From one initial project board designed to spur creativity, the Arduino movement has created new boards and add-on kits that allow you to read temperature sensors, access the Internet, and control motors and relays. (All of this from a little board that starts at about fifteen dollars!) For almost everything that you'd want to do in a brewhouse, you'll probably want to start with the Arduino Uno R3, which costs a little more. If you've got that board and a little simple coding know-how, you can start monitoring temperatures and controlling pieces in a hurry.

If you're more of a computer type, grab a Raspberry Pi, a credit card–size fully functional Linux computer for the shockingly low price of twenty-five to thirty-five dollars. Turn it on, plug it into a monitor, and you've got yourself a minicomputer.

Since these boards and computers were born from the open-source software community, there's a sharing ethos that runs through the people playing with it. That sounds familiar, doesn't it? And since many programmers run on a delicate balance of caffeine and ethanol, there's a large portion of the community obsessed with doing beer-related projects and providing plans and code for free or for a small donation.

Of course, more and more projects are coming online every day to bring sensors to the homebrew level. Here are a few of note:

- Brewtroller (www.oscsys.com/projects/brewtroller): This custom Arduino controller system and shop includes all the parts that you need to create a fully automated brewery with very slick controls. Want automated valves and recirculation? They've got them. Want to control your brewery from your phone? Done!

- BrewPi (www.brewpi.com): This project uses both a Raspberry Pi and an Arduino controller to control and log temperatures of your brews. Control and log multiple brews, check the status via the Internet, make changes and run profiles from your computer. And that PID equation from above? That's totally what this thing uses to help control the temperature!

- Kegbot (kegbot.org): Have you ever sat in a modern craft bar and lusted after the fancy computerized draft menus you're seeing pop up everywhere? The Kegbot project aims to give you that at home using an Arduino board with optional bits for an interface to a tablet or computer. It allows you to track how much beer is being poured and have your drinkers rate your beers!

- The BeerBug (thebeerbug.com): The BeerBug will provide Bluetooth signals to a computer and give you constant feedback on your beer's fermentation, including the temperature.
  Drew: Since this technology is rapidly evolving, you'll want to keep an eye on the book website (www.ExperimentalBrew.com). Denny and I will keep you up to date on the latest things we've spotted. I really geek out over this stuff!

OFF-THE-WALL TECHNIQUES

TRADITIONALLY, ALMOST EVERYTHING that went into beer went into the kettle. Even the more unconventional ingredients were subjected to a boil before the beer started to ferment. But as brewers began to think about and experiment with more untraditional flavors, they also came up with different, often more effective, ways to introduce those ingredients. Now it's common to add flavorings in the primary or secondary fermenter, or even at the time of packaging.

We'll show you a variety of ways to do that in this chapter, and we'll also cover other experiments that push the limits of your brewery. Whether you want to fake an authentic cask, make your first Eisbeer, concoct your own invert sugar, or dabble in soda-making, we bet there's something here you haven't done yet. Heck, we even have some projects for your spent grain.

FLAVOR SHOTS

Ignore the nonsense that says anything added to the cold side of brewing is cheating. Two of the most important techniques in this chapter are all about adding flavors outside the kettle. Keep in mind that while both of the techniques have the same goal—to create an intensely flavored liquid you can add to your beer—they extract different qualities from the same ingredients. For example, think of the warm, earthy cinnamon you taste in a freshly mulled hot cider. That cinnamon character is one you will only get through making a tea. If you make a cinnamon tincture, the extraction will remind you of the bright red-hot heat you experience when eating a cinnamon candy. Of course, you can create both a tea and an extract and play with flavoring the beer in different ratios to achieve a desired profile.

TEA

A flavoring tea, in this case, is a lot like making a really strong pot of tea. Go figure. You'll get the best results when the water used is hot but not boiling. The advantage of an herb or spice tea is the speed at which it's ready to use. It beats tinctures by days. However, unlike a tincture, the tea won't remain shelf stable for very long. Don't worry; it's fine once it's in the beer.

You Will Need

- 1 pint water
- 2–4 tablespoons of herb or spice (for vanilla, use 2–4 beans)
- Fine mesh strainer
- Coffee filter
- 1-pint Mason jar with lid

Instructions

1. Bring the pint of water to a boil and let it cool to approximately 180°F. Stir in the herbs and allow the mixture to steep for 15 minutes.
2. Strain the mixture through a fine mesh strainer lined with a coffee filter into the Mason jar and seal tightly. Store in the fridge and use within 2–3 weeks.

Want to sound fancy? Don't call it an herbal tea. Call it a tisane instead. This is a word derived from the ancient Greek for "barley water." Don't ask why; just be happy it's beer related!

TINCTURE

You'll sometimes hear people refer to this as an extract, but we prefer tincture since that's the precise term for an ethanol-based extract. Turns out that ethanol is a heck of a solvent and can strip most essential oils out of spice, herbs, fruits, and so on. Make no mistake: it's the essential oils that we're concerned with. Sometimes it's the cinnamaldehyde and ethyl cinnamate found in whole cinnamon bark we're after, other times it's the limonene and citral found in lemon zest. Tinctures require a little bit of time to make but produce stable and intense flavors. The goal is to make a strongly flavored shot so that you don't need to pour a ton of it into the beer.

Denny: I've gotta chime in here. In general, I don't care for alcohol-based tinctures. The added alcohol often adds a heat to the beer that I don't care for. I avoid this technique unless I have no other choice for using an additive. But that's my opinion. Many people use tinctures with no objections. The best way to find out what you like is to try it yourself!

You Will Need

- 6 oz decent vodka (not the cheapest rotgut, but nothing too expensive)
- 1–4 oz herb or spice
- 1-pint Mason jar with a plastic lid (Plastic lids don't rust like regular canning lids.)

Instructions

1. Mix the vodka and herb or spice in the Mason jar. Secure the plastic lid tightly.
2. Shake the jar at least twice daily for 4–6 days. Taste the tincture. When it's as potent as you'd like, strain the mixture through a fine mesh strainer lined with a coffee filter.
3. Return the tincture to the Mason jar and seal the lid. Store for up to 2 years and use as needed.

Variants

If you want to play with some other flavors, try rum or bourbon instead of vodka for complementary extractions, such as vanilla beans.

If you have an old-fashioned whipping siphon, you can make a tincture in under ten seconds. Load the siphon with your booze and your spice or herb. Seal the container and crack one cartridge of CO_2 or nitrous oxide into the siphon. Shake for a few seconds and then, holding the siphon with the spout facing up, press the dispense lever and rapidly vent the pressure. Open up the siphon and strain the infused vodka through a fine mesh sieve. This makes a great party trick to doctor one beer in many different ways (or if you're spiritually minded, it allows you to create an impressively varied vodka cocktail list).

STEAM DISTILLATION

So let's say you hate the effect of alcohol tinctures. It's entirely possible to make a steam distillation extract, and sometimes this method is preferable. A quick note on legality: in pretty much all parts of the world (except New Zealand) home distillation comes with restrictions; namely, no home distillation of drinking ethanol is allowed. Depending on your local laws, you can likely still distill water, essential oils, perfumes, and fuel alcohol. Just no moonshining!

We'll start with a classic: rosemary. Trying to make an alcoholic tincture with most heavily pitchy and piney things is an exercise in woe. The essential oils are protected by nasty, sticky pitch the alcohol will dissolve. Instead you need to use steam in order to bust free the aromatic power without the terpenic pitchy flavors of other extraction methods.

The process is fairly straightforward. You create a closed environment that you cram a bunch of your desired plant matter into. You run steam through the plant matter and direct the steam to an area where it can cool and condense.

You Will Need

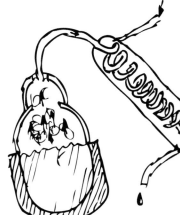

- Large stock pot with draining basket and lid
- 2 feet of copper wire
- Glass bowl
- Tongs
- Gloves
- Ice
- Water
- A few handfuls of rosemary (or other material for distillation)

Instructions

1. Add a quart of clean, filtered water to the bottom of the stock pot (this is the "retort" in distillation terms). Steam distallion is inefficient, so fill the basket with as much plant matter as you can.

2. Take copper wire and run it through a pair of the topmost holes of the straining basket. You want to have two wires running the across the center of the basket. Your glass catch bowl will sit on these wires above the plant material. Perch the bowl on the wires. Take the pot lid and flip it upside down so the peak of the lid is over the glass bowl. The whole basket, plant matter, bowl, and lid are placed over the water in the stock pot. The water will be heated to steam. This will flow through the plant matter and condense back to water/essential oil on the cold metal lid and run to the center of the lid, dropping into the glass bowl.

3. Turn on the heat and wait until you see steam escaping the pot. Add a bunch of ice to the upside-down lid. Wait until the steam is almost gone and with tongs and gloves, carefully remove the bowl. It should now be filled with a very fragrant water called a hydrosol. When you let the hydrosol cool, you'll notice a faint shimmer on the surface—that's your essential oil!

4. If you allow the hydrosol to settle and lightly freeze, you should be able to extract the oil with few problems. But doing so is not necessary for our purposes. Pure essential oils are extremely potent and not all of them are safe for human consumption in sizeable quantities. Using the hydrosol mixture as-is is safer and gives you a larger margin for error.

USING A TEA, TINCTURE, OR DISTILLATION

Whether you're planning to add a tea, tincture, or distillation, you need to wait until the beer has fermented completely and is ready for packaging. You can also use this process to add other flavorings, like liquor or coffee.

On packaging day, grab a pint of the beer in question and pour half into a measuring cup so you know you have exactly eight ounces. Add a small measured amount of the tea or tincture (~1.0 ml or smaller). Stir and taste. Repeat this process until you've achieved the appropriate taste level. Remember to top up the half pint with fresh beer if you draw down too far. You can also pour multiple beer samples and dose them each with a different amout. Then you can compare them to see which you like best.

Multiply the amount of extract added to the cup by the number of half pints remaining in the batch—or the part of the batch that you want to doctor. To save some time, you can assume you have 78 half pints remaining for a 5-gallon batch since you started with 80 half pints and used 2 for sampling. Add the amount indicated to the keg or bottling bucket and proceed with your beer transfer as usual.

Example: You have 5 gallons of wheat beer that you want to doctor with coriander and lemon peel tinctures. But you only want half of it doctored. After tasting and blending, you determine that 1 milliliter is sufficient for the coriander, but 2 milliliters are needed for the lemon tincture in a half pint. Since there are 40 half pints in 2.5 gallons, you have 38 half pints remaining in the portion to be doctored. That means 38 milliliters of coriander tincture and 76 milliliters of lemon tincture are added to the bottling bucket or keg. In English units that's roughly 1.25 ounces of coriander tincture and 2.5 ounces of lemon tincture.

FORCE INJECTION OF FLAVORS

Back on page 66 we talked about constructing your very own draft hop infuser. Its normal mode of operation is stuck at the end of a keg, just before a draft faucet. Fill it with hops, coffee, mushrooms, or whatever else you want.

It's a great gizmo, but for the average homebrewer it's not terribly practical. Outside a party situation, you have to figure out how to store the infuser (do you let the beer continue to sit in contact or do you disconnect it and drink that last pint, toss out the hops and so on, and get ready to go again?

Why not just use the infuser to infuse the beer from keg to keg? Remember, we're normally building these things out of cartridge filter housings. When filtering, you're using a fiber mesh filter to trap all the undesirable particles. You slowly push uncarbonated beer from the source keg through the filter housing and filter media and out into a receiving keg.

So what we propose is filter through your flavoring material instead of a filter straight into another keg. Boom! You now have flavor-infused beer that you never have to worry about (or waste a ton of hops) to make happen. For anyone who just heard the word *torpedo* in their head: this was inspired by Sierra Nevada's invention of their fermentation dry hopping torpedo.

You Will Need

- 1 draft infuser (See page 66.)
- 1 beverage line with a black liquid-out fitting

ONE NIGHT IN TIJUANA

By Drew

I used tinctures to great effect to rescue a beer that had been accidentally scorched in the mash, turning it from something that was trashed to something insanely popular! The beer had started life as a Golden Oat Barleywine, but a scorched character from the mash carried through and wouldn't age out. So, I hit the keg with Tequila-soaked oak cubes. After aging with the beer for a week, the smokiness of the tequila and oak successfully masked the scorch character, but it left a little too much flavor from the tequila. To correct for that, I used a few small additions of coriander, red chile pepper, black pepper, and lime zest tinctures. This not only cut the oily character, it also invoked Mexico. Thus the beer became One Night in Tijuana.

For 5.5 Gallons at 1.082, 63 IBUs, 6.6 SRM, 9.3% ABV

GRAIN BILL

12 lbs	Maris Otter Malt
1.25 lbs	Flaked Oats (toast at 325°F for 20 minutes and stir often)
1.25 lbs	Thomas Fawcett Oat Malt
1.0 lbs	Brown sugar

MASH SCHEDULE

Rest	138°F	15 minutes
Rest	153°F	60 minutes
Mash Out	168°F	10 minutes

HOPS

1 oz	Warrior	Pellet	17% AA	90 minutes
0.75 oz	Amarillo	Pellet	8.2% AA	5 minutes
0.75 oz	Citra	Pellet	13.4% AA	5 minutes

YEAST

WLP001 California Ale or WY1056 American Ale

OTHER INGREDIENTS

2 oz	French oak beans soaked in tequila (mine were soaked for many months)
2 oz	Mexican coriander extract (2 ounces of coriander by weight, roughly cracked and soaked in 4 ounces of vodka for two weeks)
1 oz	Lime zest extract (1 zested lime soaked in 4 ounces of vodka for two weeks)
20 drops	Red Pepper extract (2 tablespoons red pepper flakes soaked in 4 ounces of vodka for two weeks)
20 drops	Black Pepper extract (30 whole peppercorns soaked in 4 ounces of vodka for two weeks)

Note: For the extracts above, shake often over the 2-week infusion period to ensure you get the full flavor.

- 1 keg, filled with fermented beer (Uncarbonated makes the cleanest transfer, but some swear that carbonation helps strips volatiles.)
- 1 empty keg to receive the filtered beer
- Flavoring—hops, coffee, chocolate, fruit, herbs, spices—enough to flavor 5 gallons

Instructions

1. Remove the draft line from the output of the filter housing. Replace it with another line with a black QD fitting from your receiving keg. Sanitize the infuser.
2. Make sure the receiving keg is flushed with CO_2.
3. Fill the infuser with the flavorings of your choice. Stuff it full of hops, coffee, frozen fruit, or whatever floats your boat. With some items, like spices, you'll only need a few teaspoons. In general, look at how much of an item you'd use for a 5-gallon batch and load a little more than that in the infuser. Some ingredients, like fruit, are even better when you go bananas!
4. Hook the receiving keg up to the infuser and open the relief valve (or other quick disconnect) and let the infuser flood with CO_2. Pull the receiving keg off the infuser.
5. Hook the source keg of carbonated beer to the input of the infuser. Hook the output to your receiving keg's liquid out. This will create less turbulent flow in the receiving keg.
6. Gently release some of the pressure in the receiving keg and allow the infuser to fill with beer. Let the beer pour slowly into the new keg. Allow the pressure to equalize until the flow stops.
7. Let the beer infuse for 5 minutes before releasing the receiving keg's pressure again. Repeat until all the beer has flowed through the infuser. If you think the flavoring needs a double charge, disconnect everything, sanitize the infuser again, replace the flavorings, reconnect everything, and repeat.

CANNED STARTERS

In the case of starters, it's clear that the traditional process has its downside. You have to measure extract, boil water and mix in the extract, wait for it to cool, sanitize a growler, pitch the yeast, and so on. Well, what if we told you there was a way to make your starters superfast by concentrating most of your time well in advance?

You Will Need

- A pressure canner (23-quart size or larger)
- Mason jars: A case of half-gallon jars (6 jars) and a case of quart jars (12 jars) or a case of pint jars (12 jars)
  Note: Why two different jar sizes? Not only does it allow you to maximize the amount of wort processed at any time, but it gives you flexibility by allowing you to use a pint jar to start an old yeast culture or a slurry of yeast from the bottom of a beer without stressing the yeast out.
- 8.25 pounds of pale malt or about 6 pounds pale dry malt extract (DME)

Instructions

1. Wash all the jars. Don't worry about sanitizing them.
2. Mash 8.25 pounds of pale malt at 150°F for 60 minutes. Sparge and collect 6 gallons of wort. The gravity should be around 1.036. Note: If you don't want to spend time mashing, you can

instead directly weigh in 6.4 ounces of pale DME per quart into each half-gallon jar (3.2 ounces for a quart jar, 1.6 ounces for a pint jar), add water, seal, and shake.

3. Fill each jar to just below where the shoulder turns to the neck. Wipe the lip and add a lid. Screw down a band until it's finger-tight.

4. Stack as many jars as will fit at a time in one layer in the canner. Make sure the included jar rack is on the bottom of the pot. Jars should not sit on the pot bottom. Add water to fill the canner to halfway up the jars.

5. Read your instruction manual for your canner. Once you have it set up, bring the canner to 15 pounds per square inch (psi) and hold there for 15 minutes. Don't walk away! Turn off the heat, let the canner return to normal pressure, and carefully remove your jars.

6. Set the jars aside and let them cool. You should hear them ping as they stop boiling. Once cool, slip off the bands and check the lids. If one isn't sucked in or is popped, that jar is no good. Don't fret if you see a bunch of flaky material; that's just hot break.

7. Repeat the process with the next batch of cans as everything else is cooling off. The process takes a few hours, but you end up with absolutely sterile jars of starter wort that can hang out on the shelf for years.

That's it! When it's time to make a starter, just grab a can and a growler. Sanitize both, pop the lid, pour the wort in, and pitch the yeast! It's that easy.

BREWER'S INVERT SUGAR

Unlike the fussy Germans, the British have never exactly been afraid of adding this, that, or the other to the brew kettles if they thought it would give an appropriate kick and help keep costs low. One such fundamental ingredient is brewer's invert sugar.

Invert sugar is a syrup produced from sucrose, also known as table sugar. In the inversion process, sucrose is split into its two constituent molecules (fructose and glucose). The resulting syrup is many times sweeter than table sugar, and thanks to the structure of the molecule, it won't crystallize.

There's a debate amongst brewers whether or not it's necessary to invert sugar. Yeast produce an series of enzymes, invertases, that naturally cleave the sucrose, since fructose and glucose are more accessible to yeast than sucrose. But traditionalists argue that the flavors of specially made brewer's invert sugars can't be reproduced with simple sugar additions. Since you can't buy these syrups at homebrewer quantities, they've remained relatively unexplored at our level … until now.

MAKING BREWER'S INVERT SUGAR

Brewing boffins Nic Henke and Kristen England, big believers in this tradition, set about making their own syrups that would replicate the increasingly dark and complex flavors found in Brewers #1–4. Now typical instructions for making invert syrup require mixing sugar, an acid, yeast nutrient, and water and bringing it to a boil. Once the water's gone, you carefully raise the temperature to a fixed level for 20–200 minutes based on how dark you want it. It's a pain to get it right. For Henke and England, the key was taking advantage of a common hyperboiled sugar syrup: blackstrap molasses. By mixing small portions (1–25 percent by weight) to simple invert sugar (either homemade or with Lyle's Golden Syrup from the UK), they've reliably replicated the profiles of commercial syrups. Their approach was developed and validated by their talks with commercial producers. Not only is it easy to pull off, it's also highly consistent.

In the instructions that follow, you can either make your own invert sugar syrup by following steps 1-6, or you can buy the admittedly pricey Lyle's Golden Syrup, an invert sugar imported from the UK equivalent to Brewer's Invert Sugar #1. If you go that route, you can skip directly to step 7 and skip over the ingredients for the homemade invert sugar syrup as well.

You Will Need

- 1 small nonstick saucepan
- Silicone spatula
- Small digital scale (reads up to 500 grams)
- Invert white sugar (ingredients and instructions follow) or Lyle's Golden Syrup
- Blackstrap molasses: The key is to find a high-quality, licorice-oriented blackstrap molasses. Henke and England recommend the following, all sourced in the United States: Plantation Blackstrap Molasses, Golden Barrel Blackstrap, or other food grade blackstrap. Regardless of the variety you choose, you'll want to play around to adjust for your particular brand of molasses.

Invert Sugar Recipe

For 2.5 pints of homemade invert sugar syrup, you will also need:

- 2.5 lbs raw sugar
- 2.5 pints filtered water
- 1 teaspoon lactic acid at 88%
- ½ cup (4 fluid ounces) light corn syrup

Instructions

1. Heat the water to boiling.
2. Turn off the heat, slowly add the sugar, and stir until it's completely dissolved.
3. Add the lactic acid.
4. Immediately reduce the heat to medium-high, and set a candy thermometer alarm for 230°F (reduce your stove if you are heating more than 3°F/minute). Stir occasionally until simmering starts.
5. Once the mixture hits 230°F, set the alarm for 240°F. Slowly reduce the heat to keep the mixture's temperature stable. You want to slowly ramp up to 240°F, as once you go over it is very tough to get the temperature down.

6. Once the alarm goes off at 240°F, immediately reduce the heat to keep the mixture at 240°F. It is okay to hit 245°F, but keep under 250°F. Keep at 240°F for approximately 10 minutes.

7. Blend your invert sugar solution (left columns) or Golden Syrup (right columns) with the appropriate amount of molasses. Once you blend your white syrup with the molasses, store it in a jar in the fridge. It will last an eternity. However, you'll have to gently warm it in order to pour it.

Syrup	SRM/EBC	Invert Sugar (g)	Blackstrap (g)	Lyle's Golden Syrup (g)	Blackstrap (g)
Invert #1	15/30	495	5	500	0
Invert #2	33/65	489.17	10.83	494.17	5.83
Invert #3	66/130	478.33	21.67	483.33	16.67
Black Invert	178/350	441.67	58.33	446.67	53.33
Invert #4	305/600	400.00	100.00	405.00	95.00

FAKING A CASK

If you've never heard the term *real ale*, where have you been? Real ale is naturally carbonated by yeast in a barrel-like container and served via gravity or pump. It's lighter in carbonation, and generally served warmer at 50°F–55°F (as opposed to American standard 38°F). Cask service, at least as it's done in Britain, yields a softer, more open beer that expresses more of the yeast's esters and the earthy, floral nature of traditional British hops. Even American hops become perfumelike, with less of that harsher, piney cattiness they can express.

But here's an important thing that a good number of people get confused about, both at home and in the professional realm: sticking force-carbonated beer into a cask and serving it via a hand pump doesn't make your beer a real ale. For it to be fully real, it must be 100 percent naturally carbonated. If you skip that step, you've made faux ale.

If you look online, you'll find a single pin (a 5.4-gallon cask) with parts for gravity service costs hundreds. That's enough to stick in anyone's craw. However, if you have a keg, then you can easily fake it for a few bucks.

You Will Need

- 5-gallon corny keg
- CO_2 tank
- Priming sugar
- Dry hops (optional)
- Ice
- 2-foot serving line with liquid-side fitting but no faucet
- Soft wooden spile or cotton ball
- 2-foot serving line with gas-side fitting and cobra faucet

1. Purge your keg with CO_2. Add enough corn sugar to the keg to prime the keg for 1.3–2.0 volumes and fill it with beer. Add any whole hops that you'd like for dry hopping.
2. Attach the lid and seal it with a jolt of CO_2 at 10 psi. Lay the keg on its side, positioning the gas side connector on the bottom. Let the beer naturally carbonate for about 2 weeks by keeping it at room temperature.
3. Move the keg to the serving location and let settle for a few days.
4. The day you want to tap the keg, start by chilling the keg down with ice: Fill freezer bags with ice and drape them over the keg. Cover with towels to slow the melting. Secure a serving line to the liquid side fitting and shove a soft wooden spile or cotton ball into the end of the tube where you would normally attach a faucet. This will let the keg breathe. Attach the liquid fitting to the liquid post, which should be on top. Secure the hose to the top side of the keg. Let the cask breathe for a few hours.
5. Attach a gas fitting to the post, but instead of connecting to your CO_2 tank, connect it to a short line with a cobra faucet.

Congrats! You now have a cask of real ale and approximately three days to drink it. As the keg empties, prop the far (keg bottom) end up to ensure the flow of beer.

Alternatively, you can use a technique designed to replicate some of the impact of the real ale experience but have it last longer. Repeat all of the above. After drawing a pint or two, replace the air inlet tube with a liquid fitting hooked up to a CO_2 tank set to 1 psi. The idea is that the limited exposure to oxygen from the first two pints will slowly age the beer in the same gentle fashion as regular cask service but won't let it go too far.

ICE ICE BABY (EISBIER)

Here's a favorite technique of ours that more than likely was discovered completely by accident: eisbier. All it takes is a forgetful brewer, a few freezing-cold days, and you've got a discovery: when beer freezes, there's a liquid core of deliciousness surrounded by frozen ice walls. The technique is most associated with the Bavarian town of Kulmbach and its famous beer, the deadly smooth and sweet eisbock. Supposedly, a lazy brewer left a barrel of strong doppelbock out in the winter night. In the morning the brewer discovered the concentrated core of supermalty, superpotent superbock. The freezing had caused the beer to clear and smooth out while concentrating the alcohol.

Let's be very clear about this: eisbier is a completely different creature than the nasty "ice beer" that every major brewery came out with in the 1990s. Two Canadian brewers, Molson and Labatt, looked to other industries to speed up their production of lager beer. Remember, time is money! The faster you get beer to the shelves, the faster the money can flow in. Taking a look at what frozen juice manufacturers were doing, Labatt's patented a method of barely freezing part of their beer to create heavy ice crystals that sink to the bottom of the fermenter. In the process of forming and falling, the crystals trap and drag various haze-inducing proteins, particles, and yeast. Once safely trapped at the bottom, the still liquid beer is drawn away from the ice and reconstituted with an addition of water to bring it back closer to original strength and gravity. In other words it's partially frozen, watered-down beer that's designed to be sold fast. The thing that's kept this beer on the market is its reputation for being stronger. It provides a quick drunk that's more socially acceptable than malt liquor.

Despite the dubious quality of the mass-produced beer, the method used was sound. Besides the watering-down process, it works on a similar principle as making eisbeer. Unlike water, which freezes at 32°F, ethanol doesn't freeze until -173°F. This allows brewers to perform what is known as fractional freezing, colloquially (although incorrectly) known as freeze distilling.

When beer freezes slowly, small ice crystals form that are filled mostly with water. The ice entrains proteins, yeasts, and a very wee bit of alcohol. As you remove more water from solution, the more concentrated the alcohol becomes in the remaining beer. The trick to making an eisbier lies in the timing. Despite its low freezing point, if you leave a beer freezing long enough, ice will eventually trap all the alcohol, leaving you with nothing but a beer ice cube.

Globally there's an on-again-off-again pissing contest to produce the world's strongest beer, and it's all about this technique. For a while the record passed back and forth between Boston Beer (Sam Adams) and Dogfish Head with their Utopias and World Wide Stout pushing the boundaries of what was possible with fermentation. Utopias won out, landing around 27 percent ABV. The battle restarted when Scottish brewers Brew Dog started chasing the record, but instead of focusing on pushing fermentation, they and other brewers used fractional freezing to push to the current record of 67 percent ABV (134 proof) from another Scottish brewer, Brewmeister.

Frankly, all this is sound and fury that doesn't mean a whole lot. However, it is interesting in that it blows the bottom end of this chart of expected maximal extraction at a given freezing temperature. (But we suspect that's because Brew Dog and the others involved in the race for strongest beer are performing multiple fractional freezing steps and the chart assumes a single pass.)

Freezing Temperature (°F)	Expected Maximum ABV (%)
0	14
-10	20
-20	27
-30	30

MAKE AN EISBEER

Ready to take your own crack at an eisbeer? All it takes is a steady source of cold and patience. Okay, and a beer like the World Wide Doppelbock (page 86). Kegs make this task really easy because you can transfer the concentrated beer off the ice. No kegs? You can freeze your beer in a bucket and pour the beer through a screened funnel, but that's a pain.

What You Need

- An 8% ABV or higher beer that has finished fermentation
- Freezer
- 2 kegs and transfer equipment

- Serving line with cobra faucet
- CO_2 tank

Instructions

1. Make sure your fermentation is complete and rack the beer into a cleaned and sanitized keg. Seal the lid with 10 psi of CO_2, but don't continue to carbonate it! Turn off the CO_2.
2. Set the keg in a freezer or a cold place that will stay below 32°F (ideally around 25°F) for 24 hours.
3. Check the beer by shaking the keg. If it feels and sounds slushy, you're ready for the next step. If the beer isn't slushy, check it every 2 hours until it's ready. If the beer is frozen beyond slush, allow it to thaw at room temperature and check it every hour.
4. Push the beer that's still liquid out of the keg into a waiting keg.
5. Carbonate as usual and enjoy.

Eisbeer ABV

To determine your ABV, just use this equation:

$$ABV\ eisedbeer = (ABV_{Original} \times Volume_{Original}) / Volume_{Remaining}$$

For example, imagine you have 5 gallons of doppelbock that is 8 percent, and you want to create an eisbock. Freeze the beer and end up with enough to fill a 3-gallon keg. What's the new ABV?

$$ABV\ eisedbeer = (8.0 \times 5.0) / 3.0$$
$$ABV\ eisedbeer = 40 / 3.0$$
$$ABV\ eisedbeer = 13.33\%\ ABV$$

A word of caution: these numbers will end up a bit higher than your actual beer because some alcohol will be locked up in the ice crystals. However, you'll be close enough.

WORLD WIDE DOPPELBOCK

By Drew

For 5.5 gallons at 1.099, 47.5 IBUs, 19.9 SRM, 9.9% ABV

GRAIN BILL

20 lbs	Munich 10°L Malt
2.0 lbs	Munich 30°L Malt
12 oz	Crystal 120°L Malt
6 oz	Melanoidin Malt
3 oz	Carafa II

MASH SCHEDULE

Rest	122°F	30 minutes
Rest	150°F	60 minutes

HOPS

0.75 oz	Magnum	Pellet	14.8% AA	90 minutes
0.5 oz	Tettnager Tettnang	Pellet	4.9% AA	15 minutes

YEAST

WY2206 Bavarian Lager or WLP833 German Bock

DRY HOPS IN THE BOTTLE (OR KEG)

You can put hops everywhere else—why not in the bottle as well? It seems straightforward; just pop a few pellets into place and let 'em sit and add their magic to the beer within. Yet it's surprisingly tricky. Here's how you do it and keep your sanity. Hat tip to Scott Bert of www.BertusBrewery.com, who offered the original version of this technique as a way to test dry hops using Bud Light.

What You Need

- 12-ounce bottles of beer
- 6 hop pellets per bottle
- Extra caps
- Capper

Instructions

1. Prime and bottle your beer as usual. Make absolutely sure the beer is done fermenting before it hits the bottle. Seal and wait until the beer is fully carbonated, which is usually about 3 weeks.
2. Chill the beer to near freezing temperature. Prepare a 6-pellet dose of your favorite hop or hop blend for each bottle.
3. One bottle at a time, working quickly, follow this procedure: Pop the cap, drop 6 pellets into the bottle, recap the bottle, and invert to mix the pellets.
4. Store your newly dry-hopped beer upright for 2 weeks at refrigerator temperatures. (This reduces oxidation damage during infusion.)
5. Carefully open and decant through a sieve. Even with the beer ice-cold, you should expect some wild foaming.

Variants

Mix up the hops! Nothing says you've got to add the exact same hops to each bottle. Make one bottle all Cascade, make another all Citra, and so on. Mark the bottles well, and you'll have a tasting party in a six-pack!

Dry hopping in a keg or growler is much easier. For every gallon, add 1 ounce of hop pellets. Just make sure you have the hops well secured in a tied mesh bag. It also helps to have a screen on your keg dip tube. If not, you too can enjoy the experience of a DIPA geyser smacking you in the face after a poppet had to be removed to clear it of hop debris.

BRETTANOMYCES AT BOTTLING

Whether in the bottle or the keg, *Brettanomyces* strains can add interesting complexity—leathery, spicy, vinous, haylike aromas and flavors—with very little work from you. The secret: *Brett* can consume longer chain trisaccharides that are not accessible to regular brewer's yeast.

COSMOPOLITAN TROUT

By Drew

This beer is inspired by the monks of Orval and the crazy global nature of our hobby. It contains an ingredient from all the major brewing powers!

For 5.5 gallons at 1.058, 25 IBUs, 9 SRM, 5.9% ABV, 90 minute boil

GRAIN BILL

7.0 lbs	German Pilsner Malt
2.0 lbs	English Mild (or Pale Ale) Malt
0.5 lbs	Aromatic Malt
1.5 lbs	Belgian candi syrup (Clear or Simplicity)

MASH SCHEDULE

Mash In	148°F–150°F	60 minutes

HOPS

0.5 oz	Magnum	Pellet	12.9% AA	60 minutes
0.5 oz	Czech Saaz	Pellet	5.0% AA	10 minutes
0.5 oz	Spalt	Pellet	4.8% AA	0 minutes
0.5 oz	Fuggle	Pellet	4.8% AA	Dry hop
0.5 oz	Styrian Goldings	Pellet	6.0% AA	Dry hop

YEAST

WY3522 Belgian Ardennes for primary fermentation, then WY3112 *Brettanomyces bruxellenis* and WY3526 *Brettanomyces lambicus* in secondary

VARIANT

For a tropical version of the trout, replace the dry hop with 1.0 ounces of Citra or Amarillo and substitute WLP645 *Brettanomyces claussenii* for the *Bretts* above in secondary.

The technique can barely even be called a technique. You just add *Brett* and two ounces of sugar dissolved in four ounces or less of water to the keg or bottling bucket. (If you're bottling, just add the couple ounces of sugar, into your normal priming sugar solution.)

Note: Make sure your beer has finished fermenting! If there are still fermentable sugars, you will end up with massively overcarbed beer—and even bottle bombs—due to the *Brett*.

Then all you need to do is hold the beer warm (about 70°F to 75°F) for 1–2 months, or even longer for additional complexity. Serve the beer and be amazed! Oh and if you're looking at this thinking *these guys are nuts*, consider this: The technique comes directly from Brasserie Orval in Belgium where their classic twist on a pale ale is put through these steps before sale to the public.

BLENDING MULTIPLE BEER STYLES

When you study beer styles, you quickly learn beer styles are almost inevitably built out of other styles: the pale ale gave rise to the IPA and the Imperial IPA and the Triple IPA (and inevitably someday the Decuple IPA). Or consider the porter, which supposedly came about from a blend of common beers in the 1700s.

Whether or not that porter story is true, blending beers is an ancient and mysterious art. Sure, most of us know lambic producers blend, but did you realize that the largest breweries blend as well? Those big macro lagers all have spec sheets designed for them with aromas, gravities, and flavor compounds marked with very narrow acceptable ranges. Even as great as their process controls are, the big guys still need to blend individual batches to pull their numbers in line.

But blending's not just about numbers and old stories that aren't true. It is about exploiting those heritage lines and making new flavors sing. And sometimes it's about saving your beer, too!

We would guess that one of the least-used rescue tactics is also arguably the best. Look at your beer that needs help. What is it missing? Hops? Malt? Roast? The classic advice to fix it is brew another beer that has that needed characteristic in spades and then blend it in. Most folks don't do it, because who wants to brew another batch of beer to have something fixed? But stop thinking the usual way. Instead of thinking, *Hey, my brown ale needs hops, so I'll brew a hoppy brown and blend the two together*, think, *Hey, I need hops, I'll brew a Double IPA!* You'll end up with two drinkable beers instead of one out-of-whack beer with one fixed beer.

Let's skip away from the rescue ranger scenario and look at the creation of new flavors. This is the beer equivalent of the convenience store suicide soda. When faced with a few taps that you've already been through, you could have another straight pint, but why not mix it up? Blend a shot of something hoppy into your glass to goose the hops.

A personal favorite of ours is the dessert blend. Take three parts Imperial Stout and blend in one part fruit beer, like a Raspberry Lambic, for a dessert that beats a chocolate cake.

Do you have to do these blends right at serving? No, but you can use serving time to explore what you like. Just as with our tea and tincture instructions on page 74, keep track of the ratio that works. Then you can port the blend over to a keg, replicating what you have in the glass.

USING CARBONATED WATER TO MAKE LIGHT BEER

This technique comes from Mike "Tasty" McDole of the Brewing Network. Mike is a big fan of making bold, beautiful beers and also a fan of the golf course, but not of the two together. He prefers a lighter-weight beer on the course. Instead of sacrificing his taste buds to his needs, he simply prepares a light version of his beers using carbonated water.

By the way, this is a really great use for those 3-gallon kegs you bought on a whim that one time they were on sale.

You Will Need

- 2 gallons of 6 percent ABV or higher beer
- 1 gallon water, filtered and decholrinated
- 1 3- or 5-gallon keg

Instructions

1. Boil the water. Let it cool and transfer it to the keg.
2. Carbonate the water to match the stronger beer. (For example, if the beer is at 2.5 volumes, carbonate your water at 35°F by setting the CO_2 pressure to 10 psi and shaking for 10 minutes.)
3. Bleed the pressure from the water keg and then using a jumper transfer hose, add the 2 gallons of beer to the water keg. After transferring, close the keg up and gently rock to blend.
4. Note: We've tried the technique by just adding the boiled and cooled water to already prepared beer and then adding more carbonation. It works fine; we just don't recommend that treatment for long-term storage. After transferring, make sure the keg is tightly sealed.
5. Gently rock to blend and add a few psi of CO_2 to the keg for serving.
6. This will produce 3 gallons of beer at 4 percent. Use our dilution calculations to figure out how much water to add to reduce your beer to a target alcohol level.

$$ABV_{new} = \frac{(Volume_{beer} \times ABV_{beer})}{(Volume_{beer} + Volume_{water})}$$

$$ABV_{new} = \frac{(2 \times 0.06)}{(2+1)}$$

$$ABV_{new} = \frac{0.12}{3} = 0.04 = 4\%$$

MEASURING DISSOLVED OXYGEN

The role of oxygen to yeast health and cell growth has been well documented in the world of brewing. Oxygen is used to synthesize the sterols that make yeast cells elastic so that a bud can form. Homebrewers often discuss the merits of various aeration techniques and equipment but beyond published generalities have little idea of exactly how much oxygen they have gotten into their wort.

If you're feeling particularly chemically minded, you can find a twenty-two-step process that involves cooking, titration, and enough chemical gear and chemicals to worry your neighbors online at http://serc.carleton.edu/microbelife/research_methods/environ_sampling/oxygen.html and www.ne-wea.org/LabManual/dissolved_oxygen.htm. We suspect after you've bought all the equipment, you'll have spent almost as much as you would buying a meter, though, and you'll end up with more work.

Don't feel like jumping through all of those hoops? Well, we don't blame you, but we had to at least mention real science and titration and semi-meth lab setups! Now for the easy way. You can find dissolved oxygen kits online that contain all the parts you need. (LaMotte is one trustworthy brand.) These kits look a bit like a pool water testing kit and will allow you to test your wort fifty times for about $50. That should be more than enough for you to get your process in line.

Remember, the whole point of this process for us isn't to have a number that we write down on a spreadsheet. What we want to do is have the knowledge that our particular aeration practices are working. You want to have confidence that by mixing for a set period of time or setting your O_2 regulator to a particular flow for 30 seconds that you're achieving sufficient levels of dissolved oxygen (typically 10-15 ppm). If you're not, add more. If you're overshooting, you need to cut back because the extra oxygen isn't going to do you any good; it may actually harm your beer, causing it to stale and fade faster than you want.

YEAST CELL COUNTING

Like most things in brewing, there is debate about the proper amount of yeast to pitch in order to make the beer you desire. Of course there is a difference of opinion about the consequences of overpitching or underpitching your beer. There is even debate about what the proper pitch rate is! But let's assume that the oft-quoted figure of 100 million cells/milliliter/degree Plato is correct. How do you know how much you're pitching? You need to count the cells. And since you don't have enough fingers and toes to count that high, you need to employ special equipment to count with. The following information for this quick overview comes from Kai Troester, who has spent much of his homebrewing experience looking at the methods homebrewers use and analyzing their effectiveness. This information is based on his website (http://braukaiser.com), where you can find even more in-depth instructions.

To start, you'll need some specialized equipment. First and foremost, if you don't already have a microscope capable of both 400x and 100x magnification, you will have to buy or borrow one. You'll also need a hemocytometer, which is a grid that defines a given amount of sample and allows you to count the cells within that portion of the grid. You'll also need: pipettes, a pipette pump to fill them accurately, methylene blue stain, a small dropper bottle, and some sort of tally counter to keep track of your count.

In a nutshell, you start by diluting a sample from your yeast propagation vessel 1:20. That means you'll add 19 milliliters of water to a test tube or other container and 1 milliliter of your stirred yeast solution. Mix well, but don't shake. Some yeast strains will clump together when shaken, leading to an inaccurate count. Repeatedly pull a sample into the pipette and release it to flush the pipette.

For yeasts that are heavy flocculators, you'll need to unfloc them to get an accurate count. Since maltose inhibits flocculation, the easiest thing to do is simply add fresh wort to the yeast sediment and place it on a stirplate for a few minutes. You can also use sulfuric acid, disodium EDTA, or even PBW to do the same thing.

Transfer your sample via pipette to the hemocytometer following the manufacturer's directions on how to fill the hemocytometyer. Then place the hemocytometer under the microscope and focus on the hemocytometer grid. Count the cells in the 4x4 grids in the corners and center. Use the following formula to find the cell density with the sample dilution taken into account:

$$\text{Cell Density} = \frac{\text{Cells Counted} \times \text{Dilution Factor}}{4 \times 16 \text{ by } 16 \text{ Grids Counted}}$$

In order to get the most accurate results, be sure to count at least 100 cells. To discover the number of viable cells in your sample you must stain them with methylene blue and count the living cells. Prepare methylene blue for staining by mixing 0.1 gram of methylene blue with 100 milliliters of distilled water. Mix equal parts methylene blue preparation and diluted yeast sample. Let sit for a minute and then plate and count your cells again. Dark blue cells are dead; lighter blue or plain-looking cells are viable. Examination on a hemocytometer grid under a microscope will allow you to find the amount of healthy yeast cells in your total sample.

SODA MMM POP

One of the biggest problems facing Americans is the increasing and fractured demands for our time. Pick up the kids from soccer practice, make a nutritious and tasty dinner, answer your boss's emails at 2:30 in the morning, and so on. For homebrewers the challenge is: How do you fit the three to seven hours needed for brewing into that pell-mell?

One tactic that also allows you to involve the family is to make some soda (tonic, pop, or whatever you call it). While your local shop may sell a plethora of flavored concentrates, there's something to be said for whipping up your own batch of soda in an hour. It's inexpensive, you can tailor the drink to your own needs, and you can make it healthier than store-bought. (The average 20-ounce bottle of commercial cola contains 44 grams of sugar. That's 176 calories just from the sugar. It adds up quickly!)

Soda making also allows you to more easily incorporate some family creative time into your busy day. Kids, thankfully, don't have much interest in beer, but they do love to play around with flavors. You can turn your soda making into a guided playtime. Even better, after everything is said and done, they can enjoy a beverage they created. If you think your kids were proud the first time they made a grilled cheese sandwich, just wait until the try their very own soda! One last sneaky reason: Soda making serves as a stealthy way to test flavor combinations that you can deploy in your beer. Not all research involves beakers and chemistry; sometimes it's just exploration.

Here are few notes before you try your first recipe:

- The recipes that follow are all written for forced carbonation and kegs.
- Most soda recipes are based around a flavorful syrup mixed into soda water. So if you have a SodaStream™ or other carbonator on hand, you can add your chilled syrup into a plain glass of soda water. Just keep your syrup mix chilled in the fridge. Just pour a few glasses to dial in on a desired strength.
- You may want to keep an extra set of keg gaskets on hand to swap out after you're done with the soda. These natural sodas shouldn't taint the rubber like the more spicy commercial sodas, but it's better to be safe with it!
- Even though you're not dealing with yeast and fermentation, an infection can creep in to your soda. There's plenty of food for bugs to eat, and you're not providing any yeast and booze to crowd them out, so pay extra-close attention to your sanitation, or you may end with a glass full of nasty!
- Look at a can of soda, and you'll see one of the chief ingredients is phosphoric acid. Yet none of the sodas that follow rely on it. Why use acid of any kind? In beer we use hops and carbonation to provide a break from the sweetness of the malt. Since few sodas will use bittering hops, most depend on acid to provide the break. All soda will carry carbonic acid just from the dissolved carbon dioxide, but our sodas also rely on the acid in fruit juice. If you want to play with the big boys, you can buy food-grade phosphoric acid. However, we don't recommend it. It's nasty stuff, so stick with the easier and safer options like powdered citric acid if you want to balance a soda without any fruit juice.

TWO CENTS PLAIN

By Drew

This recipe is the basis of all soda! If you listen to enough Depression-era music, you'll hear about two cents plain. It was the cheapest thing in a soda-shop, since it was just carbonated water.

For 3.0 gallons

SODA BILL

3.0 gallons	Filtered water

INSTRUCTIONS

- Add the water to a keg. Chill the water to 35°F overnight.
- Shake the keg for about 10 minutes at 30 psi for full carbonation.

VARIANT

For club soda, boil 1.0 gram of chalk and 0.5 grams each of sodium citrate (sour salt) and kosher salt in 1 cup of water. Add the mixture to the rest of the water and proceed as above.

BLUEBIER

By Drew

It's only natural that a soda as tasty as the blueberry-ginger creation below has a beery counterpart. Think of it as a witbier with new flavors!

For 5.5 gallons at 1.036, 12 IBUs, 3.2% ABV

GRAIN BILL

7.0 lbs	Pilsner Malt
4.0 lbs	Wheat Malt
1.0 lb	Flaked Oats

MASH SCHEDULE

Rest	150°F	60 minutes

HOPS

0.5 oz	Magnum	Pellet	11.0% AA	60 minutes

OTHER BOIL INGREDIENTS

4 oz	Ginger, grated	10 minutes
1.0 Tbsp	Powdered ginger	10 minutes
½	Lemon, zested	10 minutes

YEAST

WLP400 Belgian Wit Ale Yeast

OTHER INGREDIENTS

64 oz	100% Blueberry juice (add to secondary fermenter)

DR. DREW'S BLUEBERRY GINGER REJUVENATING TONIC

By Drew

Ever since I stumbled on the idea of blueberry salsa, blueberry and ginger have been inextricably linked in my mind. This soda takes that combination in a different direction—and it's quick to make, too.

For 3.0 gallons

SODA BILL

cups	Filtered water
cups	Sugar
oz	Ginger, grated
Tbsp	Powdered ginger
2 oz	Pure blueberry juice (such as Trader Joe's Just Blueberry Juice)
5 gallons	Filtered water

INSTRUCTIONS

- Bring the sugar and 2 cups of water to a boil. Add the ginger and boil for 10 minutes.
- Allow the mixture to cool to room temperature and strain through a fine mesh sieve.
- Mix the syrup, juice, and water together inside a keg. Stir or shake (with the lid on) until thoroughly combined. Chill the mixture to 35°F overnight set at 10 psi.
- Shake the keg for about 10 minutes at 30 psi for full carbonation.

WATERMELON MINT SPARKLING FRESCA

By Drew

This recipe is inspired by the agua frescas that I find around town during the months when fruit is ripe and the weather too warm for words. It's a refreshing combination of cool, delicious watermelon with a hint of acidity and a bright pop of mint. The salt in this recipe is very important, as watermelon needs it to stand out.

For 3.5 gallons

SODA BILL

1.5 gallons	Watermelon juice (about two 15-lb watermelons)
1.5 gallons	Filtered water
2 cups	Filtered water
2 cups	Sugar
1 tsp	Salt
1 bunch	Mint, lightly crushed
½ cup	Lime juice
¼ cup	Lemon juice

INSTRUCTIONS

- Juice the watermelon flesh—not the rind—with a juicer and allow it to settle. If you only have a blender, blend it and then give it a day to settle before moving on.
- Remove the foam and decant off the fiber.
- Mix the juice with the 1.5 gallons of filtered water inside the keg.
- Boil the sugar and 2 cups of filtered water together to make a simple syrup.
- After 10 minutes at a full boil, turn off the heat and add the mint and salt. Stir to combine. Cool the mixture to room temperature.
- Strain the syrup and add it to the keg along with the lime and lemon juices.
- Chill the mixture to 35°F overnight set at 10 psi.
- Shake the keg for about 10 minutes at 30 psi for full carbonation.

SPENT GRAIN BREAD

If you've never attempted making bread due to the amount of kneading and working or you haven't been very successful in prior attempts, then give this recipe a try. It's based on a technique—no-knead baking—that was first described by Jim Lahey, owner and head baker of New York's Sullivan bakery. It hit the Internet like a storm when Mark Bittman of the *New York Times* presented Lahey's technique.

The purpose of kneading is to activate and mix two separate proteins found in wheat flour: gliadin and glutenin. Together these two proteins form gluten, a meshy, sticky protein matrix that traps CO_2 and gives bread its chewiness. The mechanical action of folding and pressing quickly causes creation and reinforcement of the gluten mesh.

Drew: Incidentally, gluten is used by vegetarians as a source of protein (in the form of seitan). However, a number of folks are exploring gluten-free diets due to physical reactions to the gluten and precursor proteins.

What Lahey discovered is that a wetter-than-normal dough will naturally form gluten if chilled and given enough time, thanks to the action of hydration and perturbation induced by the fermenting yeast.

Lahey's other fun technique is the use of a Dutch oven to recreate a professional bread oven. Spiffy commercial ovens have special features such as steam injectors, which allow a dense, chewy crust to form. By trapping a wet dough inside a Dutch oven's cast-iron enclosure, the steam naturally forming from the dough creates a similar effect.

The combination of Lahey's two techniques allow novice home bakers to easily create round boule-shaped loaves with the same intense flavors and crackling crusts that you pay good money for in a bakery. To keep this project beer-related, we'll start with every baking-oriented brewer's quest: spent-grain bread.

This recipe is based on Laheys basic no-knead recipe featured in *My Bread*. We've adapted the recipe for use with leftover grains from a batch of beer.

Ingredients

- 3 cups — Bread flour
- 1.5 Tbsp — Salt
- 0.25 tsp — Instant bread yeast
- 1 cup — Water
- 1 cup — Spent mash grains (still slightly damp)

You Will Need

- Large stainless-steel mixing bowl
- Tea towel
- Parchment paper
- 6-quart cast-iron Dutch oven

Instructions

1. Mix together flour, salt, and yeast.
2. Add the water and grains and stir to make a sticky dough. Cover the bowl and allow to rest for at least 12 hours.
3. Scrape the dough from the bowl. It will be looser than any dough you've used; that's okay.
4. Fold the dough briefly and shape into a round.
5. Move the round onto a floured piece of parchment paper and cover with a floured towel (anything but terry cloth) for 2 hours.
6. Meanwhile, preheat your oven to 475°F and add a clean, ungreased 4- to 6-quart ovenproof Dutch oven and lid at least 30 minutes before the dough is done resting.
7. Once the dough is ready, it will have doubled in size. Remove the Dutch oven, take the lid off, and quickly and gently invert the dough into the oven. Close the pot and slide it back into the oven for 30 minutes.
8. Remove the lid and bake for an additional 20 minutes to finish the bread. Remove the bread from the oven and rest it for at least 1 hour before eating.

Eat the bread within 3 days or use for additional purposes, such as . . . well, beer, of course.

SPENT GRAIN BLOND

By Drew

One of my mentors was Doug King, who tragically passed away in an accident while homebrew festival–bound. Doug had a habit of adding whatever he had to a beer—leftover tortillas, chocolate cake, and even loaves of bread. Let's keep Doug's spirit going!

For 5.5 gallons at 1.087, 68 IBUs, 6 SRM, 9.0% ABV

GRAIN BILL

17 lbs	Domestic 2 Row Ale Malt
3.0 lbs	Bread

MASH SCHEDULE

Rest	152°F	60 minutes

HOPS

1.25 oz	Magnum	Pellet	14.0% AA	60 minutes

OTHER INGREDIENTS

½ tablet Whirlfloc	10 minutes

YEAST

WLP001 California Ale
or WY1056 American Ale

ADDITIONAL INSTRUCTIONS / NOTES

Bread is assumed to provide about 15 ppg. Strike the mash as normal. Crumble or cube the bread and stir in thoroughly to wet and dissolve. Once the bread is dissolved into the mash, brew like any other all-grain beer.

FAVORITE EXPERIMENTAL STYLES

BEER IS MEANT TO BE PLAYED WITH. If it weren't, wouldn't that be horribly boring? Or to put a finer point on it: horribly German? Since we're not bound to a code of tradition or legal definitions of what a beer is, we're free to make whatever beer we want to make. Face it, though; everyone has a favorite style or two, and we're no different.

In this chapter, we'll each look at a few of our favorites. We'll provide a couple of recipes for each favorite, too. One recipe will be a base beer made for playing with the ingredients in the chapters that follow. To demonstrate the recipe's flexibility, we'll throw in a couple of simple variations that work like a charm. The second will be an experimental recipe that departs in some dramatic way from the base beer. And who knows what other shenanigans we'll talk about.

AMERICAN WHEAT By Drew

The poor maligned American Wheat. Whatever did it do to get such a reputation for being boring? Well, it was probably a little boring. Its rise started in 1986 with Rob and Kurt Widmer at their eponymous brewery in Portland, Oregon. While they called their beer a Hefeweizen, it's very clean and rumored to be brewed with an old Alt yeast strain. Because of this, it lacks the banana, clove, and bubblegum aromas of the classical Bavarian Hefeweizens. In the years since, a fair

number of craft brewers adopted this innocuously sweet and middling style of American Wheat. It gives bartenders something to offer the megaswill consumer who isn't ready for the *bold flavors* of a pale ale. But it doesn't have to be that way. Good brewers can reclaim the American Wheat! Look no further than one of America's great craft brewers, Bell's Brewery of Kalamazoo, Michigan. Oberon, Bell's summer staple, is ubiquitous across the Midwest and is both refreshing and interesting.

As part of the ongoing effort to expand the craft beer market, early micros threw everything at the wall to see what stuck. If you were drinking craft brew before 2000, you'll surely remember the endless variety of blueberry ales, strawberry ales, and so on. However, a few breweries have hit on truly sublime fruit and wheat combinations. Just try 21st Amendement's Watermelon Wheat. For a bigger, more radical version of wheat and fruit, try and get your hands on New Glarus Brewing's Wisconsin Belgian Red. The idea you should take away is more fruit, always more fruit.

In recent years, craft brewers have even figured out how to slap a few hops into an American Wheat beer, because, well, that's what craft brewers do. Time to stop in the Midwest again and mention Three Floyds' Gumballhead. It's stacked to the gills with big juicy grapefruit from the infusion of Amarillo hops. This is a real face slapper of a beer, which smartly utilizes a less harsh hop variety to great effect. While the same impact can be achieved from other low-cohumulone hops, the higher alpha varieties like Amarillo allow you to put less green matter in the kettle, meaning less chlorophyll to stand out against the sweetness of the wheat.

WHAT WORKS WELL

Adding fresh fruit to a wheat beer is your best bet. It will turn out much more nuanced and delicious than cloyingly sweet, since the yeast will eat up all that yummy fruit sugar. See page 164 for more, but whatever you do, never ever use artificial flavorings…especially cherry (unless you like cough drops). Okay, you can use artificial flavors, but use them sparingly as an enhancement to real fruit flavor instead of as the only source of it.

There are a few other things beyond fruit to consider. The sweetness of the wheat can carry an amazing amount of spice before blowing out the palate. Whether you're interested in trying black pepper, clove, or chiles, you'll find that American Wheat helps smooth out your mistakes more than other styles. Remember that traditional hefeweizens have a strong spicy phenolic character from the yeast. So an American wheat can take the punch of your spices and not seem jarring or out of place.

Unexpected roasty flavors, such as coffee, can also work. Think of that other German weizen, the dunkelweizen. In that case, the roasted malts add a cutting character to the profile. Naturally, this means you can follow the German example and use adehusked chocolate malt like the Carafa specials or reach a little and use a roasted wheat (such as Briess Midnight Wheat) or mix it up with Weyermann's Roasted Rye. Or you can throw caution to the wind. Buy a pound of a medium-roast coffee. Grind it up and throw it in the mash during your sparge.

WHAT DOESN'T WORK

With all the sweetness that the beer gets from wheat, you should avoid flavors and aromas that also play up the sweet factor: sweet chocolate, red sweet apples, caramel, and so on. Too much sweetness becomes cloying and unpleasant. You may be able to survive a glass, but you'll never make it through more. One of the worst beers I've had the misfortune of tasting was a white chocolate wheat beer. It was just sweetness built on sweetness with some extra sweetness tacked onto the finish.

BREWING NOTES

A traditional Bavarian Hefeweizen consists of around 60 percent wheat malt and 40 percent pilsner malt. In the case of an American Wheat, you need to look at what your desired flavor is. Do you want a sweet and bready base to play off some spices? Then go ahead and use 60–70 percent wheat. If you want a crisper base beer, reverse the percentages and use 60–70 percent base malt to 30–40 percent wheat malt. Domestic pale malt is a reasonable substitution here, since you really want as innocuous a base flavor as possible.

Whenever you use more than 40 percent wheat, you should seriously consider an addition of rice hulls. I generally use a pound for each 5 gallons of beer I'm making. They don't cost much and don't add flavor (assuming you're not oversparging). Rinse them well before adding them to the mash tun. Since wheat doesn't have a husk, the rice hulls help ensure that your mash doesn't become a wet ball of bread dough. It's cheap insurance to avoid a brutal day of stuck sparges. If you don't want to use them (out of masochism disguised as traditionalism), that's totally your call, but I will be decidedly unsympathetic when your story of a horrible brew day comes to light.

Looking around at older advice about brewing, there are plenty of sources that advise a protein rest (for example, a 20–30 minute stop between 120°F–130°F) when using wheat to cleave haze-causing proteins. But with the rise of well-modified malts, a protein rest doesn't carry the same impact as it used to and in fact may be detrimental to the head and body of your beer! Instead, I prefer to run a temperate mash (152°F) to create a finish that's neither too sweet nor too dry.

Hops should remain neutral; a 60-minute bittering addition is usually all you need. I like a really clean hop such as Magnum. Of course, if you're aiming to make a hoppy wheat, you need to up your game! I favor fruity, expressive hops for this sort of beer. This means varieties like the big juicy grapefruit bomb of Amarillo or the mango madness of a hop like Citra. I avoid hops like Chinook and Cascade, because I don't like the palate dissonance caused by the hop harshness and the wheat sweetness.

HUMDRUM WHEAT

By Drew

The whole point of this beer is to be inoffensive and neutral. It turns out that it's also amazingly easy to drink and makes a perfect summer beer. (Just make sure to name it something more enticing than Humdrum.) See the variations if you want to add some kick.

For 5.5 gallons at 1.057, 13 IBUs, 5.6% ABV

GRAIN BILL
6.0 lbs   Domestic 2 Row Pale Malt
6.0 lbs   Wheat Malt

MASH SCHEDULE
Rest   153°F   60 minutes

HOPS
0.25 oz. Magnum   Pellet   12.9% AA   60 minutes

OTHER INGREDIENTS
½ tablet Whirlfloc   10 minutes

YEAST
WY1010 American Wheat, WY1056 American Ale, WLP001 California Ale, or WLP320 American Hefeweizen

ADDITIONAL INSTRUCTIONS
Ferment in the mid 60°sF to reduce esters and allow wheaty sweetness to predominate. Carbonate to 2.5–3.0 volumes for maximum fluffiness.

VARIANTS
- Citra Wheat: Add 1.0 ounce of Citra hops at flameout and allow to steep for 15 minutes while you whirlpool (covered). Ferment as normal. Taste prior to packaging and if desired, add another 1.0 ounce of Citra as a dry hop for 7 days.
- Jolting Joe Wheat: Mash the beer as usual. Add 1 pound of freshly ground light city roast coffee after you finish your mash recirculation. Proceed as normal.
- Midnight Wheat: Add 0.5 pounds of Melanoidin malt to the mash and cap the mash with 0.5 pounds of Briess Midnight Wheat Malt (or Weyermann Chocolate Wheat) during the sparge to produce a hearty-looking but easy-drinking dark wheat. This beer is a great base for vanilla and spice tones, like a dark chocolate dessert.
- Smoothie Wheat: There need be nothing hard nor boring about a fruity wheat beer. I like to take 1–2 pounds per gallon of achingly fresh fruit from the farmers' market or frozen berries and purée them in a sanitized blender with juice from a freshly opened bottle. Add the purée to the beer in a large secondary vessel and allow to age for 2 weeks on the fruit. For extra kick, add a knob of ginger or fresh herbs to your blender! Feel all those invigorating healthy vitamins as you enjoy your beer!

I don't use many of the older lower-alpha European varieties that people seek out, because I think the quality available to homebrewers is unspectacular and can actively ruin a beer. (This applies well beyond wheat beers; be careful with imported hops, as many that we get seem less than stellar. Always smell your hops!)

On the fermentation front, pitch a neutral American strain and keep it on the cooler side (64°F) to avoid warm fruity esters. It's a balancing act, though; I've noticed that my wheat beers fermented colder or with lager yeasts get hammy. (It's entirely possible I'm crazy.) Don't forget to leave plenty of headspace. Wheats tend to throw more head than anything else I brew except Imperial Stouts.

The *krausen* collapsing is your cue to take to the flavoring cabinet. This is the best time to grab the fruit, the spices, the dry hops, or whatever you like. If you decide to transfer to secondary and are adding a flavoring with plenty of sugar (say, fruit purée), make sure to provide plenty of room for a lively secondary fermentation.

When it comes time to package the beer, I like to aim for 3.0 volumes to really pop the head and push the aromas of the beer.

CHILE WHEAT

By Harold Gulbransen

Drew: This recipe comes from a fellow member of the AHA Governing Committee. I judged this beer once in competition and was impressed enough to give it a medal. The amazing part is that I normally hate chiles in beer. In fact, I'd go so far as to say that hot and beer don't belong near each other except in the sentence *It was hot, so I grabbed a beer to cool down.* Turns out this beer had just enough chile heat to be interesting but not so much as to ruin a great base wheat beer.

For 5.5 gallons at 1.056, 15 IBUs, 5.6% ABV

GRAIN BILL
6.0 lbs	Domestic 2 Row Pale Malt
5.5 lbs	Wheat Malt

MASH SCHEDULE
Rest	135°F	15 minutes
Rest	150°F	20 minutes
Rest	155°F	15 minutes

HOPS
0.55 oz	Sterling	Pellet	7% AA	60 minutes

OTHER INGREDIENTS
½ tablet	Whirlfloc	10 minutes

YEAST
WLP011 European Ale or WLP029 Kolsch
Yeast in a 1.5-L starter

PRIMARY FERMENTATION ADDITIONS
15 grams	Fresh serrano or jalapeños, chopped with seeds
15 grams	Dried Pasilla chiles, chopped with seeds
10 grams	Dried chile de arbol, chopped with seeds

ADDITIONAL INSTRUCTIONS
Ferment on the chiles for 10–14 days. Check the gravity and heat level. The chile flavor should be subtle with just a hint of the burn. If more heat is desired, rack to secondary and add more chiles.

AMERICAN IPA By Denny

As we all know by now, India Pale Ale made its name as a stronger, hoppier version of pale ale. In the last twenty years, American brewers and hop varieties have taken over the style and spun off numerous variations. (Though it's questionable how many of these new styles are really IPAs. Session IPA? Really?) But who are we to look down on styles that aren't styles. Whether you're interested in a bona fide Imperial IPA, or a marginal IPA like black, chances are you're after something where the hops stand out.

From something that began as a beer that would survive a trip from England to India, IPA has branched out and evolved into many versions. Anchor Liberty Ale, introduced in 1975, is cited by the brewery as being the first modern American IPA brewed since Prohibition. It certainly set the mold for the American IPAs to follow with its use of whole cone Cascade hops all the way through the brew, including dry hopping. Since then, American IPA has seemed to be on a binge to create wilder and more extreme variations. The chart on pages 106–107 lists some of those variations along with their primary grains, hops, yeast, and any special ingredient. The specs come from the BJCP guidelines and a cross section of commercially available IPAs, but keep in mind that a lot of American IPA brewers do what they want to do, guidelines be damned! The ingredients in the chart are typical, but in no way inclusive.

WHAT WORKS WELL

There are a number of things you can try with IPA while remaining true to its origins. Perhaps the most obvious is to play with your selection of hop varieties. While American IPA has traditionally focused on the more intensely citrusy hops varieties, the newer, more fruity varieties are finding their way into IPA. Sometimes used as the sole hop and sometimes blended with older varieties, these hops can add flavors of mango, passion fruit, or strawberry to the IPA.

You can change the quality of the bitterness by adjusting your water. (See page 159.) You can also try hopping techniques like first wort hopping, hop bursting, or a hop stand.

But the malt side can be just as interesting. Changing up the grist from the typical combination of American 2-row pale malt and Crystal malts can have very positive and interesting effects on an IPA. Using 15–25 percent rye malt adds a great mouthfeel, a bit of spiciness, and a beautiful orange color. Using about 10–20 percent Victory or Special Roast malt will give the beer a really complementary nutty or toasty flavor. Using 10–25 percent of your grist as Munich malt will add to the malt backbone of your beer to balance the hops—assuming you want balance. In fact, an all-Munich grist for IPA can be a really nice change of pace. The increased maltiness and body can take an even higher hop load than you might normally consider for IPA. A little of Special B will add a bit of raisiny sweetness that really balances a highly hopped beer. Just don't overdo it. You want a complementary, not dominating, flavor from these additions.

Last but certainly not least, yeast selection makes for a fun experimental IPA. The classic choice is something clean and attenuative like WY1056 American Ale or WLP001 California Ale. However, some of the best commercial IPAs stray from Chico. Obviously WY1450 is Denny's Favorite. It provides a uniquely smooth mouthfeel while still letting the hops shine. A British strain of yeast is often used in American IPA. The slight fruitiness of some of these yeasts can complement the hoppiness, as long as the fruity esters of the yeast don't take over the beer. WY1968 is often used by breweries such as Ninkasi for their American IPA. Lagunitas uses WLP002 English Ale, which is basically the same thing. Rumor has it that Stone started out with WLP007 Dry English Ale, but it has evolved over time into something different. But you know how rumors are!

You can also go further from the norm and try a Belgian yeast strain that will change the beer radically. Pay attention to flavors created by the yeast. A fruity British or Belgian strain might not be the best choice for every recipe. For Belgo-American IPAs, I prefer a strain that's more phenolic than fruity. WY3522 Ardennes makes an IPA that has just such a phenolic edge to the flavor, which blends really well with American C hops like Chinook, Cascade, Centennial, and Columbus. Some people prefer the fruitier Belgian yeasts, like those sourced from Chimay or Rochefort. If you want to try those, consider using fruitier hops, like Citra or Mandarina Bavaria, to complement fruit with fruit. Or try splitting a batch with two different yeasts, one fruity and one phenolic, to see which you prefer.

WHAT DOESN'T WORK

First, a caveat: When it comes to flavors, it's all about subjectivity. Since I'm writing this, it comes with my taste prejudices. What I say doesn't work may well sound like IPA nirvana to you. Take that into consideration and experiment to find what you like.

Ingredients that clash with the hops in an IPA should be avoided. There are exceptions to this rule, but be wary of using a heavy hand with dark malts. Yeah, I know, there are "black IPAs" out there, but some of them are much more successful than others. Consider the integration of flavors, not just how black you can make it.

Drew: I would also advise against the use of smoked malts. I've made a number of attempts to blend smoke into a hoppy beer and have yet to find one that I feel works. The smoke phenols produce, for me, a jarring clash against the heady aroma and hop phenols of a well-made IPA.

IPA VARIATIONS

	OG and ABV	Grains	Hops	Yeast/Special	Taste	Examples
English	1.050–75 5–7.5%	Pale malt, maybe crystal or sugar	English (Challenger, Fuggle, EKG, Target, Progress)	English yeast, may be fruity or sulfurous	Hoppy, moderately strong; hop character more earthy and subdued than American styles	Fuller's IPA, Samuel Smith's India Ale, Brooklyn East India Pale Ale
Classic American	1.056–75 5.5–7.5%	Pale or pale ale malt, usually crystal malt, maybe some Munich	Cascade, Chinook, Centennial, Columbus, Citra	Clean American ale yeast, often sulfate additions to water	Decidedly hoppy and bitter; often with citrus or tropical fruit notes from the hops	Anchor Liberty Ale, Sierra Nevada Celebration
Rye	1.060–75 6–7.5%	Rye malt replaces some of the pale malt from Classic American	American hops like Classic	Clean American ale yeast, sulfates often added	Bitter, with intense American hop aroma and some spiciness from rye; rye also contributes to full mouthfeel	Sierra Nevada Ruthless Rye, Founder's Red's Rye IPA, Harpoon Rich and Dan's Rye IPA
Session	1.040–45 4–5%	Pale, pale ale or pils malt	American hops like Classic	American or English ale yeast	Lots of hop aroma and flavor but reduced bitterness to complement reduced strength	Founder's All Day IPA, Boulevard Pop-Up Session IPA, Victory Hop Ticket, Stone Go To IPA
Black*	1.050–90 5–10%	Roast barley, black patent, chocolate, or other dark malt in addition to Classic grist	American varieties	American or English yeast, sometimes sugar	Hop character typical of Classic or Imperial, roast character from dark grains	Stone Sublimely Self Righteous, Deschutes Hop in the Dark, Firestone-Walker Wookie Jack

*Cascadian Dark Ale, American Black Ale

Denny: Likewise with fruit. While I've heard from people who have used grapefruit or orange juice in an IPA to bump up the citrus qualities of the hops they used, something like a cherry or plum IPA may have you wondering what you were drinking when you came up with that recipe!

Drew: And you should be careful with hop varieties from year to year, from farm to farm, and even row to row! Hops are an agricultural product, and there can be considerable variation. For instance, that grapefruit/sandalwood scented Simcoe can instead be strongly catty and oniony in some crops from some suppliers.

	OG and ABV	Grains	Hops	Yeast/Special	Taste	Examples
East Coast	1.050–75 5–7.5%	Classic IPA grains, may use more caramel malts than other styles	American varieties	American or English yeast	Hop character very present but bitterness reduced compared to Classic or West Coast versions	Victory Hop Devil, Founder's Centennial IPA, Troegs Perpetual IPA, Surly Furious IPA
West Coast	1.060–80 5.5–8%	Classic IPA grains, sometimes crystal, Munich, Vienna or other grains	American varieties	Clean American ale yeast, sometimes one of the cleaner English ale yeast	Intense hop character almost like an Imperial IPA	Ninkasi Total Domination, 10 Barrel Apocalypse, Stone IPA, Firestone Walker Union Jack IPA
Imperial	1.070–90 7.5–10%	Pale or pale ale malt; sugar often added to reduce body and distinguish it from American Barleywine	American varieties like Classic IPA, but in larger amounts	Clean ale yeast	Bitter with big hop flavor; malt should not be cloying or intense	Russian River Pliney the Elder, Lagunitas Hop Stoopid, Dogfish Head 90 Minute IPA, Avery Maharajah
Red IPA	1.060–85 5.7–8.5%	Classic American grains with crystal, CaraRed, Muncih, Special B, others	American and Australian varieties, both citrusy and fruity, including Galaxy, Topaz, Citra	Clean American or English ale yeast	A cross between an IPA and amber ale	Sierra Nevada Flipside, Summit Horizon, Sam Adams Tasman Red
White IPA	1.060–75 6–7.5%	Pale or pils malt, wheat (malted and/ or unmalted), limited specialty malts	Both citrusy and fruity hops including Cascade, Centennial, Bravo, Citra	Clean American or English ale yeast; special ingredients may include sweet orange and coriander	A slightly subdued IPA with a soft tanginess from the wheat; some approaches fall into "Hoppy Witbier" territory	Deschutes Chainbreaker, New Belgium Accumulation, Harpoon The Long Thaw

BREWING NOTES

There are almost as many strong opinions about what American IPAs should contain as there are homebrewers making them! I think the one thing everybody agrees on is that the hop character should be at the forefront, but consensus seems to end there! Here's what I think.

The base malt should be either 2-row pale or pale ale malt, although pils malt can be used for lighter color and a less toasty flavor. Some sort of caramel malt will add body and maltiness to balance the hops. That can be anything from a very light malt like carapils to the more traditional 60L crystal, to a 120L crystal for deep malt flavor. Blending different crystal malts can add a depth of flavor. Many homebrewers feel like you should keep the cara/crystal malts to less than 5 percent of your total grist, but I don't like rules like that. John Maier at Rogue Brewing has shown that larger amounts can be successfully used if you take factors like hopping and overall beer body into account. Many of my recipes follow that lead.

American varieties should dominate the hop profile. Using British or German hops along with them can increase the hop complexity and make for a more interesting beer.

Mash temperatures in the low 150s work well for IPA, although you can go lower for a longer time for a thinner body or use higher temperatures for more body and to increase the effects of the crystal/cara malts.

BASIC IPA

This IPA recipe will provide you a base for experimenting with grains, hops, yeast, and water treatment. Or just brew it and drink it as it is!

For 5.5 gallons at 1.072, 73 IBU, 7.5% ABV

GRAIN BILL
13.75 lbs	2-Row Pale Malt
1.38 lbs (22 oz)	Crystal 60°L Malt
8.0 oz	Carapils Malt

MASH SCHEDULE
Rest   153°F   60 minutes

HOPS
1 oz	Mt. Hood	Whole	4.9% AA	First wort hop
0.85 oz	Columbus	Whole	17.8% AA	60 minutes
0.5 oz	Mt. Hood	Whole	4.9% AA	30 minutes
1.5 oz	Mt. Hood	Whole	4.9% AA	0 minutes
1 oz	Columbus	Whole	17.8% AA	Dry hop

OTHER INGREDIENTS
½ tablet Whirlfloc   10 minutes

Water adjustment as necessary to reach 250 ppm sulfate

YEAST
WY1450 Denny's Favorite or WY1056 American Ale in 3-qt starter

VARIANTS
- Wry Smile Rye IPA: Replace 3 lbs of the pale malt with 3 lbs of rye malt for a rye IPA.
- Oaked IPA (by Drew): Decrease the 60-minute Columbus addition to 0.5 ounce and ferment with a British strain like WLP005 British Ale or WY1275 Thames Valley. After primary fermentation, add 2 ounces of boiled oak cubes (French, medium toast) for 1–2 weeks. Go by taste. Package the beer at a slightly lower carbonation and you have an Englishy-oaky IPA!

HOPS ACROSS THE WATER
BELGO-AMERICAN IPA

By Denny

Not that long ago, the bitterest Belgian beer you could find was DeRanke's XX Bitter. It's a nice beer—assertive, but compared to the new IPAs flowing out of America, it's not that hoppy. No one could crack the code of how to marry aggressive American hops and Belgian yeast phenolics in a beer that really worked. Then Brassire Achouffe's Houblon Chouffe did it by ditching the prototypical American hops (Chinook, Centennial, Cascade) and going with two newer varieties: the neutral Warrior and the low-cohumulone, grapefruity Amarillo.

Today, there are a slew of new hops available that break the mold of expected hop characters. For example, Nelson Sauvin, a New Zealand variety, smells like Sauvignon Blanc, and Citra brings pineapple and mango to the party. That's not to say the usual American hops can't work for you, given a complementary choice of yeast. The big thing to keep in mind with this recipe is to think of it as an American IPA with a Belgian yeast, rather than as a Belgian beer with American hops. I don't use sugar because I want it to be more like an IPA than a tripel.

For 5.5 gallons (20.8L) at 1.080, 97 IBUs, 8.2% ABV

GRAIN BILL
16.0 lbs Pilsner Malt (use a continental brand)
1 lbs   Crystal 20°L Malt

MASH SCHEDULE
Rest   152°F   90 minutes

HOPS

Amount	Variety	Form	AA	Time
1 oz	Falconer's Flight	Pellet	10.5% AA	First wort hop
1.15 oz	Chinook	Whole	13% AA	60 minutes
1 oz	Centennial	Whole	8.6% AA	30 minutes
1 oz	Amarillo	Whole	8.9% AA	10 minutes
1 oz	Simcoe	Whole	12.9% AA	5 minutes
1 oz	Cascade	Whole	8% AA	0 minutes
0.5 oz	Cascade	Whole	8% AA	Dry hop
0.5 oz	Amarillo	Whole	8.9% AA	Dry hop
0.5 oz	Simcoe	Whole	12.9% AA	Dry hop

OTHER INGREDIENTS
½ tablet Whirlfloc   10 minutes
Water adjustments as necessary to achieve approximately 250 ppm sulfate and 50 ppm chloride

YEAST
WY3522 Ardennes in 2-L starter

ADDITIONAL INSTRUCTIONS
Ferment for about 10–14 days, starting at 63°F–65°F. Check the gravity and let the temperature rise if near 1.012. That will make sure the beer reaches the 1.012 goal. When the beer is at or near 1.012, transfer to secondary and add the dry hops for 1–2 weeks. If you keg, dry hops can also be added to the keg.

VARIANTS
- Switch-Up Belgian IPA: Try different hop combinations, but keep a distinct American C hop character. Try using a combination of a fruity hop like Citra with a pungent hop like Chinook or Columbus.
- Light IPA: Use a neutral ale yeast and make an American IPA. The pils malt and crystal 20 will give you a lighter color and body than a traditional IPA, with less toastiness from the malt.
- Belgian Rye IPA: Replace part of the pilsner malt with an equal amount of rye malt. Make sure it's at least 15 percent of your total malt bill.

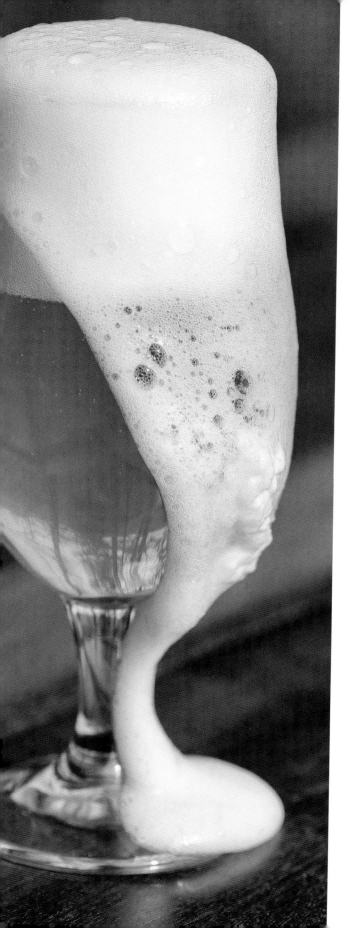

BELGIAN STYLE GOLDEN / TRIPEL By Denny

Belgian Golden Strong Ale (BGSA) and Belgian Tripel are two sides of the same coin. The main difference between them is the yeast strain used. A tripel may also be a bit hoppier, whereas Golden Strongs tend to present more phenols and alcohol tones. Both styles make a great base for an experiment because they're pretty neutral beers. The fermentables are often just Pilsner malt and sugar.

The character of both beers comes from the yeast. Even if you're unfamiliar with these styles, you're likely familiar with the yeast character in the classic examples: Duvel for Golden Strong and Westmalle for Tripel. Duvel yeast is reputedly derived from a Scotch ale yeast. Although it's developed a bit of phenolic character through the years, it has very low esters and is a relatively clean yeast. Westmalle yeast is more phenolic and a little more estery than Duvel's, but those characteristics are still pretty restrained. Westmalle's fermentation schedule, which stays in the low- to mid-60°sF during fermentation, reduces the fruitiness that the yeast can produce when it ferments warmer.

WHAT WORKS WELL

These are Belgian styles. You can pretty much do what you want to do and call it what you like. That's the Belgian beer spirit! Just remember that if you get too wacky, people may not recognize the base beer any more. And be sure to take a look at the recipe design chapter of this book for ideas on how to conceptualize what an ingredient might do when you add it.

Some Golden Strongs use Grains of Paradise for a peppery spice with a hint of fruit. White peppercorns approximate that flavor while bringing another dimension to the beer by taking that grains of paradise flavor and bumping it up a notch. Black peppercorns will add a definite spice to the beer. My favorite is a combination of red, white, and green peppercorns for a complex fruity spiciness that doesn't overwhelm the beer.

Other herbs and spices can also work well in these styles. Coriander, rose hips, cumin seeds, or rosemary can make interesting accents. The important thing to remember is to use restraint. A tripel with a hint of rosemary can be great. A rosemary tripel, not so much!

Using a clear or golden Belgian candi syrup in place of the sugar can add depth to the flavor. Golden Belgian syrup can even add a bit of honeylike flavor to your beer. For that matter, try different types of sugars: *piloncillo*, demerara, and date sugars each lend their own character to the beer.

WHAT DOESN'T WORK

Fruit is pretty risky, since it can easily overwhelm or compete with the yeast in these styles. Also, dark malts are pretty much contrary to the style if that matters to you. Even if it doesn't matter, think about how the roasty malt will interact with a Belgian yeast. If that kind of thing sounds good to you, consider brewing a Dubbel or Belgian Stout instead of trying to put roasted grains in a tripel or BGSA. Using a fruitier yeast that is typical for those styles will complement the roast malts.

BREWING NOTES

BGSA/Tripel recipes should be based on good pils malt. It doesn't necessarily have to be a Belgian pils malt. If you have good German Pils malt on hand already, that will be perfectly fine. With most modern malts, a protein rest isn't necessary. You can do a step mash if you feel there's a benefit. (Hey, that sounds like an experiment on page 210.) I simply use a 90-minute rest at 148°F. The longer-than-usual mash time assures full conversion at a lower-than-normal temperature. The temperature makes sure you get a very fermentable wort, producing a beer with the digestibility that Belgian styles are noted for.

Sugar is a necessity for both of these styles in order to keep the fermentability of the wort high. Don't fall for the old line that sugar will give your beer a cidery flavor, whatever that's supposed to mean! The sugar can be added at the beginning of the boil (my preferred method), the end of the boil, or even in the fermenter. As discussed on page 143, different sugars will give you different effects. But don't be afraid to use good old table sugar, either cane or beet. There's really no difference in the final product between those two, and they're what Belgian brewers usually use. We don't recommend the use of rock candi sugar. It offers no advantages over table sugar and is much more expensive. Candi syrups, on the other hand, are a great way to add flavor and fermentability to the beer.

Many people don't realize that tripels are hopped to a fairly high bitterness level. I shoot for about 30 IBU in my Westcoastmalle Tripel. A too-sweet tripel is hard to drink!

It used to be thought that Belgian beers are fermented at high temperatures. That's not exactly true. Most BGSA/Tripel styles will benefit from starting the fermentation in the mid-60°sF and holding that temperature for 3–7 days. After that, temperatures can rise to the mid-70°sF to ensure complete fermentation. Remember, we're going for digestibility, so we don't want a thick, sweet, underattenuated beer.

On the yeast front, after years of fighting the "make a starter, dammit" battle, there are still some brewers trying to use yeast pitching rates to affect the final character of the beer. The belief is that by pitching reduced amount of yeast, you'll create a stronger ester and phenol profile in comparison to pitching at traditional ale rates. There's truth here in that additional reproductive stress will cause an increase in stressor chemicals, but most homebrewers are already actively pitching at levels below what's ideal, even when they use a starter. Remember that as a beer's gravity goes up, so does the amount of yeast required. By the time we're in beers of these strengths, it's almost impossible to pitch too much yeast by making a starter.

As for trusting online yeast calculators—which a number of brewers use to plan their yeast starter sizes and timings—please remember that those calculators are helpful, but they're estimations

WESTCOASTMALLE
TRIPEL

By Denny

Here's my basic recipe for tripel, which I call Westcoastmalle. As you might guess, it's my homage (I don't use the word *clone*) to Westmalle Tripel.

For 5.5 gallons at 1.081, 34 IBUs, 9.4% ABV

GRAIN BILL

12.0 lbs	Pilsner Malt (continental, not domestic)
2.5 lbs	Table sugar (cane or beet)

Note: Add sugar any time after boil starts.

MASH SCHEDULE

Rest	148°F	90 minutes

HOPS

1 oz	Czech Saaz	Pellet	4.3% AA	First wort hop
1.25 oz	Hallertauer	Whole	4.8% AA	60 minutes
0.5 oz	Tettnanger Tettnang	Pellet	4% AA	30 minutes
1 oz	Czech Saaz	Pellet	4.3% AA	5 minutes

OTHER INGREDIENTS

½ tablet	Whirlfloc	10 minutes

YEAST

WY3787 Trappist High Gravity in 2-L starter

ADDITIONAL INSTRUCTIONS

Ferment for about 14–21 days, starting at 63°F–65°F. Check the gravity, and if it's near 1.010, let the temperature rise. That will make sure the beer reaches the 1.010 goal.

VARIANTS

- Kentucky Revival Tripel by Drew: Soak 1 ounce of American oak cubes in enough Bourbon to cover for at least 2 weeks, although longer is preferable. When the primary has completed, transfer the beer to a cold space (50°F) and add the oak for 2–4 weeks. The result is a smooth vanilla-and-bourbon tropical custard in your glass!

- Sugar Sugar Tripel: Replace the 3 pounds of table sugar with an equal amount of demerara, *piloncillo*, or date sugar to deepen the flavor and add fruit notes. You can also caramelize some honey, agave syrup, light candi syrup, or even liquid malt extract in a sauté pan and add that. Boil down the syrup or honey until it turns a little darker and is reduced by about 25 percent, then add it to the kettle at the end of the boil.

based on presumed normal factors. The right answer if you want to do this is to grab a microscope, a hemacytometer, and some methylene blue. We cover this technique on page 91.

So unless you're ready to perform viability counts, you should stick to the principle of more yeast and a complete ferment. Little is worse than a sickly sweet underfermented strong ale. You can also brew a smaller beer (OG <1.055)—say Belgian Blonde—and use that batch's yeast cake to power your main ferment.

CARAMELIZED HONEY PEPPER TRIPEL

By Denny

This recipe will yield a richly flavored tripel with a hint of spice on the finish. However, it's still a highly drinkable beer due to the overall amount of sugars promoting great fermentability. You'll also notice the bitterness is just a bit lower than the Westcoastmalle Tripel so that it doesn't compete with the white peppercorns. A word of warning: Don't enter this into a competition as a tripel. The honey and and peppercorns take it way out of style. That's OK, though. You'll want this one all to yourself anyway!

For 5.5 gallons at 1.081 OG, 24 IBU, 9.4% ABV

GRAIN BILL

12 lbs	Pilsner Malt
2 lbs	Honey, caramelized (see Additional Instructions)
1 lbs	Demerara sugar, 10 minutes

MASH SCHEDULE

Rest	148°F	90 minutes

HOPS

.5 oz	Horizon	Pellet	12% AA	60 minutes
.5 oz	Tettnanger Tettnang	Pellet	4% AA	20 minutes

OTHER INGREDIENTS

½ tablet	Whirlfloc	10 minutes
15	White peppercorns, coarsely cracked	2 minutes

YEAST

WY3787 Trappist High Gravity in 3-qt starter

ADDITIONAL INSTRUCTIONS

You can use any type of honey you like; it doesn't have to be expensive specialty honey. While the mash and boil are going on, add the honey to a wide pan and put on medium low heat. You want to reduce the honey by about ⅓–½, or until it begins to darken and become caramelized. Heat slowly to avoid scorching and keep an eye on it. It can go from golden brown to burned in just a few seconds. When you see it begin to change color, remove it from the heat immediately. Add the caramelized honey to the kettle at flameout. Chill wort to 62°F. Ferment at 65°F for 7 days, then let temperature free rise for another 10–14 days or until done.

MILD By Drew

To the modern American brewer completely divorced from the realities on the ground in the United Kingdom, the mild remains a mystery. Yet the modern dark mild is worth getting to know. It is a fine balancing act of malty sweet and just a modicum of roast with no overt hop character to get in the way. Then there's the pale mild: subtract the roast and rock on.

At first glance, a beer best known for sessionability may not seem like the best style to play with, but the easy-to-quaff factor is actually a big reason I recommend it. A beer of low carbonation that is sweetish, but not cloying; toasted, but not acrid; rich, but not heavy; soft, but not wimpy can be a thing of beauty. In other words, it is a beer of such balance that it becomes a perfect canvas for flavors and techniques that are on the less extreme end of the spectrum.

In a time where music plays as loud as possible and even potato chips are battling a war of "xtremez," it's easy to forget that more does not necessarily mean better. Look at a modern song's volume amplitudes, and you'll see that the song's dynamic range (difference of low volume to high volume) is tiny, and the sonic envelope is flattened into a dreadful buzz. Try the newest flavor of nacho-cheez-blasted corn chip and try to taste any hint of corn—or actual cheese. My point is that you can and should experiment with beer without overpowering your senses and sensibilities. Sometimes turning the volume down is the best way to fully appreciate a flavor or aroma.

Oh and there's another great reason to brew a mild: speed. If you have kegs and can force-carbonate the beer, then you can put a mild on tap in as little as four days.

WHAT WORKS WELL

If you can imagine a coffee with the flavor you're exploring, then you can incorporate it in a dark mild without much problem. Sweet flavors work especially well, including things we perceive as sweet—think Christmas cookie spices or a vanilla chocolate mild. Unlike many of the other styles in this chapter, a mild works really well with these sweet flavors.

A mild can also work well with warm spices, such as curry, Chinese five spice powder, or cinnamon. For best results with these hotter spices, you'll want to make sure you retain a fair amount of body either with a less attentuative yeast strain or with the addition of flaked barley or oats. Alternatively, if you're working at the upper end of the mild spectrum, you could add strong fruit, like sherry-soaked raisins or currants, to give a little winter warmth.

The pale mild category is a bit of an ahistorical odd duck; does it exist or is it just a fresh and less hopped bitter ale? We'll leave that matter to our friends who are righteous experts in the practical history of the styles, like Ron Pattison of the *Shut Up about Barclay Perkins* blog (and author of *The Home Brewer's Guide to Vintage Beer*). What we do know is that a pale mild is a hell of a treat and can be doctored with a number ingredients. Careful with spices, though, unless you want someone to confuse it for a strange witbier.

WHAT DOESN'T WORK

The biggest thing to keep in mind is that anything can ruin a mild if you use too much of it. Avoid going over the top with your additions and changes to the base recipe. While the malt flavors give you some buffering capacity, you don't have nearly the margin of error that you do in a bigger beer.

Session Beers

In the world of online arguments amongst beer-minded folks, one of the most amusing is "What is a session beer?" Traditionalists will say that anything over 3.5% or 4% ABV is way too strong to be a session beer. Macho drinkers scoff and say that any beer is a session beer if you can keep drinking it and drinking it.

The term is nominally British and comes from the concept of the session at the pub with your buddies. Here in the US, drinking tends to be an individual sport even when you are partying with pals. We all proceed at our pace, buying our own drinks. In the UK, pub time is centered on the round. When you gather with friends, it is understood that you drink together and that each person stands their round (aka you buy the drinks for everyone, and they likewise will buy drinks for you). Since it is a horrible breach of etiquette and pub life to skip out on your round, you're going to be at the pub for a while. As you can imagine, if you have a sizeable group it takes a number of drinks to get to your turn. If you're sitting there throwing back even moderately-rated beer (at 5.0% ABV), you'll get drunk quickly—hence the need for session-strength ales. A mild or bitter at 3.2% will let you pop off to the pub with your mates and still be reasonably functional after multiple rounds spent watching the match.

But it's not just the Brits that enjoy a low ABV beer. The Belgians may be known for their uber-strong exports, but they also have a tradition of more modest-strength beer referred to as tafelbier.

SCHOOLHOUSE TAFELBIER
by Drew

This recipe was inspired by a proposed plan by the Belgian government to replace soda machines in their schools with machines that served tafelbier (table beer), which used to be served to children at meals. Please note, even though the recipe is built for 5.5 gallons, it's really a lot easier to make as a double batch due to the small amount of grain!

For 5.5 gallons at 1.025, 7.2 IBUs, 1.7% ABV

GRAIN BILL
3.75 lbs Belgian Pilsner Malt
1.0 lbs   Caravienne Malt
4 oz   Aromatic Malt

MASH SCHEDULE
Rest   155°   60 minutes

HOPS
0.5 oz   Czech Saaz Pellets   3.2% AA   60 minutes

OTHER INGREDIENTS
1/2 tablet   Whirlfloc   10 minutes
1 tsp   Freshly cracked black pepper   5 minutes

YEAST
WY1214 Belgian Ale

ADDITIONAL INSTRUCTIONS
- Capture the first gallon of runnings and boil in a separate pot until reduced in half. Take the remaining runnings and proceed as normal. Add the cracked black pepper and the boiled runnings syrup in the last 5 minutes of the boil.
- Ferment cool and carbonate to 3 volumes to fluff up the body of the beer.

Two specific things to avoid are sour flavors and anything tannic. Bright acidic notes tend to clash and overaccentuate the roasted malts, which throws the palate sensations completely out of whack. This also applies to tannic flavors, so use a very light hand if you plan to use oak or any other woods.

EXPRESS MILD
By Drew

This is a beer I've turned around quite successfully in just four days from brew day to people's glasses. If that's not outrageous enough, just look to the variants.

For 5.5 gallons at 1.036, 12 IBUs, 3.2% ABV

GRAIN BILL
6.5 lbs	Maris Otter Malt
1.0 lb	Flaked Oats or Oat Malt
8.0 oz	British Crystal 55°L Malt
8.0 oz	Carafa II Special Malt

MASH SCHEDULE
Rest   154°F   60 minutes

HOPS
0.25	Target	Pellet	11.5% AA	60 minutes
0.12	Progress	Pellet	8.1% AA	20 minutes

OTHER INGREDIENTS
½ tablet Whirlfloc   10 minutes

YEAST
WY1275 Thames Valley or WLP022 Essex Ale

ADDITIONAL INSTRUCTIONS
Ferment cool and carbonate to a low volume (1.5–2.0). Serve quickly and enjoy fresh.

VARIANTS
- Cherrywood Smoked Mild: Substitute 3 pounds of the Maris Otter Malt with Briess Cherrywood Smoked Mild Malt. Drop the Progress addition and ferment and package as normal for a lightly smoky session beer. Try other smoked malts to see their flavors (except Peat malt, which doesn't belong anywhere near a beer).
- Cocoa Insanity: Substitute Pale Chocolate Malt for Carafa II in the grain bill and add another half pound of oats. At packaging, add homemade vanilla extract and our defatted cacao extract (see page 179), to taste.
- Old Time Mild: Increase the Maris Otter Malt to 14 pounds and up the hop additions to 1.0 ounce Target and 0.5 ounce Progress. This pushes the beer into more traditional mild territory of the 1700s, when milds weren't weak! (For a commercial example similar to this, hunt down Original Sarah Hughes Dark Ruby Mild from the United Kingdom.)

CURRIED OAT MILD

By Drew

Curry, particularly tikka masala, is widely considered the modern national dish of Britain. Why not make a beer that celebrates the complex relationship between East and West? This beer is based around a spice load that contains many of the pungent aromatics of Northern and Southern Indian curries, including the ubiquitous and ever-changing North Indian garam masala. Since different brands of garam masala can vary, find a brand that works for you. (I use a garam masala blend from a local spice house.) This beer also uses one my favorite and less celebrated ingredients: Oat Malt (see page 141).

For 5.5 gallons at 1.036, 14 IBUs, 3.5% ABV

GRAIN BILL
6.0 lbs	Maris Otter Malt
2.0 lbs	Flaked Oats or Oat Malt
8.0 oz	British Crystal 55°L

MASH SCHEDULE
Rest	152°F	60 minutes

HOPS
0.25	Magnum	Pellet	12.9% AA	60 minutes

OTHER INGREDIENTS
½ tablet	Whirlfloc	10 minutes
1 knuckle	Ginger, peeled and sliced	15 minutes
½ tsp	Freshly ground cumin	0 minutes
½ tsp	Freshly cracked Indian coriander	0 minutes
½ tsp	Garam masala powder	0 minutes
¼ tsp	Rough cracked black peppercorn	0 minutes
¼ tsp	Paprika	0 minutes

YEAST
WY1275 Thames Valley or WLP022 Essex Ale

ADDITIONAL INSTRUCTIONS
- Ferment cool and carbonate to a low volume (1.5–2.0). Serve quickly and enjoy fresh.
- If you want more color, prepare a 4-ounce vodka tincture (see page 75) with 1 teaspoon each of paprika and turmeric. Strain through coffee filters and add to the beer.

BREWING NOTES

With a low original gravity (1.030–1.038), the mild requires nothing but the best ingredients in order to stand as a platform for your tests. This begins with your choice of base malt. While that American 2-Row looks tempting and cheap, for the love of all that's holy, use a proper premium British Ale malt like Maris Otter or Golden Promise. Supplement that with a solid British medium crystal for a touch of sweetness. If you want a body boost, an addition of oats (flaked or malted) will do the trick. Finally, we come to the dark part of the equation (for dark milds). Traditionally you'd use a British chocolate or black malt and call it a day, but I prefer using the softer, less acrid Weyermann Dehusked Carafa II malt for color and a light roasted toffee character. For a pale mild, just leave the roasted malts in the bin.

Mash the grain on the warm side, at least 152°F–154°F, to create those extra dextrins. A simple single infusion mash is both practical and traditional. When you first make a beer with this little grain, you may want to plan for an efficiency drop. If you want to play it safe, boost the malt bill and then dilute with water to achieve your target gravity if needed—on the upside, more beer! It is also paramount to watch your pH and keep it from rising too high in the sparging steps, since the tannins will be extra noticable in this smallish beer.

For hops, go traditional with British strains like Fuggles or EKG throughout. You can also use a British bittering hop like Progress or Challenger. Keep the IBUs unconsciously low from an American perspective at around 12. Use one or two charges and enjoy the time spent brewing without dashing to the kettle every five minutes for hop additions.

Choose a yeast that accentuates malt, such as WY1275 Thames Valley or WLP022 Essex Ale. Ferment cool and allow it to finish out. Voilà, you have a session ale that's ready for quaffing! Before you start sipping, you'll need to carbonate it, but keep the carbonation low. Somewhere around 1.5–2.0 volumes of CO_2 is to style. This is a traditional English session ale after all!

AMERICAN ROBUST PORTER By Denny

American Robust Porter is bigger and has more flavor than a brown or English-style porter. This extra flavor makes it a great base for your experiments. No matter what you decide to add, the underlying porter flavor doesn't get lost as it might with a beer with less body or flavor.

I love to experiment with this style because the basic flavor profile reminds me of chocolate. Just think of all the things that go along with chocolate.

WHAT WORKS WELL

Speaking of things that go with chocolate, coffee is a real treat in a robust porter—especially if you happen to be one of those overachievers who roast their own coffee! Believe it or not, blueberries work great in a porter, too. They are pretty subtle, so I'd recommend you use more of them than you might for a lighter-flavored beer. The upside of that subtlety, though, is that the blueberry flavor integrates wonderfully when you get it right. While a strongly flavored beer like a porter can stand up to strong flavors, don't completely abandon the idea that it's great to land your flavors to be right on that edge of "what's that?"

I would be remiss if I didn't mention that the base porter recipe on page 122 was developed for a Bourbon Vanilla Imperial Porter. The combination of the chocolaty porter with vanilla beans and bourbon is a real wintertime treat.

WHAT DOESN'T WORK

There are lots of things that wouldn't work in this beer: lemons, beef, pickles, and aspirin, for instance. But that's all obvious stuff, right? The following recommendations are based on my own tastes. If you disagree, be my guest.

A lot of people like chocolate and mint together, but adding mint to a beer like this can make it taste a lot like cough syrup. Chocolate and peanut butter? Also not for me, thank you. But if it sounds good to you, take a look at Drew's information about powdered peanut butter on page 133.

I would avoid the fruitier hops, like Citra and Meridian, as the sole hops for this style. Although blueberries might be great, too much tropical fruit flavor will clash with the chocolate and roast flavors in this recipe. If you want to use those hops, be sure to blend them with something that will temper their impact.

No matter what specialty ingredient you choose, be aware that you can easily go over the top with bitterness in this beer style. If you add something like coffee, you might even want to experiment with reducing the bittering hops to compensate for the bitterness from the coffee.

WHY NOT RYE PORTER

While a rye porter isn't as off-the-wall as some of the other recipes here, it's an unusual style that you don't see too often. The rye adds a real smoothness to the mouthfeel. You need to take a careful approach to both the grist and the hopping, though, so that the spiciness of the rye and the roastiness of the malt don't result in a sharp and biting flavor. In this recipe, the hops are cut back a bit from what I use for other porters, and the use of Munich malt smooths out the flavor. The Special B adds some sweetness and raisiny flavor to offset the dark malts.

For 5.5 gallons at 1.073, 40 IBU, 8% ABV

GRAIN BILL
11.0 lbs 2-Row Pale Malt
1.75 lbs Munich Malt (10°L)
1 lbs Crystal 60°L Malt
1 lbs Flaked Rye
14 oz Chocolate Rye Malt (350°L)
8 oz Special B Malt
1 oz Black Patent Malt

MASH SCHEDULE
Rest 154°F 60 minutes

HOPS

0.75 oz	Tettnang	Pellet	4.6% AA	First wort hop
0.6 oz	Magnum	Whole	14.6% AA	60 minutes
0.75 oz	Cascade	Whole	6% AA	10 minutes

OTHER INGREDIENTS
½ tablet Whirlfloc 10 minutes

YEAST
WY1450 Denny's Favorite or WY1056 American Ale in 3L starter

ADDITIONAL INSTRUCTIONS
Ferment for about 10–14 days, starting at 63°F–65°F.

BREWING NOTES

The original gravity of this beer is fairly high, and the final gravity is, too. That's intentional to give it a chewy body. The Munich malt and two different crystal malts contribute to that. The brown malt is an essential for this recipe. Be aware that different maltsters have very different ideas of what brown malt is! For the purposes of this recipe, you want a brown malt that's about 70°L.

The hops should be supportive, not take center stage. I use Magnum for the smooth bittering they give you and finish with just a bit of East Kent Goldings, which have a candylike character.

If you're going to add flavorings to the base recipe, keep the yeast neutral. Something like WY1056 American Ale or WY1450 Denny's Favorite works well. The latter will accentuate the smooth mouthfeel of this beer.

Be aware that the final gravity of this beer flies in the face of the low numbers that homebrewers strive for. It will finish in the 1.020–25 range. Don't think you have a stuck fermentation! The recipe is designed for that FG.

BASE IMPERIAL PORTER

By Denny

Don't be fooled by the name. While this was designed as a base beer, if you don't add anything at all, it's still a very tasty brew! Do note that this beer has a high final gravity; don't worry if it doesn't get as low as you're used to.

For 5.5 gallons at 1.086, 40 IBUs, 8.7% ABV

GRAIN BILL

12.0 lbs	2-Row Pale Malt
2.75 lbs	Munich Malt (10°L)
1.6 lbs (26 oz)	Brown Malt (70°L)
1.38 lbs (22 oz)	Chocolate Malt (350°L)
1 lbs	Crystal Malt (120°L)
8 oz	Crystal Malt (60°L)

MASH SCHEDULE

Rest	154°F	60 minutes

HOPS

0.75 oz	Magnum	Whole	14.6% AA	60 minutes
0.5 oz	East Kent Goldings	Whole	4.75% AA	10 minutes

OTHER INGREDIENTS

½ tablet	Whirlfloc	10 minutes

YEAST

WY1450 Denny's Favorite or WY1056 in 3-L starter

ADDITIONAL INSTRUCTIONS

Ferment for about 10–14 days, starting at 63°F–65°F. Check the gravity and let the temperature rise once you're getting close to the 1.030 mark.

VARIANTS

- Bourbon Vanilla Imperial Porter: This porter was originally devised to have bourbon and vanilla added to it. When fermentation is complete, split 2 vanilla beans lengthwise. Scrape all the seeds and gunk from them and add the scrapings to a sanitized secondary fermenter. Chop the beans into 2- to 3-inch-long pieces and add them, too. Rack the beer onto the vanilla in the secondary. Leave in secondary 10–14 days, then taste. You want the vanilla to be a bit on the strong side, since it will fade. If the vanilla flavor is adequate, rack to bottling bucket or keg and add approximately 375 milliliters of Jim Beam Black Bourbon. You don't need to use an expensive bourbon, and you don't want to add a lot. The beer shouldn't scream, "BOURBON!" at you. It should have an integrated flavor of chocolaty porter, vanilla, and bourbon. This beer does not benefit from extended aging. I prefer it within a few months of brewing.
- Coffee Porter: Add a sanitized muslin bag with about 5 ounces of coarsely cracked coffee beans to a secondary fermenter once fermentation is complete. Rack the beer into the secondary and let that steep for 5–7 days for a great aroma and a bit of flavor. Then when you bottle or keg the beer, add strong brewed coffee to taste.
- Blueberry Porter: If you want to add blueberries, use at least 1.5 pounds per gallon for this beer. The best way to add blueberries is to freeze and thaw them before adding them to a sanitized secondary fermenter and racking the beer onto them. The freeze-thaw process breaks down the cell walls and allows you to extract more juice. Leave the beer in secondary 1–2 weeks, then taste. Package when the blueberry flavor is the strength you want.
- Banana Porter: If you like bananas and chocolate, try fermenting this porter with a German Hefeweizen yeast. Ferment in the low 70°sF to increase the banana flavor.

SAISON By Drew

Saisons are a class of farmhouse ales steeped in romantic legend. The story says that in days of yore, farmers needed to slake the thirst of their laborers. Since plain drinking water was often unsafe, they would make beer during the off-season and crack open the barrels and bottles to ease the long hot work of farming. The beer provided was part of the pay for the field hands, but it was also part hospitality. At one point, providing booze as the only pay to farmhands was so widespread that laws forbidding the practice were put on the books. (In the United Kingdom, for example, it wasn't farmhouse ale, but cider that had to be curtailed.)

While that's a great story, as near as I can tell, it's a load of pucky when it comes to the modern notion of saison. When Belgian brewing scientist extraordinaire Jean De Clerck wrote his comprehensive *A Textbook of Brewing* in the late 1940s, he made no mention of saison as a style. It's likely that the whole modern take on saison was inspired by the exemplar of the style, Brasserie Dupont. In Belgian practice, which largely ignores style, Dupont's beers would have been considered as *ambrées*. Where then did the notion of the formal category arise? More than likely it was the original evangelist, Michael Jackson, who sought categories to help readers understand the wide varied world of beer.

Saisons these days come in two strength categories: normal/table or super. The normal version provides 4–6.5 percent ABV, while the super saisons can climb into the teens. Which you choose to make is up to you, but remember that the higher the gravity, the trickier your ferment will be.

Speaking of which, saison is all about the yeast selection and fermentation. No other style of ale is as driven and defined by the yeast you use. Fortunately for homebrewers, an ever-increasing variety of style-specific strains is available to make your beers sing. In 2011, when I first performed a saison yeast comparison, ten strains were commonly available to homebrewers. Since then a new raft of varieties have hit the market. Today you can find yeasts from Brasserie Dupont, Brasserie Thiriez, Brasserie Blaugies, Fantome, and others dug out of old banks. See page 156 for my cheat sheet on yeast selection.

WHAT WORKS WELL

The usual additions of Munich malts and wheat or other adjuncts provide enough body to support almost anything you throw at it: spices, hops, fruits, tea, or the kitchen sink. There's very little that doesn't work in the framework of a saison. The main thing to watch for is the interaction of your target flavor with the spice phenols produced by your yeast. Of the myriad strains of saison yeasts available, WY3711 French Saison provides the cleanest saisonesque backdrop with which to play. There are enough phenols to establish saison provenance, but not enough to interfere with most other ingredients. By itself, however, I feel that a better straight saison can be had with many of the other more finicky strains.

The blend of maltiness and dryness in saisons makes them ideal candidates for fruit. Also, despite the dryness, saisons have enough malt character to stand up to a high level of hopping—especially with noble or fruity new hops.

Where a number of the classic Belgian IPAs are based on Belgian Golden bases, there's a real history in the saison world of hoppy beers. You need look no farther than the 1970 creation of Avec

Les Bon Voeux de la Brasserie Dupont, or as most Americans say, Avec. This beer, translated as, "With the best wishes of the Dupont Brewery," started as a New Year's present to friends of the brewery. But it caught on and became a year-round beer! It comes in at 9.5 percent ABV with a brisk tropical fruit character broken by the grassy spiciness of noble hops. Unusual for a Belgian beer, it's also dry hopped. Where did Belgian IPA start? Looks like we have a good candidate!

So far we haven't talked about the use of *Brett* and other "wild" creatures in a saison. A trend that I see is a number of increasingly funky wild saisons. The operating theory is that how sanitary would a farmhouse be? I strongly prefer any wild character in a saison to be a secondary note and will almost always reach for the spicy, fruity *B. claussenii* over the funkier, earthier *B. lambicus* or *B. bruxellensis*. Added to the secondary or later in ferment with a little extra food, *B. claussenii* provides bright, spicy notes that integrate well with existing saison aromas.

WHAT DOESN'T WORK

Candy-sweet flavors are best avoided. While there's someone out there right now ready to argue the merits of their awesome Milk Chocolate Caramel Saison, I politely disagree. Sweet things need to be considered very carefully when played against the backdrop of the bone-dry saison.

Too much sweetness will make a clashing, cloying, muddled mess of a beer. This includes not just sugary things, but too much of any spice or flavor that triggers sweet associations in the brain. For instance, substantial vanilla will cause your palate to hunt out any signs of sweetness. However, a hint of vanilla can provide a rich top note to your saison.

White or Common Horehound (*Marrubium vulgare*)

A favorite candy flavor of mine is horehound, an old medicinal plant used since Roman times for a diverse set of maladies, including sore throats and digestion. I blame my grandfather for giving me horehound drops from the five and dime in his little New England village. Of course I tried to use horehound candy in a saison, and oh boy was it terrible. The combination of the candy sweetness and the high herbal tones clashed over the background of the saison's earthiness.

Not to be deterred, I tracked down an actual horehound plant. It's a gray and furry-leafed perennial herb related to mint. In fact, it smells like an earthy, leathery mint. The flavor is intense. The right approach was to dose a beer after the ferment when I could taste it in portions. I don't tend to like mint extracts, as they miss the earthy base notes of the plant and instead give you those high oils we perceive as sweet. Since horehound is delicate, I steeped it for ten minutes in water just off the boil. In a 500-milliliter graduated jar, I poured a carbonated sample of the saison and pipetted small amounts of horehound tea until I discovered that for that beer and that strength horehound tea, I needed 5 milliliters of horehound tea to hit the right balance. You'll need to do the same procedure, since your horehound tea and beer will undoubtably be different from mine.

SAISON EXPÉRIMENTAL

By Drew

In 2011, a beer like this was brewed at Eagle Rock Brewing Company and pitched with thirteen different yeast strains for presentation to the attendees of the 2011 American Homebrewer's Association National Homebrewer's Conference. It was quite eye-opening and was an experiment that I encourage you to repeat. Of course, whatever experiment you want to get up to is off to a perfect start with this brew. It is dry, crisp, and refreshing as all get-out.

For 5.5 gallons at 1.048, 22 IBUs, 4.7% ABV

GRAIN BILL
8.75 lbs Pilsner Malt
8.0 oz   Flaked Wheat
8.0 oz   Table sugar

MASH SCHEDULE
Rest   150°F   60 minutes

HOPS
0.35 oz Magnum Pellet   12.9% AA   60 minutes
0.45 oz Saphir Pellet   4.4% AA   10 minutes

OTHER INGREDIENTS
½ tablet Whirlfloc   10 minutes

YEAST
WY3711 French Saison for flavor experiments or WLP565 Belgian Saison I for straight or spicy saisons

ADDITIONAL INSTRUCTIONS
Don't forget to chill the beer into the lower 60°sF before pitching the yeast. Once the yeast is in, keep the beer chugging along in the high 60°sF for a day or two and allow it to rise naturally into the low 80°sF. You'll end up with a spicy, but not headache-inducing, beer this way.

VARIANTS
- Jasmine Dragon Saison: My wife loves Jasmine-infused green tea, so one year as a treat for her, I combined my love of saisons with her love of tea. To make it, take a simple saison like the one above and add a tea tincture made by soaking ½ cup of jasmine dragon pearl tea in 1 cup of vodka for a week. Shake routinely and add to the keg by taste. Also, enjoy the show as the pearls blossom into beautiful tea flowers.
- Saison Sangreal: California runs amok with produce, and one of my favorite seasonal pieces is the late winter arrival of Moro blood oranges. Drop the Saphir from the recipe above. Make at least 3 liters of blood orange juice; that's usually 20–25 pounds of oranges. Freeze the juice. Zest 3 of the oranges and add to the kettle whirlpool. After primary fermentation subsides, add the thawed blood orange juice and complete the fermentation.
- Saison Vin: I like associations and stories with my beers, and this one is as simple as French style name + the French love of wine. This is also the only way you'll see me using a superconcentrated canned wine kit. They cook the grape must into a thick syrup that is used as brewers use liquid malt extract. Unfortunately, the must ends up tasting cooked and stale, unlike liquid malt extract. For this variant, scale up the pilsner to 10 pounds and the wheat to 1 pound, and drop the sugar. Once the *krausen* rises in primary fermentation, add one can (48 ounces) of Merlot concentrate. Swirl the fermenter gently and allow the fermentation to complete before adding 2 ounces of French Oak cubes that have soaked in red wine for at least 1 month. Leave the oak in contact for a minimum of 2 weeks.

CITRA SAISON

By Drew

Denny has a strong dislike of all tropical hop beers, but this is the beer that should shut him—or any hater—right up. Magnum doesn't provide much flavor, just a nice clean bitterness.

For 5.5 gallons at 1.058, 51 IBUs, 6.5% ABV

GRAIN BILL
6 lbs   Pilsner Malt
4 lbs   Wheat Malt
0.5 lbs   Munich Malt
0.7 lbs   White table sugar

MASH SCHEDULE
Rest   149°F   60 minutes

HOPS

| 0.7 oz | Magnum | Pellet | 12% AA | 90 minutes |
| 1.8 oz | Citra | Pellet | 11% AA | 5 minutes |

OTHER INGREDIENTS
½ tablet Whirlfloc   10 minutes

YEAST
WY3711 French Saison

ADDITIONAL INSTRUCTIONS
Ferment using our saison profile: cool and then warm up. Before you package the beer, give it a taste and see what you think of the Citra flavor and aroma. If you want more Citra, then add 1 more ounce of Citra as a dry hop. Be careful, though, because Citra is intensely aromatic and can become jarring when used in excess. Adding too much may render the beer overly intense, overwhelming its "saisonness."

Stop Saison Stalling

If you find you're having problems time after time with saison strain stalling, there are three primary culprits:

Not enough yeast

Not enough heat

Too much pressure in the fermenter

That last one may surprise you, but the scuttlebutt says that the two primary saison strains (WY3724 Belgian Saison and WLP565 Belgian Saison) originally came from red wine yeast. Wine yeasts are incredibly pressure-sensitive and will stall out under pressure that doesn't bother most ale yeasts. To solve that problem, I use a piece of sanitized foil slapped over the top of the fermenter instead of an airlock during most of the fermentation. When the beer approaches completion, I'll add the airlock. Since switching to the foil, I haven't had a saison stall on me in years!

In fact, I strongly encourage brewers to embrace simplicity in making saisons. Even amongst commercial brewers, I see a ton of overreaching combinations of things like Pineapple Upside Down Cake Golden Raisin Bourbon Oaked Saison. Focus your flavors, people! Your saisons will be better for it.

BREWING NOTES

Start with a base of clean, crisp pilsner malt. You can use a European variety like Weyermann or Best Pilz or turn to a domestic variety like IdaPils. Make sure it's fresh and firm before use! On top of the pilsner, consider a portion of Munich if you want a slightly orange color and a hint of toasted biscuits in the brew. To round it out, add a portion of wheat malt. This will provide a lingering sweetness that isn't cloying and will preserve a little body to avoid straight-razor dryness from the fermentation. Want to play with other grains? Remember that the Belgians are big fans of oats, and I think oats work well here to provide a little roundness. If you want to make a super saison, increase the pilsner malt poundage and add a pound or two of sugar as well. My rule of thumb no matter the gravity is sugar below 10 percent of fermentables, oats between 10–15 percent, and wheat for up to 50 percent.

For chilling, you'll want to get the wort good and cold, about 63°F–65°F, before pitching the yeast. The yeast should have been grown into a 2-liter starter or pitched from a previous batch of beer. Saison yeasts can be temperamental beasts; don't start them off in a weakened state! Allow the yeast to reproduce cold for 24 hours and then allow it to naturally ramp in a water bath into the low 80°sF. Let it hang there and ferment until the gravity is below 1.010. If the yeast stalls, be patient. If it still hasn't finished in a month, pitch a neutral yeast and allow it to finish the ferment.

What is the most common flaw amongst homebrewed saisons? It's sweetness—not just from sweet-intensifying flavors, but from poor yeast performance and high final gravities. Before you do anything funky odd with a saison, you really must strive for a complete fermentation—one that drops the final gravity below 1.010.

BEER

1.00 l

CONVENTIONAL BREWING INGREDIENTS

IF YOU'RE GOING TO EXPERIMENT with beer, you definitely need to take some time to master the ingredients that form the foundation of all beers. Although different beers can have a lot of different ingredients, from fruit to spruce, there are four main ingredients that you're sure to see: grains, hops, yeast, and water. These are the components that every brewer must consider when making or drinking beer. And then there's the matter of oft-maligned sugar. It may not be beloved by the Germans, but virtually every other brewing culture out there has discovered great uses for it. From British Bitters to Belgian Dubbels to American Imperial IPA, sugar is everywhere you turn. You just have to know how to use it.

GRAINS

Grain is the heart of a beer. In fact, the fermented grain we know as malt is what separates beer from fermented fruit beverages such as wine and cider. Before we look at specific grains, let's first look at the process that allows grain to be made into malt.

MALTING

The malting process starts the activation of amylase enzymes in the grain, which eventually convert the grain starches to fermentable sugars. First, maltsters dampen the grain to a specific moisture level. The moisture is maintained at a specific temperature until the grain begins to germinate.

You'll often hear brewers talking about modification. It's this germination process they're referring to: The sprout coming out of the end of the grain is referred to as an acrospire, and the amount it grows reflects the amount of modification of the grain. The longer it sprouts, the further the activation of grain enzymes has gone. This activation, in turn, is an indicator of how easily the grain can be mashed. As the acrospire grows, the protein levels of the malt reduce, the starches are released from their protective matrixes, and the plant begins to consume them. However, if the maltster lets the process go on too long, they end up with either new barley grass or grain that's too mealy and mushy for proper use in the brewery.

Note: In the past, malts generally only achieved a low level of modification and had to be mashed using tedious processes that took the grain through a series of temperature steps, each of which activated different enzymes. (The enzymes reduce haze, increase foam production and retention, and control the body of the beer. Which enzymes are activated to work on the malt depend on the rest temperatures and the impact on the time a step is held.) Modern malts are generally highly modified, though, meaning that they can, and should, be mashed at a single temperature for the best results. In fact, if the malt is very highly modified, step mashes can actually be detrimental. If you use the wrong temperature step or hold a step for too long at a low temperature, you can ruin the foam or body of a beer!

Once modification has reached the maltster's preferred level, the grain is dried to halt further acrospire growth. The grain is then put in a kiln and heated to both dry and achieve a specific color (which translates to flavor), depending on the type of malt being produced. How the malt is treated during this drying stage (extra water, multiple temperature steps, and so on) affects not only the color but also the flavor.

Malt color is measured on the Lovibond (°L) scale. It covers the yellow-to-copper-to-red-to-brown/black range that you find in all malt beers. The scale was invented by a British brewer, Joseph William Lovibond. He developed a device made of stained glass (originally liquid-filled jars) called a tintometer to describe beer color. He was driven to develop this device because he was convinced that a golden amber color was a sure sign of a high-quality beer. Eventually his tintometer would be replaced by frequency analysis of light, but the Lovibond unit is still in use.

You will sometimes see malt color specified in standard reference method (SRM) units. In fact, the Lovibond ratings of modern malts are back-calculated from worts made with them in the lab passed through SRM analysis. Usually a standalone SRM measurement refers to the color of the finished beer. Practically speaking, SRM and °L are identical.

A competing version of SRM is European brewery convention (EBC). The measurements and calculations are almost identical. Both required turbidity-free wort in a fixed sample cell. Labs then measure the reaction to a stimulating light at 430 nanometers. The number is converted and ultimately multiplied by a different number (12.7 in the SRM/°L system, 25 times in EBC).

To convert any EBC measurements into SRM, divide the EBC by 1.97:

$$SRM = EBC / 1.97$$

To convert SRM to EBC, you just multiply:

$$EBC = SRM \times 1.97$$

For on-the-fly conversions, simply multiplying or dividing by 2 will get you into the ballpark.

Malt Genetics

We're about to fall into a world of malts. It is important to understand that these types are generic terms for a general characteristic style of malt. Lying underneath all these comments of pilsner malt and pale malt, two-row and six-row is the notion of strain variety.

In the United States you'd have a hard time knowing about strain variety because domestic malts are usually sold to homebrewers by general style monikers. German malts usually are sold by the generic type as well, but if you look at British malts, you'll see the varieties poking out.

For instance, Maris Otter is not a pale malt toasted in a particular fashion; it is the strain. It was developed in the late 1960s in Britain as a high-yield winter barley variety for cask beer makers. Because the strain is nearly fifty years old, it's been passed in yield and stability by newer strains and is hanging on just barely, because of its flavors. You'll see others from Britain as well: Pipkin, Optic, Halcyon, Golden Promise, and so on (see page 195 for tasting notes). Just about the only European malt you'll ever see explicitly referred to by strain is Moravian, the traditional malt of the Pilsen region.

Every great once in a while, you will see recipes still refer to American strains such as Klages, Harrington, or even B1202. Klages is no longer commercially grown, and even Harrington, once the king of American malts, has faded. Modern varieties such as Tradition, Lacey, and AC Metcalfe have taken their place.

Here's the question, then: Why don't we know about these varieties? It's a not a nefarious conspiracy; the truth is that buyers are usually interested in the variety as much as the data. Barley variety development at several US Department of Agriculture (USDA) Agricultural Research Stations (and similar institutions around the world) is driven by the demands of the biggest customers, the mass breweries. Comparatively, craft brewers are just now getting some sway while we homebrewers are the gleaners of the industry.

What do the big brewers want? More than anything, they want consistency, low cost, and low protein with high enzymatic content and starch content. That translates to less room taken up in the mash tun and stronger, clearer, smoother, and more stable wort. The farmers—who already lose a ton of money to barley not fit for malting and beer making—want to increase their product yield that fits the numbers needed for malt. Less than a quarter of the world's barley growth meets the statistics for the higher-price malting barley category. The rest goes to cheap farm feed.

So farmers want consistent yields, but brewers need consistent numbers for repeatability. How does a maltster faced with a naturally varying agricultural product deal with this dilemma? Maltsters blend—and that is the reason your malt isn't coming to you as "Tradition" Pale Ale Malt. By blending multiple varieties, a maltster can dial in their numbers (unless the growing season has been truly terrible).

Malt Numbers

Unless you've been buying sacks of grain, you've probably never realized that each bag of grain is tagged with lot numbers and tracking data. Some bags come with a malt analysis card, and for others, you can use the lot number on the maltster's website to download the data. What each company provides is different, but there are a few numbers you should pay attention to:

- **Color:** Unsurprisingly, this is the color rating of the malt—in SRM, Lovibond, or EBC. The value is determined by analyzing the wort produced by a Congress mash (see page 133).
- **Diastatic power (degrees Lintner):** This is the measure of the enzymatic power of the malt.
- **Extract, fine grind, and coarse grind:** This indicates how much starch we should predict being available to us from a malt. The different grind types reflect perfect lab conditions with no concerns about slow lautering (fine) and real-world brewery conditions (coarse). You'll notice that the coarse numbers are always lower and only available for base malts. Specialty malts typically grind finer than base malts, thanks to the extra kilning. Look for the "as is" rating; that's

Congress Mash

Named for the European Brewing Congress, not the U.S. legislative body, a Congress mash is a standardized lab test for producing wort for malt analysis that is in use by brewing chemists worldwide. In this test, 50 grams of malt is mixed with 400 grams of water and run through a series of mash rests: 45C for 30 minutes and then stepped by 1C every minute until the temperature hits 70C, where the soup sits for one hour. The separated wort is then weighed and measured. Follow-on tests may require the wort to be boiled and measured again.

Everything about this test is specified in the guidelines adopted in 1975: the water, the strike temperature, the milling size, the method of filtration, the pH, and so on. All our analysis numbers come from this crazy superspecific process (actually annoyingly precisely pedantic science). Oh, and to make sure the numbers are right, the test has to be run multiple times on the same lot of malt.

the percentage with the moisture weight calculated in. The primary thing to watch for is that the numbers should be in the high 70s and 80s. You can multiply this by 46 (sucrose weight) to determine the maximum gravity you get from a perfect mash. Malt with an as-is basis of 80 percent would provide a maximum of 36.8 points per pound of malt. You then multiply that by your efficiency to see what you would actually get: 36.8 × 70 percent = 25.76. If the maltster provides only a dry basis number, subtract the moisture content from the percentage before using. (For example, if the dry basis coarse grind number is 84 percent, and the malt has 4 percent moisture, you'd calculate using 84 percent − 4 percent = 80 percent.)

- **Moisture:** Moisture affects the storability and milling characteristics of a malt. If the kernels are too dry, the malt will shatter and absorb more of your mash liquor. Moist malt, on the other hand, can gum up the mill and not crack cleanly. Moister malts also have shorter storage lifespans. Be careful with your malts and allow them to breathe from time to time if storing in an airproof vault. Moisture that leeches out in the drier environment can sit on the kernels and rot them.

- **Protein:** Modern brewing malt development has been driven in part to reduce the amount of protein in the kernel. Excess protein levels can cause stuck, gummy mashes; darker beer; and most importantly, harsh, hazy beer that has particulates (proteins) settling out in the bottle or keg. You wouldn't think this would be a problem normally, but you can save yourself some heartache by paying attention to this number. A few years back, several maltsters' supplies of Maris Otter had higher protein levels, leading some of us to have harsh, cloudy batches.

BASE GRAINS

Base grains are just what they sound like: the base fermentable upon which you build your beer. The most common base grain is barley, although wheat or other grains can also be the base of a beer. Most base grains are malted, although unmalted grains can be used as well. They're kind of a special case, which we'll cover in a dedicated section (page 141).

Barley grows in two forms, commonly referred to as two-row and six-row (the number of rows of kernels you see on the head of the barley). Six-row barley used to be the standard variety grown in the United States for brewer's malt due to its hardiness. It traditionally had a higher protein (and thus, enzyme) content than two-row barley. It therefore was more suitable for using in beers that contained adjuncts like rice or corn, which are unmalted and have no enzymes of their own. They relied on a surplus of barley enzymes to convert the starches in them to fermentable sugars.

These days, barley breeding has produced two-row barley that has nearly the same enzyme (or diastatic) power as six-row malt has traditionally had. There is no longer a reason to use six-row malt just to convert adjuncts at normal amounts.

In addition, six-row barley has a slightly grainier flavor that can be objectionable in some styles. Some brewers perceive an extra astringency from six-row's greater quantity of husks. Lighter styles with nothing to cover the flavor of six-row are usually not appropriate for it, although it's a welcome addition to styles such as cream ale or Classic American Pilsner. Six-row can be fine for some specialty malts in which the flavor is more defined by the level of roasting rather than the flavor of the barley itself. Additionally, the extra husk material can be a boon to those who make beers high in huskless adjuncts such as wheat, rye, corn, and oats.

Diastatic Power

Diastatic power (DP) is a measure of the amalyse content of a grain and therefore of the grain's ability to convert complex starches into simple, yeast-consumable sugars. If your mash doesn't have a high enough DP level, then you'll fail to convert all the starch. This leaves your beer with residual starch, which serves as a weird sensation and as bacteria chow. It's typically measured in degrees Lintner in the United States and in Kolbach units in Europe.

To convert from Kolbach to Lintner:
$$Lintner = (Kolbach + 16) / 3.5$$

To convert from Lintner to Kolbach
$$Kolbach = 3.5 \times Lintner - 16$$

Practically speaking, you want to keep your average Lintner rating for your mash above 30–35 or 40 to be really sure. In other words, take each grain in your mash and find its Litner rating. Multiply by the weight of the addition and then average the sum across the weight of the entire mash. If that remains above 40, you're golden.

$$Mash\ Linter = (\textstyle\sum (Weight_{Grain} \times LitnerRating_{Grain}) / (\textstyle\sum Weight_{Grain})$$

Many maltsters simply call their light-colored (approximately 2 Lovibond) base malt two-row. That can be misleading, since almost any malt you buy is made from two-row barley. A more accurate designation would be two-row pale malt or even simply pale malt. Just be aware that all of these can refer to the same thing.

Pilsner Malt (1.2°L–1.8°L)

Pilsner malt is the lightest-colored of all the malts. Pilsner malt is also sometimes referred to as lager malt. This is the preferred malt for very light colored beers, such as . . . well, pilsner! It is also typically used for tripel, Kolsch, blond ale, and cream ale, among other styles. Its light kilning means that you get the full malt flavor, unobscured by any toasty flavors created by the kilning. The one possible downside of the light kilning is that there is an increased chance of having a finished beer with DMS (dimethyl sulfide). This gives the beer a kind of cooked-corn aroma. All malt contains a precursor to DMS called SMM (S-methyl methionine). SMM can be limited to some extent by slightly undermodifying the malt or kilning at a higher temperature. The SMM present in malt means that DMS will always be produced, but since it's a fairly volatile chemical, a large portion of it can be driven off by a vigorous boil. This is the basis of the recommendation to do a longer boil with pilsner malt than with pale malt. The longer boil will drive off more DMS. It's also the reason it's recommended to boil with an uncovered kettle. You want the DMS to be able to escape.

It used to be thought that pilsner malt always required a multistep mash, including a protein rest. That's because traditional pilsner malt (such as Moravian) was undermodified. These days you have to look really hard to find a pilsner malt that requires a step mash. It's modified just as much as pale malt, and almost any pilsner malt can be used with a single-infusion mash. If you're in doubt, you can check the website of the maltster to see what they recommend. Or you can do an experiment and decide for yourself.

Pale Malt (1.8°L–2.2°L)

Pale malt is kilned a little darker than pils malt so that the malt just starts to take on a little toastiness in flavor. Pale malt is the base of many ales, from American pale ales to British bitter. It can be mashed with a single temperature mash. Because it's kilned at a higher temperature than pilsner malt, the risk of DMS in the finished beer is greatly reduced. A 60-minute boil is sufficient for DMS reduction in pale malt.

Pale Ale Malt (2.6°L–3.5°L)

Pale ale malt is a lot like pale malt, but kilned just a bit darker to get an even more toasty flavor. Pale ale malt is especially well suited to British styles due to its deeper flavor compared to pale malt. The difference, though noticeable, is subtle. While it will add depth of flavor to a beer, pale malt can be used as a substitute.

British pale ale malts are usually made with different varieties of barley than US pale ale malts. One barley variety commonly used is called Maris Otter. It has been said that British malts in general, and Maris Otter in particular, have a richer, maltier flavor than their American counterparts. That can work well in some beers but can also be inappropriate for American style ales.

Vienna Malt (2.8°L–3.9°L)

Going a little darker, we have Vienna malt, named for its city of origin. Vienna malt can be used in combination with other malts to provide a maltier, toastier profile, or as 100 percent of the grist for the Vienna lager style. In the mid-1800s, lagers were just beginning to be understood, although there is evidence they had actually been brewed far longer. Owing to the technology (or lack thereof) at the time, all malts were dark. When Anton Dreher began brewing his lagers in 1841, Vienna malt (who knows what it was called then) was the lightest malt available. Today's brewers are uncertain exactly what color the original Vienna lager was. Some say reddish; some say a very dark gold. Since no original examples remain, it's purely speculation at this point. But most agree that this darkish malt was the base of those beers. Besides its toasty, malty flavor, it's been noted to impart a dryness to the beer that can enhance drinkability.

Munich Light Malt (5.1°L–7°L) and Munich Dark Malt (8°L–10°L)

Munich malt has a very rich, sweet, malty flavor with a noticeable toastiness. Either variety can be used as 100 percent of the grist of a beer, or used in conjunction with other malts to deepen flavor.

Base Grain Taste-Off

Nathan Rice is a member of the HomeBrewTalk forum who was curious about how the flavors various malts compared. Using one American malt and five British malts, Nathan brewed a standard recipe with hops only at 60 and 30 minutes. All grains were mashed at 150°F for 60 minutes. Wort was boiled for one hour to end up with a 1-gallon batch of each beer. Each batch was chilled and transferred to a 2-gallon bucket and was pitched with 2 grams of Safale S-04. Fermentation went for seven days at 68°F. After fermentation, Nathan bottled all the batches and gave them 12 days to carbonate. Below are Nathan's tasting notes. While this was not a blind or triangle tasting (see page 199), this is still interesting and informative data.

AMERICAN 2-ROW PALE
(often a blend of spring barley types)
OG: 1.058 FG: 1.010
Bready. Very light. Very slightly sweet with a smooth, light graininess. Very faint twang, probably from the yeast. Serviceable if a bit nondescript. It's amazing how you can tell this is the base malt for a lot of commercial beers. It tastes familiar.

GOLDEN PROMISE
(single variety 2-row spring barley)
1.061 FG: 1.012
Very mild aroma. Flavor is slightly sweet. Cracker sort of breadiness. Grainy. Sweetest of the six. Pleasant

HALCYON
(single variety 2-row winter barley; a cross between Maris Otter and a barley variety called Warboys)
1.065 FG: 1.012
Light nuttiness in the aroma. Grain is very present. Subdued caramel. Maybe a bit like the crusts from white bread. Really clean. Light nuttiness is nice. Very mild.

MARIS OTTER
(single variety 2-row winter barley)
1.061 FG: 1.013
Toasty on the nose. Much nuttier than 2-row. Slightly sweeter and more caramel in flavor as well. Toasty sweetness comes through. Toasted bread

For example, using Munich malt along with wheat malt is the grist bill for a classic dunkelweizen. Using Munich as 10–25 percent of the grist for an American IPA works great as a backdrop for the high hop rates of that style. You can even make a great American IPA using Munich malt as 100 percent of the grist. Although altbier traditionally uses little to no Munich, a great altbier variation can be made with an all-dark Munich grist, coupled with Spalt or Mt. Hood hops.

Wheat Malt (1.7°L–2.4°L)

Not many malts are so special that they get whole classes of beer all to themselves, but that's how fundamental wheat is and has been to brewing. Two primary varieties of malted wheat are available: white and red. The difference is in the bran coating the kernel. It's no surprise that red wheat is darker and more common, whereas white wheat was developed from albinolike versions of its older cousin.

In tasting, white wheat is generally considered to be sweeter and more breadlike, while red is more hearty and earthy. The debate over which variety to use rages on. The debaters point out the advantages and flaws of each type.

OPTIC
(single variety 2-row spring barley)
1.061 FG: 1.010
Very little nose. Slight oat aroma. Flavor leans toward the sweet grain side. Maybe a little rougher than the others and almost grassy. I like it, though.

PEARL
(single variety 2-row winter barley)
1.064 FG: 1.010
Slight sweetness and caramel on the nose. Faint green, almost vegetal aroma—not unpleasant though. Medium caramel flavor with the smoothest mouthfeel of the group. Sweetness carries through.

The three that stood out for me as the most distinct from each other were Maris Otter, 2-Row Pale, and Optic. The Optic smelled like a clean barn (not a barnyard though). It reminded me of good horse feed and had a definite rough graininess that I could see complementing some styles very well. Maris Otter was definitely the most toasty of the group with some deep, rich flavors.

2-Row Pale was, like I said, kind of familiar tasting. There's a reason it's the base malt for so many good beers. It's pleasant, unobtrusive, and doesn't assert itself in any particular way.

All that being said, however, I think my favorite was the Golden Promise. The residual sweetness resulted in a fuller mouthfeel without being too much. The cracker like breadiness gave it a crisp flavor that balanced out the sweetness nicely. I still think there are some styles that would benefit from this kind of flavor more than others, but in the right place, this seems like a really nice malt.

You may also see mention of spring and winter wheat. Winter wheat, which is planted in the fall and is harvested at the break of spring, is almost always a red wheat. It is considered more robust than spring wheat, which is planted in spring and harvested at the end of summer.

In beers, such as the revitalized Bavarian Hefeweizen, malted wheat can make up 70 percent of the grain bill. This indicates that the malt carries sufficient enzymatic load to self-convert. In fact, it is possible to make a 100 percent wheat beer, if you can figure out how to lauter the wort away from the doughy mass. In other styles, like Belgian Witbier, you may see 40 percent. American Hefeweizen (or American Wheat) ranges to the 50 percent mark. Traditionally, both British and British-inspired American Pale Ales and IPAs saw charges of wheat of nearly 20 percent, in the belief that the extra protein from wheat contributed to positive foam characteristics and head retention.

It turns out that wheat doesn't have significantly higher protein levels compared to barley, but due to solubility factors, it leaches more protein into the wort. According to a recent study from Leuven, Belgium, wheat provides some better foam stability characteristics, but only for brews with highly modified malts and only in the higher-gravity versions and only when gassed with nitrogen instead of CO_2. Even better: we know that wheat is supposed to induce hazy, cloudy beers, right? The effect of wheat protein haze is more pronounced at lower overall levels of wheat in the mash; that is, a beer brewed with 20 percent wheat will be hazier than a beer brewed with 40 percent wheat. According to the researchers, this is due to the more aggressive breakdown of the large protein strands in the 20 percent wheat beer. This more aggressive breakdown leads to smaller particles, which are less likely to settle out.

What's the verdict, then, on wheat malt and foam and haze? It seems that for all of our best wishes, these perceived effects are tricky and intertwined with a number of factors. One thing not to discount, however, is the increased viscosity of the wort having an impact on mouthfeel.

Rye Malt (2°L–4.3°L)

We're putting rye malt in the base grain category because it really doesn't fit anywhere else. It's probably not a great idea to use rye malt as 100 percent of a beer's grist. It can be done, but it can be difficult to lauter that much rye, and the beer produced can be viscous to the point of seeming oily. Rye malt is a great complement to other malts. The seldom-seen roggenbier style uses rye malt as about 50–60 percent of the total grist, with most of the rest being made up of Munich, pale, pilsner, and/or wheat malt. Rye malt is a great addition to American IPA or pale ale styles at amounts from 20–60 percent of the total grist bill. It gives the beer a full, smooth mouthfeel, and a beautiful red-orange hue. It's generally regarded as adding a slightly spicy finish to the beer, which is a wonderful complement to the American hops (see page 108 for Denny's Wry Smile recipe).

CRYSTAL AND CARAMEL MALTS

Crystal and caramel malts are used to increase the body of the beer and provide flavors not available from base malts. These flavors can range from a nearly imperceptible sweetness from very light crystal malts (such as carapils at 1.5°L) all the way to the raisiny flavors you get from Special B (135°L), with a range of toffeelike flavors in between. Crystal malts are typically produced at colors of 20°L, 30°L, 40°L, 60°L, 80°L, 90°L, and 120°L. The exact colors available will vary depending on the maltster. When you look at crystal malt, you'll notice that it's a mix of lighter and darker grains. The color is specified by an average of the grain colors.

While crystal and caramel malts are essentially the same thing, some maltsters make a subtle distinction between the two based on the process used to produce them. For more information, we turn to Dave Kuske, director of malting operations at Briess Malt & Ingredients Co:

> The difference between caramel and crystal malts involves both terminology and chemistry and production differences.
>
> As for terminology, the European maltsters landed on crystal malt as the descriptor of malts that go through a conversion step where starches are rapidly (typically within forty-five minutes) converted to sugars, and the sugars are then crystallized at high temperatures in a roaster. Somewhere in our distant past, it was decided that our crystal-style malts produced in the same manner were given the name caramel malt.
>
> The term *caramel* really refers to the process of pyrolisis of sugars. When I give presentations on the process, I encourage the audience to envision a candy thermometer. There are different temperature breaks where different types of caramel are produced, and each has unique physical and flavor properties. Crystal-style malt is in reality the end process of achieving high enough temperatures to produce a hard crack–type caramel inside of each malt kernel, which results in a hard, glassy endosperm. This crystallization lends unique properties to the flavor and functionality of the malt. In order to achieve crystallization, the actual kernel temperature must exceed 300°F, which requires much higher applied temperatures only achievable using a roaster, which has the burner capacity to reach in excess of 700°F if needed.
>
> There are caramel malts on the market that are produced using a kiln. The green malt is heated at minimal airflow and is held at high moisture content for an extended period of time (more like hours than minutes) on the upper kiln to stew the malt to allow the enzymes to break the starches into sugars. It is a tricky step on the kiln because it is difficult to get the wet malt heated up to the enzyme-optimum temperatures (60°C–70°C or 140°F–158°F) without drying the malt in the process, which slows the enzymatic breakdown. I liken it to trying to heat up a wet bath towel. After stewing, the malt is heated at the highest temperature possible on the kiln, which is not hot enough to actually crystallize the sugars due to maximum temperature limitations on the kiln. In most cases, 220°F–240°F burner temperature is as high as one can achieve on a kiln, which falls far short of crystallization temperature of the predominant sugars. There is some caramelization that occurs at the lower temperatures, but the majority of the color and flavor development is due to the Maillard reaction (sugar + amino acid), which provides a different flavor profile and a mealy or powdery endosperm.

Many maltsters have come up with their own trademarked names for their versions of crystal/cara malts. We'll look at a few of those, along with other crystal/cara variations, below.

- Golden Naked Oats (4.3°L–8.1°L), from Simpsons Malt, are a huskless crystal oat malt. This malt gives the beer a flavor sometimes referred to as nutty. It also increases the body. Although it's technically a crystal, homebrewers have been known to use larger amounts of it in a batch

than normally would be used for crystal malts. Amounts around 30 percent aren't unusual to see in some recipes.

- Caramunich I (31°L–38°L), Caramunich II (42°L–49°L), Caramunich III (53°L–60.5°L), Caraaroma (115°L–150°L), Carabelge (118°L–13.7°L), Carabohemian (64°L–83°L), Carawheat (42°L–53°L), Carapils (1.5°L–2.9°L), Carahell (8.1°L–11.8°L), Carared (16°L–23°L), Caraamber (23°L–31°L), and Cararye (57°L–76°L) are names trademarked by Weyermann for their line of caramel/crystal malts.
- Carastan is the name Baird's gives to its crystal/cara malts.
- Caravienne (21°L) is a light crystal malt originally produced by the Belgian maltsters Dewolf-Cosyns. After they closed around 2001, it has been produced by a number of other maltsters. If you can't find it, we've found that 20°L crystal is a really close substitute.

DARK ROASTED GRAINS

Dark roasted grains span a wide spectrum of colors and flavors. They can be made from either malted or unmalted grains. They can be used in amounts as small as an ounce to color a beer or in larger amounts to give the beer roasty flavor and aroma notes of coffee or even hints of chocolate. In general, the darker the grain, the less of it you use.

Some maltsters have found that by removing the husk of the grain before kilning, they can make dark malts that have less bite and a smoother flavor. These can be great in porters, where the reduced bitterness from the roast malt lets your hops shine through. (See the last two entries that follow for examples.) Here are some of the dark roasted malts, a range of color for them, and ideas for their use:

- Chocolate (300°L–350°L), chocolate wheat (300°L–450°L), chocolate rye (180°L–300°L), and chocolate spelt (170°L–240°L) are most often used in styles like porter. Their roasty coffee and cocoa character plays off the base malt to create a rich flavor profile. Adding some Munich or crystal malt along with the chocolate malt accentuates the chocolate flavor and tones down the roastiness a bit. Non-barley variations maintain some of the character unique to the grain they were made from, as well as having the moderate roast qualities of chocolate malt.
- Dark chocolate malt (420°L) has a more intense coffee character than regular chocolate malt. Pale chocolate malt (180°L–250°L) is perfect for those who find chocolate malt too strong. As you might expect, it is a touch lighter and can benefit some styles where you don't want the roastiness or acrid acidic bite of chocolate malt.
- Roasted barley (375°L–450°L) and roasted rye (188°L-300°L): These malts are used to impart a roasted coffee character and dark black color to the beer. Roasted barley is often cited as the ingredient that distinguishes a stout from a porter. (The actual historical record says otherwise.) The classic dry stout recipe uses about 10 percent of the grist bill as roasted barley. Roasted rye does about the same thing while retaining a bit of the rye character. Due to the dark roasting, though, much of that flavor is lost.
- Carafa malts are trademarked by the German maltster Weyermann. They come in three color variations: I (300°L–375°L), II (413°L–450°L), and III (488°L–563°L). They also come in two varieties: regular and special (aka dehusked). These malts can be thought of as chocolate malts in terms of flavor and color, although the darkest carafa is closer to roasted barley than chocolate malt in color. A primary use of carafa malts is for color in a beer. An ounce or two in a 5-gallon

batch of homebrew will give the beer a reddish hue. Larger amounts start to impart a chocolate and toffee flavor, but without some of the harsh roastiness of roasted barley.

- Dehusked and debittered Blackprinz (500°L) and Midnight Wheat (550°L) malts are trademarked by Briess Malt & Ingredients Company. Like Weyermann Carafa Special malts, both Blackprinz and Midnight Wheat are dehusked malts. Briess points out that the husk is mainly, but not completely, removed. Since it's the husk that develops bitter notes during roasting, the dehusked version (called Carafa Special by Weyermann) contributes a smoother flavor with less astringency than the variety that retains the husks.

FLAKED, UNMALTED, AND OTHER SPECIALTY GRAINS

- Flaked barley (1.5°L), flaked wheat (2°L), flaked rye (2°L), and flaked oats (1°L) are often used to increase body as well as head formation and retention. A high level of protein promotes those effects. Flaked maize (1°L) and flaked rice (1°L) can be used to lighten the body and increase the alcohol content of your beer. Flaked maize can add a little sweet, corny flavor. Flaked grains have not been malted and therefore have no diastatic power to convert their starches to sugar. They need to be mashed with grains that have ample diastatic power, like pale malt, so that the flaked grains can hitchhike on the enzymes. Pale malt has enough enzymes to convert itself and at least its own weight of another grain.

  Note: You will sometimes see recipes where flaked grains are steeped. While that may get you some of the properties of the grain, you will also be adding unconverted starch to your beer. That unconverted starch will create haze, not to mention that wild yeast and bacteria just love to eat unconverted starch while they ruin your beer! It's never a good idea to use flaked grains without some sort of base malt to convert those starches.

- Oat malt (4°L) is produced by Thomas Fawcett & Sons in England. It is intended to enhance the body and flavor of porters, stouts, winter warmers, and other robust English ales. It provides a nutty, rich silkiness to beers and serves as a great replacement for flaked oats. Due to the tiny kernel size, it is a bit trickier to mill, but generally works fine with your standard mill gap as long as it is mixed with regular malt. For extract brewers, oat malts are self-converting and can be steeped for 30 minutes on their own at 148°F–160°F to complete the starch transformation. In other words, you can steep and get the effects of oats without introducing a bunch of starch as you do if you just steep flaked oats. Note: While only one maltster makes malted oats today, malted oats played a major role in the brewing world until the turn of the twentieth century. There were a number of great beers that were golden, strong, and almost entirely made of oats, both in the UK and continental Europe. (See the Haarlem Bokbier variant on page 32 for an example.)

- Melanoidin malt (23°L–31°L) is produced by Weyermann, who say it adds flavor stability and fullness to a beer. In addition, it produces a red color. Keep in mind that melanoidins are a color, not a flavor, although the Maillard reactions that create melanoidins also create flavors. Savvy, lazy brewers like Drew use Melanoidin malt to simulate some of the flavors produced by crazy decoction mash brewers. Gambrinus Malting produces a Honey Malt (aka Brumalt) that provides some of the same flavor impact, but with increased honeylike sweetness. Aromatic malt is another malt variety with similar impacts. You can think of them as super Munichs, so a little goes a long way.

- Briess Victory, Dingemans Biscuit, and Malteries Franco-Belgies Kiln Amber (15°L–28°L): These are all lightly roasted malts that carry a similar toasty, biscuity bread quality. Again, these are potent malts suitable for about 10 percent of the mash and can impart tremendous warmth to a beer when used judiciously.

Smoked Malts

Until recent times, all malts carried a smoky flavor due to kilning over wood fires. Given people's continued affinity for smoked meat products (bacon or barbecue, anyone?), it's safe to say that smoke is something people love. They're just not used to it from their beer.

- Rauchmalt (2°L–5°L) is the German answer to the smoke question. The whole Bavarian town of Bamberg is Bam-nutty about its Rauchbier. (The word *Rauch* means "smoke" in German.) The majority of the German rauchmalts are smoked over beechwood fires. They can be used in amounts up to 100 percent of your grist to impart a intense, smoky (some say bacony) flavor to your beer. It works wonderfully when put into a beer with a sturdy malt backbone, such as a Marzen or bock. Weyermann also has produced a special edition Oak Rauchmalt.

- Peat (2°L–3°L) malt is the approach to smoked malt that takes its cue from Scotland. Maltsters produce, mostly for distillers, intensely smoky, almost iodiney, malts over burning piles of peat. What is peat? It's a mass of decaying vegetation held together by dirt and moss. It slowly forms around bogs and has been an important fuel source in Northern Europe for . . . well . . . forever. The smoke varies wildly based on what's in it, but you can be assured that it's tough stuff. Peated malt is very strong, and caution is advised in its use. Usually a small amount (2–4 ounces per 5 gallons) will impart an intense smoky flavor and aroma to the beer. It's been said that it can give you iodine or seaweed flavors in larger amounts. It seems to be a thing that brewers either love or hate. **Drew: There has been a debate about the use of peated malt in Scotch ales. Some say it gives the beer the smokiness that the style needs. Others say that it throws the beer out of style, is unpleasant, and has no place in a wee heavy. Like all things in homebrewing, it's up to you to decide. But at least in my case, I prefer peat to stay in my scotch. And I know Denny doesn't use peat malt or drink scotch!**

- Other smoked malts are worth exploring, since other countries have histories of smoking their malts over diverse woods like spruce and fir. The most popular commercially made American smoked malt available to homebrewers is Briess's Smoked Malt (5°L) that's fired over Cherrywood. It's not as intense as the peat-smoked and is not far off from the Rauch malt. It can be used to great effect to lend character to milds and dark ales. Note: If you're like a great many brewers, you've probably dabbled with the notion of proper barbecue, and maybe you've invested in a smoker. Making your own smoked malts is a simple as exposing lightly misted malt to a smoky fire for 20–30 minutes. You can do this with a couple of takeout tins or a proper cold smoker arrangement, or you can make like Alaskan Brewing and take over a salmon smokehouse to produce the Alderwood smoked malt they use for their world famous Alaskan Smoked Porter. This is one area in which we encourage playing around; just remember to give your freshly smoked malts some resting time (1–2 weeks) before using.

SUGARS

Sugar, honey, and other rich sugar sources such as dates have historically been added to beer since the times of the Sumerians. In modern times, many styles of Belgian beer and more than a few British beers include sugar additions.

Sugar briefly fell into disrepute during the early days of homebrewing, when the typical recipe was a kit and a kilo—meaning a kit with 3.3 pounds of liquid malt extract and a dodgy packet of dry yeast to which you added a kilo of table sugar. The extract had often been sitting on store shelves for long enough to go stale and become oxidized, and the sugar, intended to up the alcohol content, did nothing to hide the flavor of the stale extract. The sugar was wrongly blamed for the poor, cidery quality of the beer. Even today, you'll hear that too much sugar yields a cidery beer—and now you know it's not true.

By adding sugar to an existing recipe, you boost its alcohol content, since sugar is highly fermentable. Replacing a portion of malt with an equal number of gravity units of sugar is a common way for brewers to lighten the body of a beer, because the sugar ferments out completely. The beer feels drier because it doesn't contain the additional longer-chain carbohydrates (dextrins) and proteins that malt leaves behind when it ferments.

An important point: you'll hear a lot of brewers say, "Well, I wanted it drier, so I boosted it with sugar," or, "My ferment stalled out, so I tried adding sugar to dry it out." It really doesn't work that way. Your sugar additions most effectively dry a beer when used to replace base malt, not to undercut existing malt gravity.

Of course, some brewers also use sugars because they're after a particular flavor—or in the case of lactose or maltodextrin, a particular change to both sweetness and body. As you'll see on the following pages, sugar gives you a few ways to play with your beer.

SUGARS FOR ALCOHOL

Any of the sugars on the pages that follow can be used to increase the alcohol content and/or thin out the body of a beer. However, the ones in this section add no flavor to the beer, and the primary purpose of using them is for adjusting alcohol and body. As a general rule, you can assume most dry sugars have a gravity impact of about 45 points per pound per gallon (PPG). If you want to thin body without increasing alcohol, substitute one of the sugars for an equal number of gravity points of grain. To increase the alcohol, add sugar rather than substituting it. One pound of dry sugar will add about 9 points to the original gravity for a 5-gallon batch of your beer. In general, it's best to keep sugar additions to less than 30 percent of your total fermentables.

- **Corn syrup:** Corn syrup is a mix of maltose, sucrose, and fructose generated by enyzmatic conversion of dent corn. It's America's favorite sweetener and humectant (a substance that retains moisture). Commercial consumer-grade corn syrups are typically a blend of corn syrup and its cousin, high-fructose corn syrup. Because the consumer-grade syrup is blended with salt and vanilla, we don't recommend it for heavy use in brewing. A brewer's corn syrup is available, but it's hard to find. As its name implies, you can use that one in your beer.

- **Corn sugar (dextrose):** Corn sugar is a simple monosaccharide consisting of glucose. Its simple nature, yeast digestibility, and predictability is why you see it used so extensively for bottle priming when the yeast are in their most stressful environment (full of alcohol, CO_2, and pressure).
- **Rock candi sugar:** Rock candi sugar consists of large chunks of refined table sugar. It offers no additional flavor and no difference from table or corn sugar, and thus is not worth the price. Darker or other colored forms of candi sugar can add slight smoky, spicy tones to a beer, but the overall impact from the small amount usually used in brewing is minimal.
- **Table sugar:** Table sugar is plain white sucrose (disaccharide of fructose and glucose) derived from sugar cane or beets. Arguably it is one of humankind's most important and dangerous discoveries. Regardless of the source, it produces the same results. It adds no flavor to your beer. It is a great choice to add alcohol and/or lighten the body of your beer. Don't believe us? Take a simple wort of DME and water. Make two sample batches of ½ liter. Into one batch add cane sugar syrup; into the other batch add beet sugar syrup. Ferment out, chill, and taste. If you can taste a difference due to the sugar, our hats are off to you.

SUGARS FOR FLAVOR

While the previous sugars are all highly refined, and thus vanish like a ghost, the "dirty" sugars that follow can leave behind aromas and flavors that you can't get any other way. What makes them dirty? Well, it turns out that for much of recent human history sugar making was a simple process. Take sugar cane, squeeze the juice out of it, and boil or evaporate the liquid. The crystals were thus coated with various byproducts of the process and plant that carry other flavors.

The best way to retain the flavor of sugar in the brewing process is to add it as late in the process as possible. Why? Just like any other addition, the aromas and flavors we sense are due to potential volatile compounds. Chuck them in too early, and your brewery will smell great while your beer is bland. This is true of a great many things; the better your brewery smells, the less scent your beer will have at quaffing time.

Adding sugar late in the boil or after the bulk of fermentation has occurred works well, although some of the very dark candi syrups stand up well when added earlier in the boil. Most dry sugars will yield about 45 ppg, and liquid sugars will yield around 32 ppg.

- **Agave:** As you might expect, this liquid sugar comes from the agave cactus and is not refined into crystalline form as other sucrose sources are. It tastes a little less sweet than other sugars, and the darker varieties can have a smoky flavor. Be wary, though; with the recent rise in popularity of agave as a low glycemic index sweetener, the commercial market has expanded with some questionable providers.
- **Candi syrup:** Traditional candi syrup is a byproduct of the molasses production pipeline, but it was never seen in the United States for brewers until the early 2000s, when Brian Mercer of Dark Candi began to bring it in and repackage it. Overnight, everyone's understanding of making Belgian dark ales such as Westvleteren 12 was shattered. Before this, people used a mixture of

WeightSugarAddition = 50 / 45
WeightSugarAddition = 1.11 lbs

Therefore, in order to replace 10 points of gravity in this example, you remove 1.88 pounds of malt from the recipe, leaving 13.12 pounds, and add 1.11 pounds of sugar.

malts, such as Special B, Carafa, high Lovibond crystals, and dark brown sugars to capture the plum, raisin, and rum characters of those special beers. It worked, but never quite matched the inspiration. Once we got our hands on the dark syrups, that world became unlocked to us! New suppliers, including some domestic producers, have sprung up in recent years. We don't use the clear syrups, but the amber and dark syrups have become indispensable—especially when you want to make two radically different batches from a pale mash just by adding a candi syrup to one portion.

- **Demerara sugar:** Some natural brown sugars have particular names and characteristics, and are sold as turbinado, demerara, or raw sugar. Turbinado is made by crystallizing raw sugar cane juice, then spinning it in a centrifuge to remove water and some impurities. Demerara and raw sugar have less molasses than light brown sugar, but added near the end of the boil or to the fermenter, it can add a honeylike flavor to your beer.

- **Honey:** Honey provides a vast array of flavor possibilities. If you've never explored honey beyond the squeeze bottle on your grocery shelf, you're missing out. That stuff is the honey equivalent to American Light Lagers. Instead, find your local apiarist (beekeeper) and explore his or her wares. You'll find varietal honeys produced from a singular crop such as blueberry, almond, cherry, and so on. Even the wildflower and clover honeys will punch above their weight. As an added advantage, if you buy local and know your apiarist, you can avoid buying honey that's tainted with heavy metals and chemicals illegal in the United States, but legal in China and India (homes of cheap honey production), and you can be assured that your honey is all honey and not honey with added corn syrup. To see an example of strange honey in practice, see the Saison Guacamole on page 175, which uses intensely molasseslike avocado honey. Please note that because of its delicate aromatics, honey is best added late in the fermentation process.

- **Invert sugar syrup:** Invert sugar syrup is a simple syrup made by boiling sucrose and water in the presence of an acid (citric, ascorbic, or tartaric). The heat and acid cause the sucrose molecules to break into fructose and glucose in a chemical process called hydrolysis. The result is a thick syrup that can be added readily to beer. In theory, inverted sugar is easier for the yeast to ferment than a noninverted sugar. Practically, during the ferment, yeast produce an enzyme, invertase, that naturally inverts the sugar. As long as you have healthy yeast and aren't breeching 40 percent sugar, your yeast will handle it. To see how to make your own invert sugar syrup, refer to page 80.

- **Maple syrup:** Almost everyone is very familiar with this concentrated sap from the maple tree. And we're talking the real, honest-to-goodness stuff from the cold northern region of North America. If you're looking at the cheap syrup you used as a kid, stop. That stuff is doctored high-fructose corn syrup and has as much to do with maple trees as our left feet. In the past, we'd tell you to skip over the Grade A maple syrup for the far better Grade B syrup, but the International Maple Syrup Institute is encouraging a change in the grading process. Gone are the Grade B slots. Everything is Grade A, but with a spectrum of Golden/Delicate to Dark/Strong. Under the new scheme, we recommend Grade A Dark/Robust. In order to maintain the most flavor from the delicate syrup, it's best to add it late in the fermentation process. Even then, it's possible for the flavor to ferment out. Too much maple syrup can add an almost woody flavor to beer. Start by using maple syrup as 8–10 percent of your total fermentables. After you taste a beer made that way, you'll have an idea of what your taste threshold is and how much you want to use in the future.

- **Molasses:** Molasses, called treacle in the United Kingdom, is a byproduct of cane or beet sugar refining. The juice is boiled to concentrate it. The first, least sweet, boiling is known as cane syrup. The second boiling is usually just referred to as molasses. The third, strongest-flavored boiling is called blackstrap molasses. Molasses can add a very distinctive flavor to a beer and is best used in moderation. It is also recommended that you stick to varieties that are unsulfured to avoid adding sulfurous characters to your beers—unless you like the idea of a fire-and-brimstone ale.

- ***Muscovado* (also *moscovado*):** This unrefined, dark brown sugar of the Caribbean has much smaller crystals than turbinado sugar. The sugar cane extract is heated to thicken it, pan-evaporated in the sun, and pounded to yield an unprocessed, damp sugar. Think moister than fresh brown sugar (which is really just white sugar with molasses added). Muscovado has one of the largest mineral loads of commercial sugars and is a key ingredient in making rum. Unsurprisingly, the flavor impact is reminiscent of molasses and rum.

- *Panela, piloncillo, raspadura,* **or jaggery:** The first three are names for an unrefined sugar mostly made by boiling sugar cane juice in South and Central America. Jaggery is made from cane, dates, and palm sap in East Asia. Instead of aiming for crystals, concentrated cane juice is allowed to cool and harden in thin pans. Once cooled, but while still plastic, the sugar sheet is pressed and shaped and dried into various blocks or cones. To use, the solid mass is traditionally grated. We just need it broken up and dissolved. In the United States, we most commonly see the cone-shaped Mexican piloncillo. The flavor characteristics depend largely on the color, but the usual flavor is somewhat between muscovado and golden invert syrup with strong caramel components.

Sugar Additions the Easy Way

We learned this trick from Dave Mathis of American River Brewing Company. Instead of doing the whole dump-and-frantically-stir method of sugar additions to a roiling boil, just take your sugar and add it to a nylon mesh bag. Tie the bag to a mash paddle or spoon—anything that will allow you to suspend the bag in the boil. Instead of futzing with stirring or creating a syrup with wort, you allow the natural cavitation of the roiling wort to gently dissolve the sugar and directly incorporate it. Just add the bag about 20 minutes from the end of boil, and you'll be set!

SPECIAL SUGARS

There are two remaining sugars we need to talk about. They don't boost the booze, they don't add flavor, and unlike the other sugars we've talked about, they actually add body instead of cut it. These sugars are for special cases when you need to retain mouthfeel or create richer body in a beer.

- **Maltodextrin:** Maltodextrin is good for adding mouthfeel and body to extract brews without affecting flavor, because it adds no sweetness. Maltodextrin is added to the wort at the same time as the extracts, or it can be boiled with a little water and added later in the process, even up to packaging. Maltodextrin is only 3 percent fermentable by brewer's yeast. It adds 40 ppg. Another use for maltodextrin is in the creation of a finer, longer-lasting head.
- **Lactose:** Lactose is a milk-based sugar (glucose and galactose) that is not fully fermentable by beer yeast. It adds body and sweetness to sweet stouts or other beers. Add to the boil for 30–35 ppg. For a 5-gallon batch, the typical dose in a stout will be 1 pound, to lend that richness that can cut off the acrid notes of a dark stout. Many homebrewers look to lactose as a way to sweeten an overly dry beer by adding a freshly boiled lactose addition to the finished beer. The problem is that lactose is 6.25 times less sweet than table sugar!

HOPS

One of the first things new brewers learn is why hops are used and the different effects they have on beer depending on their usage. The rule of thumb is that hops added early in the boil provide bitterness (due to the isomerization of alpha acids) to balance the sweetness of the malt sugars. Hops added later will contribute less bitterness, but more of their volatile essential oils will remain to add flavor and aroma to the beer.

Generally, you will extract most of the bitterness in the first 60 minutes of boiling the hops. Boiling them longer results in little further isomerization. In fact, boiling hops longer than 90 minutes can lead to a degradation of the bitterness already extracted. Hops added in the last 20 minutes of the boil will add hop flavor to the beer, and hops added in the last 5 minutes or less of the boil give the beer hop aroma.

In addition, hops have been touted as having preservative qualities. More than any other factor, this is probably what drove their adoption by brewers. With no refrigeration and no knowledge of sanitation, unhopped beer spoiled rapidly within a week or two. Those bitter iso-alpha and other compounds stave off two of the most common beer spoilage organisms: *Lactobacillus* and *Pediococcus*. Both are gram-positive bacteria, and iso-alphas' bacteriostatic effect interferes with their reproduction. Hops, however, have no effect on gram-negative bacteria or our funky yeast cousins, *Brettanomyces*.

Fun fact: Hops are also a natural soporific, meaning they are conducive to sleepiness. If you're suffering the occasional bout of sleeplessness, toss a few hops in a pillowcase or potpourri sack and stick it under your pillow. You'll be asleep in no time at all!

TRADITIONAL CONTINENTAL HOPS

Traditonally, most European hops were grown in England, Germany, and nearby areas. Generally, these traditional British and German hops have a lower alpha acid content than more recently developed American varieties. That means for high levels of bitterness, you have to use large amounts of them, which could lend a vegetal character to the beer. On the other hand, some of these hops, such as East Kent Goldings and Saaz, have delicate, enticing aromas when used in moderation.

Some of the best known English varieties are Fuggle, East Kent Goldings, and Northern Brewer. English hops get described in very different terms than American varieties. Fuggle has been called earthy or even dirtlike. (It's a description, not a value judgment!) East Kent Goldings are noted as having a candylike aroma.

A subset of German and Czech hops that are low in bitterness and high in aroma are often referred to as noble hops. They have a high amount of the hop oil called humulene. Humulene gives an earthy, woody, or herbal quality to the hops. Additionally, the spicy character that people detect is a case of good oxidation. The compounds that form these aromas are believed to come from the oxidation of beta acids. These noble varieties are Hallertauer, Hersbrucker, Czech Saaz, Spalt, and Tettnang. Fuggle, Goldings, and East Kent Goldings are sometimes referred to as English noble hops. In the United States, you'll sometimes hear varieties such as Crystal, Liberty, Mt. Hood, Santiam, and others referred to as American nobles.

Why all this emphasis on being noble? Outside of our craft beer and homebrew bubble, the world is absolutely ruled by lager breweries making their pilsners of varying quality. Given the number of these brewers either founded by Germans and Bohemians (or paying fetishistic homage to them), it makes sense that they would all go for that vaunted noble label. If you're trying to make money at growing hops (good luck!), you're going to go where the large segment of the market lies: big alpha and noble aromas.

A reminder about imported hops: Since we're not making like a big brewer with crews flying over to Germany to judge the recent crop, what we see as homebrewers is typically the unspoken-for hops that may be of lesser quality. Don't be seduced by the notion of having to use a particular variety. It's far better to choose a fresher hop with similar qualities than a degraded sample of the right hop.

TRADITIONAL AMERICAN HOPS

American hops growers have taken traditional European hops and built new varieties by crossbreeding them with wild hops found in America. These native hops had higher levels of alpha acid and aromas of citrus fruits such as grapefruit and lemon, or intense flavors and aroma of pine. Unlike the European hops, which gently tickled your senses with lightly oxidized noble oils, these American varieties were more of a slap in the face. (And I mean that in a good way.) The hop breeding program at Oregon State University leads the way with varieties such as Cascade and Willamette. Other well-known and much-used American hops include Chinook, Centennial, and Mt. Hood. Later American varieties, some discovered growing wild, include Columbus, Amarillo, Summit, and Simcoe. A lot of these hops have flavors and aromas reminiscent of citrus fruits. Grapefruit, lemon, and tangerine are flavors often used to describe them. Others, descended from

First Wort Hopping

An exception to the conventional usage, First Wort Hops (FWH) arose in the 1990s after a paper was published in Brauwelt International revisiting the procedure (which was apparently common in the late 1800s). FWH are added to the kettle as the mash is being run off and remain in the kettle throughout the boil. Although the mechanics of FWH aren't completely understood, the theory is that certain chemical changes, possibly related to the pH of the wort and protein binding, take place as the hops steep in the wort. This results in a smoother, more agreeable quality of bitterness, even though the measured IBU level in FWH beers is about 10 percent higher than those using conventional hop additions. While previous testing has shown that tasters are able to detect the difference and usually prefer the added flavor and smoother bittering from FWH, there is not complete agreement.

German brewers used the technique for those reasons and to produce what they described as a more intense, pleasant hop aroma. It appears though that the practice has been abandoned commercially there. Many other brewers have found that FWH produces more hops flavor than a conventional flavor addition, but little to no contribution to aroma. This sounds like an experiment waiting to happen. See page 221 for suggestions on how to conduct your own FWH experiment or page 204 for our results.

continental hops, retain more of their parent's character. Willamette is bred from Fuggle and has some of the same earthy notes. Likewise, Mt. Hood's lineage traces back to Hallertauer hops. It has some of the same noble hops flavor and aroma and makes a great substitute for German Hallertauer hops.

As craft brewing has grown in popularity, and the IPA has become the current king of craft beer drinking, demand for American hops has skyrocketed globally. This has led to increased hop shortages and has left hop farmers racing to catch up. The problem is one of lag. It takes three years for a field of a new hop variety to reach sustainable levels of commercial-grade hop production. For years, hop growers were focused on yielding the highest amount of alpha acid for the megabreweries. Aroma and flavor characteristics took a back seat in crop selection. Now, while alpha acid is still a primary focus, more and more aroma varieties are being brought online.

An added complication today is the number of proprietary strains that exist from commercial hop breeders. That's why you see basically the same hop under three different names (Columbus, Tomahawk, and Zeus) and why hops like Simcoe and Citra are in short supply and high demand. And of course, new varieties are constantly being grown. On the pages that follow, we'll cover the major categories and some of the most popular hops that are likely to stay in production for decades.

NEWER HOPS

The latest wave of hops to hit the market have largely been bred for fruity aromas and low cohumulone levels. It has opened up a wave of experimentation about what can be done with hop flavor.

Flavors and aromas in the newest hops range from blueberry and passion fruit to eucalyptus and peppermint. Hop varieties such as Citra, Calypso, El Dorado, and Mandarina Bavaria still exhibit the citrusy or piney character of the previous generation, but many times those flavors are blended with tropical fruit flavors. For example, Mosaic hops can come across as a combination of the dankness of Columbus and the mango-passion-fruitiness of Citra.

Why low cohumulone levels? It was long thought that higher cohumulone amounts created a sharp, intense bitterness, and lower levels equated to a smoother, more subdued bitterness. This theory has been called into question the last few years after testing done at Oregon State University, based on work done by Dr. Thomas H. Shellhammer, (Nor'Wester Professor of Fermentation Science, Associate Professor of Brewing and Food Engineering, Department of Food Science and Technology, Oregon State University, Corvallis, Oregon). Although the low-cohumulone theory may be in doubt, that hasn't stopped hop farmers from growing lower-cohumulone hops or stopped brewers from getting excited by them.

OUR FAVORITE HOPS

You'll notice that we're not grinding out a list of hops for you to look through. The problem is that with such rapid development of new cultivars, any list we'd make would be out of date within moments. So instead, we've focused on general characteristics, but that doesn't mean we don't have our favorites! In no particular order, here are the hops we find ourselves grabbing time and time again. No doubt if you ask in a year or two, we'll have new favorites!

Drew

- **Magnum and Warrior:** Magnum is my all-purpose bittering hop. You will see this crop up time and time again. I like the clean, neutral bittering that it gives, and it provides an excellent base for the rest of the beer. Warrior is my other bittering hop. I tend to use Warrior in my big hoppy beers like my DIPA/TIPAs. However, neither of these hops blow me away in other parts of the brew day (dry hop, late hop, etc.).

- **Amarillo:** One of my favorite hops to use as a singleton addition and particularly makes a fantastic American Saison or Hoppy American Wheat Beer. Provides big grapefruit with minimal cattiness although it can taste like baby aspirin if used too heavily.

- **Cascade and Centennial:** I lump these two together because they are classics and the original name for Centennial was "Super Cascade." These are the citrus cat bombs that have defined so much of what is American craft brew. One of the originals—New Albion Pale Ale—used nothing but Cascade, and it has never surrendered its place of importance.

- **Columbus/Tomahawk/Zeus:** If you've ever giggled at Rob Schneider saying "You put your weed in there" or watched Cheech & Chong, then the triumvirate of C/T/Z are for you. Actually they're for you if you just like an aggressively piney deep earthy hop character that coats your mouth.

- **Citra:** The little hop that could. It only recently appeared on the market and is a proprietary hop. Where it usually takes years for a hop to launch, Citra burst on the scene and captured brewers' hearts with its big blast of mango. I love this hop for defying expectations.

- **Challenger and Target:** I strongly dislike the majority of the Fuggles and Goldings hops I've run into here in the US, mostly because of the quality of what we get here in the US. Instead of floral and earthy, what I've always gotten is mulched grass and tea, so my two British mainstays are a little off the beaten path. Challenger is a dual use hop that is semi-earthy and semi-citrusy. It's a good bridge hop for those used to an American presentation. Target is a higher alpha British hop popular in the early '90s. The aroma and flavor profile is very clean with a nice twinge of citrus from heavy myrcene content. Think somewhere between Magnum and Warrior.

- **Styrian Goldings:** Despite the name, this hop descends from Fuggles. It is an old spicy, slightly woody hop originally from Austria. It is my go-to hop for my Belgian beers since it's heavily used there.
- **Saphir:** This new variety of hop out of Germany is all about the aroma. It has a low alpha acid content of 2-5 percent. What it lacks in IBU potential, it more than makes up in aroma. It is another European hop that is picking up the citrus idea from American hops. Very smooth and lightly tangerine.

Denny

- **Magnum and Horizon:** Both of these have a smooth, clean bitterness that blends in and supports the beer without shouting at you. I find the two very much alike. These are my favorite bittering hops for Belgian-style beers, especially tripels. I don't care as much for them in hoppy American styles such as APA or AIPA, because they just don't give me the hoppy slap in the face I'm looking for in those beers.
- **Columbus/Tomahawk/Zeus:** These are different names for the same hop. It has an intense, dank aroma with hints of citrus. It's a great hop for bittering, flavor, or aroma and is one of my favorite dry hops.

- **Amarillo:** Amarillo was discovered as a wild hop and subsequently domesticated. Its lemon and orange notes make it a great flavor or aroma hop, either alone or combined with other hops with similar qualities.
- **Cascade:** I live in the Pacific Northwest, and Cascade is one of the signature hops of this region. Developed at Oregon State University and first released in 1971, the grapefruit flavor and aroma have led to it being one of the most popular hops in the world. Although it's being slightly overtaken by newer varieties, Cascade hops are one of my go-to hops. In addition, Cascade's vigor and disease resistance makes it popular both with commercial and home hop growers.
- **Mt. Hood:** Another hop bred and grown in the Pacific Northwest, Mt. Hood is a mainstay for me in both German and Belgian styles. It has a lovely, slightly herbal aroma, with some light floral notes. I'll take fresh Mt. Hood over old, imported Hallertauer any day.

YEAST

There's an old saying that brewers make wort, but yeast makes beer. The role of yeast in making beer goes way beyond simply fermenting the sugars into alcohol. Yeast is a primary flavor component of beer. Even a yeast that doesn't add any of its own flavor helps define the beer by letting the other ingredients shine through. Choose the proper yeast, treat it right, and you'll be rewarded with a delicious brew.

ATTENUATION AND TEMPERATURE

Many times we've heard people ask if their beer is done fermenting, because it hasn't reached the amount of attenuation they expected based on the attenuation rating of the yeast. That rating is used to compare the attenuation of one strain to another using a standardized wort. It doesn't necessarily reflect the amount of attenuation you'll get with the yeast. That depends pretty much on the composition of the wort. Using the same yeast rated at 75 percent attenuation, you might get 85 percent in a very fermentable wort (mashed long and low, with sugar added) or 65 percent for a more unfermentable wort (mashed at a higher temp with significant amounts of crystal malt). Be sure you take the type of wort you've made into account when trying to decide if fermentation is finished.

Fermentation temperature plays a large role in the performance and flavor of a yeast. Generally, higher temperatures promote faster fermentation and more ester or phenol production. Temperatures that are too high can promote the formation of fusel alcohols. These smell like nail polish remover and can give you a headache that might make you wish you'd never drink again—okay, maybe not quite that bad! Yeast companies will give you a suggested range of temperature for the yeast, but don't think you have to stick strictly to that range. Often, the suggested temperatures will be higher than those that make the beer taste the way you want it to taste. We have found that we usually prefer beers that are fermented at or slightly below the lower end of the suggested temperature range. As with everything else in homebrewing, experiment and decide what's right for you.

FORM (DRY AND LIQUID)

Yeast for brewing comes in liquid or dry form. Each form has its own advantages and drawbacks. Dry yeast is very easy to use. Simply open the packet, rehydrate (or not), and pour the yeast into the wort. Dry yeast makes an excellent choice for doing experiments because of the consistency. If you acquire two packs of dry yeast with the same date, you can be pretty certain that there will be the same number of viable cells in each pack. Because dry yeast packs contain so many more cells than liquid yeast packages, you don't need to make a starter to increase the cell count as you usually do with liquid yeast. The major drawback of dry yeast is that there is a limited number of strains available. Not all yeasts take well to drying, so your selection is more limited than if you use liquid yeast.

Rehydration gets a bit of a mixed reaction from brewers. Some object that it complicates the process of brewing and that dry yeast works just fine when they snip open the packet and dump it into the freshly cooled wort. Why bother with rehydrating? The problem with not hydrating the yeast first is that the mummified granules lack any defense against the toxic levels of sugar in fresh

Embrace the Funk

Brandon Jones of Nashville, Tennessee, is one funky brewer. And as certain as we are that he's tired of hearing people say that, it still needs to be said. Brandon loves funky beers … you know, the kind made with exotic strains of wild yeast and bacteria. He runs the Embrace the Funk program at Yazoo Brewing in Nashville, as well as a website devoted to his endeavors (embracethefunk.com). We asked Brandon to talk about what he does at Embrace the Funk and some of the strains he's worked with. Here are Brandon's notes:

Most of my experiments at Yazoo go two ways when working with a new microbe:

1. I usually find or hear about a strain of Brettanomyces or bacteria via a lab like ATCC or another brewer. If the microbe is from a lab, I order it freeze dried so it comes as a pure seed that just needs to be woken up, plated for purity, and stepped up to proper cell count. That's all fairly easy ,and it provides sure-fire results.

2. The other way, which I think is more fun, is when we isolate and grow up microbes we have captured. Isolating and stepping up from the great spontaneously fermented beers of Brussels or using your own local flora can yield some pretty awesome results.

If I'm on a treasure hunt for a new microbe, I will either plate directly or pour a small amount (about 25 mililiters) of unhopped wort (at about 1.020 original gravity) into the bottle of dregs or a pint mason jar. I let it sit covered in a warm environment inside for 3–4 days. Then I will swab the liquid and plate. (If you're trying to collect local flora, an easy way is to use unhopped wort (10–16 ounces) in a jar, then let it sit with cheesecloth over the top for 8–12 hours before plating.) Try placing jars around different fruit trees or bushes. From there we can look at the morphology to see yeasts or bacterias then pick colonies to step up.

Some microbes from known sources might have a known character or two I can play off of immediately, so I could take those into a darker wort or step up the IBUs. However, I'd say most of the time I use our hefeweizen wort to do an initial 5 or 10 gallon test. It's a good, versatile wort to use with an unknown microbe. Also, the IBUs aren't too high, and the gravity of the wort isn't anything that should give the yeast or bacteria any growth problems. Once in a while I'll add wort. Over half the viable population dies before it can get to work. A quick 5–15 minute soak in warm water with a pinch of yeast nutrient gives your yeast time to restore their strong, flexible walls and modulate their intake of sugar. Take a moment and ensure they're ready to go.

Liquid yeast gives you a wide variety of yeast strains to choose from. Because there are fewer cells in a package than dry yeast, you will usually need to start by pitching the yeast into a low-gravity wort to start the yeast and build up the cell count. Some yeast packaging will give you a chance to proof the yeast first, which is great for ascertaining its viability. But don't be fooled into thinking that this proofing is equivalent to a starter. There is very little food for the yeast in the pack, meaning that there is virtually no cell growth. You still will usually need to make a starter, even after smacking the pack to proof the yeast.

A quick word about yeast suppliers. Until recently, homebrewers have had a relatively small number of yeast suppliers to choose from: Red Star, Lallemand, White Labs, and Wyeast. But over the past few years, new boutique suppliers have appeared, challenging the market by pushing new, different strains on the world. Take a look around and explore the options provided

some wood cubes, spices, dry hop, fruit, or even blend with another project. But the main thing I do at this stage is learn what the microbe will give me under my normal pitch rates (sometimes I will do a side by side and under pitch a second carboy by 25 percent), normal O_2, and normal pitch/ferment temps. Once I have a good idea of how a microbe performs I'll mark it in my library as a possible primary or secondary fermenting microbe. Sometimes two microbes I've marked as secondaries are good as mixed culture primaries together.

Here are a couple of the neat microbes I've played with:

- *Saccharomyces paradoxus: This is a really neat strain and a true paradox of character. It's actually naturally occurring in many parts of the world and found on tree bark! I believe the history on ours is it was isolated from a tree in South America. For beer, it produces what some perceive as a sour and tart aroma in malt-based beers but with a Sacch strain. Since it has good pectinase activity—meaning it can break down pectin—if you are using fruit in your beer, it can help clear the beer and break down the fruit quicker, which should translate to better fruit character in your final beer. As far as a beer with no fruit, this one is good as a single strain or a secondary addition. The 100 percent fermentations show the aroma does not match the flavor though. It has a lactic/lemon sourness in the aroma, but the flavor is peppery, tart, and rustic. In my experiences, it has 97 percent attenuation when pitched at 65°F with a free rise to 71°F, with a final pH of 4.1. Pitched in secondary or alongside of a saison strain, it would probably make a killer beer!*

- *Lacto Brevis: I really love this Lacto. It is IBU and alcohol tolerant, but the best part is this bacteria is heterofermentative! That means it can create alcohol with bacteria, and it happens fairly quickly, too. I haven't used any O_2 when pitching, but have pitched at 64°F, 70°F, and 85°F. My preference so far leans towards pitching at 70°F and letting it free rise into the mid 70°Fs. I've been able to get a peachy and somewhat green apple character from it going into the mid to upper 70°Fs. I has attenuation of 90 percent and a final pH of 3.3, which is really sour even for me. It turned a bit too cidery for me when pitched in the upper 80s. This is a good one for both primary and secondary additions*

by companies like East Coast Yeast and others. Who knows, you may have a new microbiologist in your backyard.

TYPES

Yeast can be grouped into two main classes. Each class contains several subclasses.

Ale yeasts generally work best at temperatures from the low 60°Fs to the mid-70°Fs. They are sometimes referred to as top fermenting yeasts. Their flavor impact can range from virtually none, as in many American pale ales, to a flavor that pretty much defines the beer, like German Hefeweizen or most Belgian styles.

There is less variation in lager yeasts than in ale yeasts. Lager yeasts should be very clean. They ferment at lower temperatures than ale yeasts, generally in the 45°F–55°F temperature range (although there are ale yeasts that ferment very well into the mid 50°sF). The main differences between lager yeasts are those that leave the beer with a sharp, crisp mouthfeel and those that give a maltier flavor and chewier mouthfeel. But remember, there's a lot of crossover and not a huge amount of difference. A yeast from one group may work great for a style in the other group.

Clean Ale

Clean ale yeasts are the choice for many American styles of beer. These yeasts have very low levels of esters (the fuity aromas and flavors you get from some yeasts). While some people refer to clean ale yeasts as boring, in reality, these yeasts allow you to experiment with malt and hops without interference from yeast flavors. Yeasts such as WY1056 American Ale, WLP001 California Ale, or Fermentis Safale US-05 are great examples of clean ale yeast.

Estery Ale

Estery ale yeasts pack their own distinctive flavors. Usually when you hear the word *ester*, brewers tend to go straight to the world of faults. After all, many American beers' distinctive aromas come from the hops, and to a German lager brewer, an ester in the brewhouse is a deeply troubling failure. However, to a British or Belgian brewer, esters are welcome companions.

Mostly formed during the lag phase, ester compounds provide strong organoleptic sensations. These usually include fruit notes of apple, pear, banana, clove, or cherry. But the range can run to flowers (geranyl acetate) or the dreaded nail polish remover (ethyl acetate). The amount in your beer is driven by the yeast health, the presence of precursors, yeast stress, and most importantly, temperature. The warmer your ferment, the more ester production you will see.

British brew strains tend to showcase a number of the fruity tones that American brewers avoid. The strains were chosen for a number of factors, including flocculation, stability of the yeast cake, and yes, the estery character that blended well with native ingredients—especially the earthy and floral hops grown in the British Isles.

Belgian or French Ale

Belgian yeasts are pretty much the definition of estery yeast. The fruit flavors, coupled with phenolics that range from spicy to smoky, bring a huge depth of flavor to most Belgian styles. There are liquid yeasts available that are sourced from Trappist monasteries that have been brewing beer for centuries. With these yeasts and a carefully constructed recipe, you can pretty accurately create the same flavors that the monks do. WY1214 Belgian Abbey / WLP500 Trappist Ale (Chimay) and WY1762 Belgian Abbey II / WLP540 Abbey IV (Rochefort), used in the right temperature range with the right recipe, allow you to create beers that would cost a fortune if you bought them.

> **Denny:** One of my favorite beers is Rochefort 10. I once calculated that the 5-gallon batch of a similar recipe that cost me about thirty-five dollars to make would cost over six hundred dollars if I bought the same amount by the bottle.

WY3522 Ardennes is an example of a Belgian yeast that favors phenolics if fermented at lower temperatures (60°F–65°F) and fruitier characteristics fermented at temperatures of 68°F and above. At the low end of the range, it makes a wonderful Belgo-American IPA.

The saison and farmhouse yeasts of Northern France and Southern Belgium are usually a little less estery and more phenolic than other Belgian strains. It will depend on the exact strain and how you use it. We'll let Mr. Saison tell you a little more about those on page 158.

Wheat/Hefeweizen (Ale)

In Germany, a country with a history of strict beer laws that tightly regulate everything about a beer, the Bavarian hefeweizens stick out like a weird sore thumb. Like saison, a wheat beer is just a wheat beer without the appropriate yeast to make it a hefeweizen.

The few strains that exist for hefeweizen are prodigious producers of clove phenol (4-vinyl guaiacol) and a banana ester (isoamyl acetate). This is the classic push-pull of a Bavarian hefe. The general rule of thumb is lots of yeast, ferment cooler (64°F–65°F) if you want to promote the clove, and ferment warmer (67°F–68°F) if you want to push the banana.

You'll also notice some American Wheat strains, those very neutral ale strains that don't impart the same loveliness that a true hefeweizen does. You can safely ignore them if you wish.

Sharp Lager

Sharp lager yeasts yield a very clean, crisp beer. They are generally best suited to German or Bohemian pilsners, as well as Dutch pils, Helles, Dortmundern, and even American lagers. Examples of these yeasts are WY2000 Budvar Lager, WY2001 Urquell Lager, WY2007 Pilsen Lager, WY2035 American Lager, WY2042 Danish Lager, WY2124 Bohemian Lager, and WY2278 Czech Pils.

Malty Lager

Malty lager yeasts leave the beer with a smoother mouthfeel that favors malt characteristics. They are best used for fuller-bodied lager styles, such as Munich dunkel, Maibock/Helles bock, or doppelbock. Look for WY2206 Bavarian Lager or WY2308 Munich Lager.

Saison Yeasts

By Drew

At once simple and frighteningly complex, sweet and dry as a bone, refreshing and challenging, the saison has become a beloved style for craft brewers due to its wide range of flavors and experiences that it can deliver. More than any other style, saison is yeast driven. You can take a bonafide recipe, straight from the records of Dupont and brew it, but if you don't pitch a saison strain, you won't get a saison. Because of this, there are more style specific strains for saison than any other style

There are three strains that every brewer should know: WY3724 Belgian Saison, WLP565 Belgian Saison I, and WY3711 French Saison. The first two are, in theory, from Brasserie Dupont, the progenitor of the modern saison. The third is from a French brewer of Farmhouse ales.

WY3724 and WLP565 have gained a reputation for being difficult amongst brewers. They ferment hot and produce big phenols, but then stall out for a while. Fortunately that's easy to avoid (see page 127). WY3711, on the other hand, is trusty and a monster in Internet parlance. In my view, I like WY3711, but it produces subdued saisons. If you can wrangle the others, they can give you more saison-y characters.

But of course saison doesn't stop there. Here's a listing of what I've found in my saison travels. Unless otherwise noted, all wort was chilled to 64°F–65°F, pitched with yeast, and allowed to free rise to ambient (75°F–80°F):

WYEAST

WY3522 Belgian Ardennes: Subtle nose, dry, spicy, and tropical with a touch of ham

WY3711 French Saison: Leathery, big fruity nose, spicy (black pepper, cardamom) but approachable—flavors are better when it's fermented cooler

WY3724 Belgian Saison: Phenols, fruit in balance, beautifully dry

WHITE LABS

WLP565 Saison 1 (Heated straight to 85°F): Deep, dry spice, black pepper, dry as hell, slightly medicinal

WLP565 Saison 1 (free rise to ambient): Fruit, cherries, subdued spices, more balanced with a sneaking of malt... still dry, but not overly so

WLP566 Saison 2: Surprisingly neutral, light phenol, spicy sandalwood flavor

WLP568 Saison Blend: Phenolic nose, beer comes in balance, but muted...less saison and more Belgian

WLP585 Saison 3: Fruit driven nose, lactic (yogurt), ginger, sweetest perceived finish—a definite favorite

EAST COAST YEAST

ECY08 Saison Brasserie: Cinnamon, pear, berry, mellow, feels fluffy, nice finishing zing but not harshly dry— another favorite

ECY03 Farmhouse Brett: Horsey, leathery, horehound, crisp pop, earthy, mushrooms, but not muddled thanks to some tartness on the finish

WATER

Water treatment is one of the last things that homebrewers should tackle in the effort to tweak their beers to perfection. Our experience is that if your water tastes good, then you can usually make good beer without treating your water. That said, water treatment will help you get that final 5 percent of homebrew deliciousness that we all crave. As a general rule, keep a few things in mind:

- Getting the pH right (5.2–5.6) is key. Too high a pH will encourage the extraction of tannins, which can give your beer an undesirable dry mouthfeel and the perception of harsh bitterness. Also, correct pH can increase your mash efficiency.
- Higher levels of sulfate can enhance the bitterness of the beer by increasing the dryness of the finish, which can be desirable in styles like IPA. This dryness is unlike the puckering dryness you get from tannins as a result of your pH being too high.
- Higher levels of chloride will enhance the perception of malt and sweetness in a beer, as will higher levels of sodium. Sodium is tricky, however, and too much will give your beer a strange malt flavor, not to mention saltiness.
- Proper levels of calcium (50–100 ppm for ales and 20–50 ppm for lagers) promote both yeast health and clearer beer.

If you're an extract brewer, consider using distilled or reverse-osmosis water if you don't think your own water quality is up to par. When extracts are made, the producers make sure they have the correct minerals for the type of extract being produced. Since the minerals are already there, you can use water with no mineral content and still be assured that your wort will have the proper mineral content. The caveat here is that you may still want to do some adjustments for flavor enhancement.

GETTING STARTED

In order to properly manipulate your water, you have to know your starting point by getting a water analysis. If you're on a municipal water system, you might be able to get the information you need from your local water department. Often, though, those reports lack the information about minerals that are crucial to homebrewers. Instead, send a water sample to an independent lab for testing. You can find one local to you or use Ward Laboratories (www.wardlab.com). Many brewers have found their service to be complete and accurate. However you get your information, make sure it includes concentration numbers for sodium, calcium, magnesium, sulfate, chloride, carbonate, bicarbonate, total hardness as $CaCO_3$, and total alkalinity as $CaCO_3$.

Okay, so you've got your water analysis information. Now, what the heck can you do with it? There are several fine, free resources to help you calculate mineral additions. Look for calculators from Martin Brungard (Bru'nwater) or Kai Troester (Brewer's Friend), among others. Plug in the numbers you get from water analysis and pick a water profile. Some of the calculators have profile lists right in them, though you can also refer to a book or the Internet.

You will usually have better luck choosing a profile based on the color and flavor, or style, of your beer (like amber bitter) than by choosing a profile from the city where the beer is traditionally brewed. Water profiles for various cities are usually no more than a snapshot from a particular

time and may change after the profile was published. Also, many breweries adjust their water to accommodate the beer they're brewing, so simply knowing the water profile from a particular city may not tell you what the treated water they use is really like.

ADJUSTMENTS FOR pH AND FLAVOR

There are two main reasons to adjust the water you use for brewing: pH and beer flavor. Adjustments for pH are usually made in the mash, although pH can be adjusted in the kettle as well. Correct mash pH, generally 5.2–5.6, can improve the efficiency of your mash. In addition, correct pH can effect the utilization of your hops and even the final color of the beer.

Sometimes, even though your pH is correct in the mash, you want to add mineral salts like chlorides or sulfates to enhance beer flavor. You can add these to the mash for pH and flavor adjustments, unless they would adversely effect the mash pH you've worked so hard to get right. In that case, these minerals can be added directly to the kettle for flavor.

Denny has pretty good water, and for most mid-colored beers, his mash hits the correct pH with little to no adjustment. Calcium, present in both of the most common water treatment minerals—gypsum ($CaSO_4$) and calcium chloride—will lower the pH if added to the mash. If that's what you need, simply add them to the kettle as the wort is boiling. The effect on the kettle pH is minimal, and the flavor enhancement works great.

SULFATE AND CHLORIDE

Knowing how sulfate and chloride relate to beer flavor gives you some options in adjusting your beer. For a more bitter beer with a drier finish, increase the sulfate. The dryness of the finish enhances the perception of bitterness. For a beer that tastes maltier, increase the chloride. In general, you can think of the ratio of sulfate to chloride as being assignable to each beer style you brew.

That works pretty well, but sometimes you have to toss that aside and concern yourself with the absolute numbers. For instance, assume you're brewing an IPA and have decided that a sulfate:chloride ratio of 1.2:1 is works well for you. But after a few batches, you've found that it just isn't giving you the hop kick that you'd like it to have. You want a drier finish and more in-your-face bitterness, which you can get by increasing the sulfate. But to maintain the ratio, you also need to increase the chloride. It's recommended that the chloride level should stay below 100 ppm, so if you try to maintain the ratio, you could go above that. At that point, forget about the ratio! What matters is the amount of sulfate you need. Keep the chloride amount constant and start trying increases in the sulfate level. It will throw your ratio off, but it may just get you the beer you want to drink.

Note: Gypsum and calcium chloride can also be added directly to a glass to taste-test the effect they have on the beer. This is a good way to see if you want to use them in the next batch. Go easy … start with small amounts and scale up from there.

THE IMPORTANCE OF ALKALINITY

Alkalinity is a measure of the buffering capability of water and its ability to resist pH change. Alkalinity is usually due to the level of carbonate and bicarbonate in the water. Those things make it more difficult to lower the pH of the water. Grain has a natural acidifying effect on the water, which will lower the pH under most circumstances. Too much alkalinity will make that impossible and have a negative impact on beer flavor. Some amount of alkalinity is necessary to keep beer pH from falling too low and giving the beer a winelike character, but too much alkalinity will mute hop expression and make the extraction of undesirable amounts of tannins from the hops and grain more likely.

EXPERIMENTAL INGREDIENTS

TO SAY HOMEBREWERS are a creative group is an understatement. We've all seen posts like this on brewing forums: "I want to brew a Dijon mustard red wine celery beer. How much red wine should I use? Should I add the celery to the boil or dry celery in secondary?" Just as you're about to post an answer to the effect of, "On what planet would this be considered a good idea?" someone will post a reply saying, "Well, when I used Dijon mustard, red wine, and celery, I did it like this." So, in the spirit of keeping an open mind, this chapter will look at some ingredients you may not have considered and the ways they can be used in your beer.

GET YOUR PRODUCE ON

Fruits and vegetables exist primarily for one purpose: to ensure the spreading of a plant's genetic material (seeds). Lucky for us, they do so in packages that exhibit diverse flavors and aromas. The trick is how to get the flavors and aromas into your beer.

Needless to say, you should start with the best sources of produce. Hit the farmers market late in the day to strike a deal and choose produce not for looks, but for flavor. If the brew day is imminent, look for fruit so ripe it's about to turn south. Don't have a farmers market handy? Don't fret. Despite the fresh is best mantra of the culinary media, individually quick frozen (IQF) techniques have ratcheted up the quality of frozen fruits and vegetables in the past decade. When a particular fruit or vegetable is out of season, frozen is not only easier, it's also cheaper and tastes better than those god awful specimens that fly thousands of miles and are picked by dint of being able to survive the trip.

Before we get into the how much question, let's tackle how to use produce:

1. You must wash your produce. Some fruits and vegetables, like apples and cucumbers, come coated in a food-grade wax that serves both as a protectant and beautifier. The rule of thumb is if it's pretty and glossy, it's coated. Simply wash with cold water and use a clean produce brush on your shellacked produce.

2. If the produce is large, or if the flesh isn't exposed, it's time to chop. Use a clean knife and cutting board and tackle the fruit or veg. Don't worry about cutting a perfect brunoise—give everything a good chop to get it into ½ to 1-inch pieces.

3. Unless you're dealing with fresh, leafy items, give everything a freeze. The average home freezer is horribly inefficient and we're going to take advantage of that. When water in the produce is frozen slowly, it has time to form large crystals. These crystals pierce the cell walls of your produce. When you thaw and the crystals disappear, the juices and other interior goo will rush out of the mangled cells, giving you better flavor extraction. Vacuum packing will help encourage full goo-ifcation of your source matter. Alternatively, if you have a home juice machine that works by pulverizing the produce, you can create your own fruit and vegetable juice for use. Just make sure the machine is cleaned and sanitized before using (or freeze the juice before adding it).

   Note: If you feel the need to sanitize the fruit before adding it, avoid heating it. That can set the pectin in the fruit and make it a gooey mess in your beer. Instead, soak the fruit in vodka to sanitize it. Or give the fruit a light spray of a sanitizer like Star San if you must. However, the two of us usually depend on the alcohol content and lowered pH of the fermented beer to keep things safe.

4. That's it for the prep work for almost all fruits and non-starchy vegetables. We'll cover the exceptions in a moment, but let's finish this happy path with a trip to the fermenter. Although you may not normally use a secondary fermenter, this is one time that a secondary can be valuable. Adding fruit will often trigger a true secondary fermentation. Using another primary fermenter for your secondary is not a bad idea. Be sure that whatever venting mechanism you're using—airlock, blowoff tube, etc—won't clog. If your excitable ferment throws raspberry flesh into the airlock port, it could jam the airlock, creating a truly explosive situation. You do not want to come home to a wall full of glass shards or a ceiling full of Raspberry Imperial Stout!

   Note: Some folks like to use big mesh bags to hold their additions to retain clarity. However, we generally prefer to add the produce directly. If you want clear beer, then you'll need to be vigilant and patient enough to allow the beer to settle or be annoyed enough to filter. Truth be told, the mesh bags won't spare you this pain either.

OTHER PRODUCE PROCESSES

Citrus zest is a great way to add citrus fruit flavor. In fact, almost the entire orange flavor that we picture when we think of a fresh orange is locked in essential oils like limonene in the outer peel. Use a fruit zester or microplane grater to create citrus zest. Start with the zest of two fruits before adjusting up or down. It can either go in during the last 2–3 minutes of the boil or be added to the fermenter after fermentation has died down.

Remember that the zest is the outermost part of the fruit rind, where the oils are concentrated, and not the white, bitter pith. However, you can take a cue from brewers like Mark Jilg of Craftsman Brewing, who uses the whole orange—including the pith—to provide an extra bitterness to his fruity and hoppy Orange Grove Pale Ale.

Dried fruits and vegetables can be another great way to skip the annoyance of fresh produce, and they don't add any moisture to the brew! Using them is as simple as opening a bag and dumping them into the beer. You're effectively using the beer to rehydrate them and create an alcoholic tincture. Use roughly the amount called for in the table (see 166).

Be careful when buying dried fruit; make sure to grab unsulfured varieties. You don't want to add sulfur compounds to your beer, do you? From a visual perspective, the unsulfured version isn't as bright and fresh-looking, but fortunately you'll be drinking it, not staring at it. With dried vegetables, make sure you're buying dehydrated vegetables and not oil- and salt-coated roasted vegetables. That would be bad juju for your beer.

Roots like potatoes, carrots, beets, or parsnips should be cooked first and smashed to ensure complete access to their goodness. Mashing starchy vegetables helps you avoid flooding your beer with starches.

PRODUCE QUANTITY

Now you get to see why we seemed so obsessive about cost. To get fruit flavor in a beer, you need a lot of it. For a 5-gallon batch, we're talking a minimum of 2.5 pounds of cranberries on the low side to nearly 20 pounds of apples on the high side.

The general rule of thumb with fruit is to use 1 pound for each gallon of beer, but for very subtly flavored fruits like blueberries or blackberries, you might want to increase that amount to 2 or 3 pounds per gallon. If you're wondering about the impact on your beer's gravity, you have to remember that a good portion of fruit is water. The rough average of fruit juice gravity is in the 1.040–1.050 range.

Vegetables are a little trickier to gauge. Many of them contain green flavors like chlorophyll (spinach) or sulfur compounds (garlic), which are less-than-desirable in a finished beer. Others, like chile peppers, will punish you horribly for overuse. Sometimes a single pepper (such as a ghost pepper) is enough to drive a full batch into hotter-than-hell territory. To determine a dosing rate that's appropriate for your needs, create a purée or juice and then follow our sample calculation rules with a pint of similar beer.

Think about increasing the amount even more if you're adding it to a strongly flavored beer like a stout or porter. One pound of blueberries per gallon in a porter produces a very restrained blueberry flavor and virtually no aroma. To really make them stand out, using 2 pounds per gallon of finished beer isn't out of line.

To use the following charts, know that the amounts are listed per gallon. The low number is intended to be for a more subtle flavor. The high number is for when you want to leave no doubt in your drinker's mind as to what you've added. Think of it as: "Would you like some beer with your raspberry?" Also, don't forget: these fruits have endless subvarieties. Take a chance on a new variety you've never tried before, like the freaky Buddha's hand citron or a candy cane beet. These are guidelines, after all, not Procrustean strictures.

Fruit Additions: Whole, Chopped, Puréed, or Juiced

type	Pounds Needed per Gallon (Low to High)	Average Gravity	Notes

apple | 1–4 lbs | 1.057

One of humanity's oldest fruits, apple shines best in simple beers. Try crabapples for their intensity.

apricot | 1–3 lbs | 1.057

Apricot is difficult to capture. It's delicate and fades quickly. Artificial apricot flavor will help.

blackberry | ½–2 lbs | 1.040

Tart and tannic with a bright berry aroma and flavor, blackberries are a crowd favorite.

blueberry | 1–3 lbs | 1.057

Blueberries are delicate. Use the smallest berries you can find. (Wild is best.) A great blueberry is all about the pepper bite.

cranberry | ½–2 lbs | 1.044

These are tart and tannic fruit bombs. Begin with just a touch and then add more once you understand their intensity.

cherry | ½–2 lbs | 1.079

To avoid blowing your head off, use less of the sour cherries found in Michigan than the ubiquitous sweet varieties like Bing and Rainer.

coconut | ¼–½ lb | 1.053

This one's a little unusual, since it doesn't really have a juice. Add toasted coconut flakes (unsweetened) into the secondary. Toast in a 300°F oven for 10–15 minutes until golden.

dates | ½–1 lb | 1.074

Dates have been part of the beer-making process since the Sumerians wrote the "Hymn to Ninkasi." Chop these up fine in order to maximally extract their sweetness.

figs | ½–1 lb | 1.074

Figs were another ingredient found in early beer making as well. Make sure you get super ripe figs that fall apart when you look at them.

grape | 1–3 lbs | 1.083

Take a clue from wine makers and find smaller grapes; like blueberries, the juice will be more concentrated and flavorful. No wine grapes in your area? Raisins are an interesting alternative.

grapefruit | 1–2 lbs | 1.040

Everyone's old-school bitter breakfast fruit has changed. Use varieties like the giant pomelo or ruby red for a softer grapefruit flavor. The pith is extraordinaly bitter.

| lemon | ½–1.5 lbs | 1.036 |

There's a reason you see lemons used all the time in cooking. Their bright aroma and acid wake flavors up. Varieties like Meyer lemons are softer and less acidic, so you can push them more.

| lime | ½–1.5 lbs | 1.036 |

Like the lemon, the lime wakes up your aroma and flavor, but lime is more aggressive. Key limes offer a softer flavor than the classic Persian lime.

| mango | ½–1.5 lbs | 1.070 |

Earthy, acidic, and a little funky, these can make an interestingly sweet-tart addition to your beer.

| melon | 2–3 lbs | 1.057 |

Who doesn't love a sweet, crisp, fruity melon? It's easy to make a purée: blend honeydews, cataloupe, and so on for a more complex profile from the delicate aromas.

| orange | 1–2 lbs | 1.048 |

The classic citrus bred from the original citron. Oranges can vary in tartness and sweetness, so taste first!

| passionfruit | ½–1.5 lbs | 1.061 |

The tropics captured in a fruit. Deeply odd and intoxicating with just a little bit of tartness.

| peach | 1–3 lbs | 1.048 |

Like apricots, peaches are fleeting, so be prepared to boost the flavor.

| pineapple | ½–2 lbs | 1.057 |

Look up how these grow, and tell me we haven't mistreated this wonderfully bright fruit with all the canning we do to it!

| plums/prunes | 1–2 lbs | 1.057/1.079 |

Since we already find this flavor in so many of our darker Belgians, it shouldn't be surprising it works well in beer.

| pomegranate | ½–2 lbs | 1.074 |

Pomegranate is loaded with antioxidants and an acidic punch.

| raspberry | ½–2 lbs | 1.044 |

Lend a great big punch of color and acid to your beer with black or red raspberries. They're quite possibly the most popular fruit flavor in beer!

| strawberry | 2–4 lbs | 1.061 |

Everyone wants to make a strawberry beer, but it's an elusive flavor to capture. If you want strong strawberry flavor, use more than you'd ever think necessary or get your hands on flavoring extracts.

| watermelon | 1–3 lbs | 1.061 |

We prefer purée and juicing the fruit fresh, but be careful not to get any of the rind, which will taste like jalapeños mixed with grass. The flavor is potent and will ruin all the other flavors.

Vegetable Additions: Whole, Chopped, Puréed, or Juiced

type	Amount Needed per Gallon (Low to High)	Must Be Mashed? (Yes or No)	Notes

You'll notice we didn't provide any ppg for the vegetable chart, and for good reason: You're not going to get much of a contribution. Aside from carrot and corn (.012–.015ppg), you're looking at about .08ppg or less. So think of vegetables as a flavoring and not a fermentable. So why mash them? Even though you'll get little fermentable sugar and mainly flavor, you still need to mash them to convert starch in them to sugar. Otherwise, the starch can provide food for bacteria and increase the likelihood of an infected beer. For vegetables with no starch content (like cucumbers or spinach), those can be added like fruits as juices, purees, or chunks into the secondary!

| aloe | ⅛–½ lb | N |

Aloe vera juice has a very distinctive bitter bite that usually is found in digestifs. It should be added late in the boil to allow the gooey aspect of the juice to dissolve.

| beans | ½–2 lbs | Y |

No amount of Internet searching turns up a beer made with beans, but that doesn't mean you can't make one. Beans are mainly a starch with a bit of protein. That means that a mash can convert the starch to sugar. If you use fresh or canned beans, rinse them well, then smash them up thoroughly before adding them to the mash. Dried beans should be lightly broken up or coarsely milled before adding them to the mash.

beets | ¼–½ lb | N Lend a purplish pink (mostly pink) color and a sweet earthy flavor to your beer with fresh steamed beets. Make sure to trim the beet and peel the root before adding.

carrots | ½–1 lb | N Carrots are best done either as a juice or as a mash addition to help break up the hard root. Peel the carrots before processing to avoid extra earthiness.

celery | ½–1 lb | N Celery is the vegetable that always gets beaten up in school. That's a shame, because celery is actually a wonderful vegetable with aromatic properties that puzzle the drinker.

chili peppers | ¼–4 pieces | N (The number of pieces depends on heat and taste.) Peppers can be tricky to prepare. Go easy until you get a sense of them, and use deseeded, deveined, sliced peppers in the secondary or keg. Go easy to avoid blasting off your friends' faces.

corn | ¼–2 lbs | Y Corn has a long history in the brewing traditions of the Americas, from the Chicas of South America to modern lager brewing practice. They're light and sweet with a soft impact, but a big body reduction. Use cornmeal, fresh corn, frozen corn, even corn tortillas or chips (low salt, please).

cucumbers | ¼–1 lb | N Cukes have a surprising amount of bitterness in the peel. Juice, washed skin and all. Blend into a light fruity beer for a beery Pimm's cup!

lettuce | 1–2 lbs | N Lettuce in beer? Yup. It's been known to happen. Lettuce—particularly darker varieties—carries some potent bitter compounds that really jump out at you. It does take a lot to carry an impact, though, and really: avoid the iceberg.

peas | ¼–1 lb | Y Believe it or not, English peas are a traditional ingredient in beer, dating back hundreds of years. Either fresh peas or dried split peas can be used. Smash up fresh peas before adding them to the mash. The pods can be used as well as the peas themselves.

potatoes | 1–4 lbs | Y This seems like a joke, but potatoes and sweet potatoes are another product that has been used to make beer. Because it's a hardy crop, you could always count on its availability. A word of warning about making a potato beer: not only does the potato need to be cooked first, but potatoes contain a huge amount of water. You might want to run this as a secondary American cereal mash to control your liquid levels.

pumpkin / squashes | ¼–½ lb | Y/N Everyone's favorite fall flavor, pumpkin was a staple of the American craft beer scene for years and years before coffee shops got involved. What most people really mean when they say they want a pumpkin pie beer is that they want the mélange of pie spices (cinnamon, nutmeg, allspice, ginger, mace). Pumpkin (and other squashes) are best roasted in an oven to bring out a caramel sweetness. For pumpkins, avoid the common jack-o'-lantern pumpkin and buy pie pumpkins. (As a cheat, canned pumpkin works in a pinch and can go straight into the boil.)

spinach / kale / chard | ¼–1½ lbs | N These leafy greens pack a hell of a punch. Not only do they contain assertive flavors, but they also contain a fair amount of minerals. Be careful and give them a sample in a previously created beer first to see if the mineral richness agrees with you.

tamarind | ⅛–¼ lb | N A popular, citrusy sweet-sour fruit that's usually sold as a paste and used extensively in Latin and Thai cuisines. Use it at the last minute in the boil to great effect in a pale beer or use more to provide pop in a darker brown beer.

MEAN GREEN BEER

By Drew

Before we leave the world of vegetables, can we talk about the atrocity that's foisted on the American public every March 17? We know it; you know it: it's the scourge of green beer. If you're lucky, it's Harp with green dye injected into the keg. If you're not, it's some outstandingly bad American lager with the same green dye. Walk away from the green dye, people. Instead, take a chance and bulk up a golden ale with some body components like oats or wheat, and then hit it with fresh cucumber, spinach, and kale juice. Add some ginger to pull focus from the green, and voila, Irish eyes are smiling with a real Mean Green Beer.

For 5.5 gallons at 1.057, 27 IBUs, 3.8 SRM, 5.9% ABV

GRAIN BILL

11.0 lbs	2-Row Pale Malt
1.5 lbs	Flaked oats
1.5 lbs	Flaked wheat

MASH SCHEDULE

Rest	155°F	60 minutes

HOPS

0.50 oz	Warrior	Pellet	15% AA	60 minutes
1.00 oz	Columbus		14% AA	0 minutes

YEAST

WY1272 American Ale II

OTHER INGREDIENTS

1 bunch kale
2 bunches spinach
4 large English cucumbers
1 knuckle sized piece ginger, peeled

ADDITIONAL INSTRUCTIONS

On the day of packaging, take all of the extra other ingredients and juice them. Add the juice to the keg or bottling bucket and rack in on top of it. Carbonate to 2.5 volumes and enjoy!

RAID THE SPICE CABINET

While herbs and spices are usually added late in the boil, 5-10 minutes before flameout, we recommend experimenting by adding them to the fermenter or at packaging via a tea or tincture (see page 74). No matter how you add them, think about the effects carefully before adding spices or herbs to a recipe. Just because you like to eat a pickle when you drink beer doesn't necessarily mean that a pickle beer will be great!

But if you think a pickle beer is what you want, sneak up on it. Start on the low side (¼ teaspoon for most spices, ⅛ teaspoon for anything particularly pungent) with the herbs and spices. Brew a batch and assess it. Brew again and add or subtract herbs and spices based on what you tasted in the first batch. Our experience is that these additions can be tricky and this is where repeated test batches can really help.

Another word of advice: make sure you're using fresh herbs and spices! Their aromatic and flavor powers come from volatile essential oils that dissipate over time. Shy away from those packs of brewers' spices that have sat in your homebrew shop for who knows how long and avoid the grocery store for the same reason. Buy fresh spices from a reputable spice shop like Penzey's or the Spice House. Whole is preferred over pre-ground for flavor preservation. Grind just before use! You can pick up a cheap coffee grinder to grind the spices into powder if the mortar and pestle is too much work.

Watch out for certain super-potent spice oils like anethole (licorice) and eugenol (clove oil). Both can so easily override other tastes in your beer. In fact, clove oil is used as a dental anesthetic.

Here are several spices you can try:

- **Anise** is one of the many plants that carry the essential oil anethole, which is perceived by the palate as black licorice. A little goes a long, long way. Extracts work very well here. Note that star anise, which is even more potent and commonly used in Chinese cooking, is a completely different plant.
- **Black pepper** is one of the most significant spices in history. This Indian spice was the thing kings sent ships around the world to find. Even today it is one of the most widely traded spices globally. It can lend an instant vicious heat to beer, but after a short time aging, the effect of its piperine fades into a deeply earthy flavor.
- **Caraway seed** is technically a caraway fruit, a close relative of the carrot. Caraway pairs beautifully with rye to invoke the familiar Jewish deli bread.
- **Cardamom** is a strange little package of seeds within another seed. Cardamom is a warming, supremely aromatic spice that remains subtle and unidentifiable, despite being a key component of Indian cuisine and western Christmas desserts. Christmas ales are the most obvious application, but think of anything you'd want to have an ineffable spice quality—like a completely blasphemous German winter doppelbock. Start with just 0.2 ounce of cardamom and adjust in the next batch if you think the beer needs it. Too much cardamon can make your beer taste like cola!
- **Chamomile** is the well-known "secret" ingredient of the famous Belgian white beers. Found in both German and Roman varieties, the flavor is of apple and flowers, and it provides a lightly sweet note that helps reinforce the orange of the coriander and orange peel.

- **Cinnamon** is another spice widely prized and fought over in the past. Today, cinnamon is available in seemingly endless quantities. There are two primary varieties: cassia (*Cinnamomum cassia*) and true cinnamon (*C. verum*). Both are evergreen plants that have their inner bark harvested for the potent punch of cinnamaldehyde and ethyl cinnamate. Most of what the world knows as cinnamon is actually the thick and pungent cassia, originally from China. True cinnamon or Ceylon cinnamon is a subtler creature with less direct fire but more complex aromatics. Which you want is up to you! Why not mix them together for greater coverage?

- **Clove** pieces as we know and love them are the buds of the *Syzygium aromaticum* tree, and they're incredibly strong. The primary oil, eugenol, numbs the taste buds; therefore, you really must use clove sparingly. We generally recommend no more than ⅛ teaspoon for 5 gallons as a start.

- **Coriander** is the fruit of the leafy herb cilantro. It's one of the fundamental spices of humanity, going back to the Neolithic period. Of the many varieties, the best advice we can give you is to try and find the slightly longer Indian coriander and not the typical grocery store Mexican variety. The latter tends to be less complex and more citrus-flavored.

- **Cumin** is a parsley cousin with ties to the ancient Greeks. The dried fruit gives no hint of cumin's powerful impact until it's crushed. Major components are cuminaldehyde and cuminic alcohol, safranal, and pinene. It is the world's second most popular spice, only behind black pepper.

- **Fennel** can be used as both the wispy leaves and the seeds of a fennel plant. The seeds are hardier, and their licorice-like flavor is less likely to get lost. Like anise and star anise, fennel provides a punch of anethole, but it's not nearly potent as that of anise or star anise.

- **Fenugreek** is an Indian plant used in multiple dishes, especially curries. In Western food processing, fenugreek seed is used for the chemical soloton ($C_6H_8O_3$), which is commonly used as a maple substitute.

- **Galangal** and **ginger** are both rhizomes of the Zingiberaceae family. You'll recognize the taste and smell of ginger from Christmas cookies or any Asian cuisine. Galangal is closely associated with Thailand. We put these together because of their close-cousin status, but be aware that the flavors of galangal are stronger when fresh, as galangin is potent raw. However, ginger picks up its potency when cooked or dried, because its supply of gingerol is transformed to zingerone (cooked) or shogaol (dried). Gingerol is a closely related to both capascian (chiles) and piperine (black pepper).

- **Grains of paradise** are another member of the Zingiberaceae family. The grains are actually seeds that combine an intensely peppery flavor with a hint of citrus. In recent years, they've become popular in witbiers. Lightly crush them and toss them in at the end of the boil for a few minutes.
- **Jasmine** is an intensely aromatic flowering plant found worldwide. It is closely associated with the Chinese, who make a green tea perfumed with jasmine blossoms. If you want to use your own jasmine bushes, take a lesson from the Chinese and harvest your blossoms in the early evening, when they've just opened and the aroma is most intense. Since the many compounds in jasmine are particularly fragile, it would be best to avoid a high heat; whirlpool the flowers only in an off-boil kettle of wort. Alternatively, you can find jasmine syrup to use as a late addition to the kettle or even the fermenter.
- **Juniper berries,** the primary flavor of gin and Finnish sahti, contain a number of oils similar to those found in hops, both the piney pinene as well as the myrcene and limonene found in many American-style hops. Maybe this is why some of us hopheads also like gin!
- **Lavender** is a wonderfully soothing herb, prized by herbalists as a mild anxiolytic. Despite its calming nature, lavender has a strong flavor; you must use it sparingly to achieve a pleasing effect.
- **Lemon verbena,** or *Aloysia citrodora,* is a member of the verbena family, which, like our favorite hops, is rich in citral (lemon/citrus), nerol (fresh rose), and gerianol (floral, like geranium). The leaves carry the oils and perfume the air when bruised, so rub them a little before adding to the kettle or to a tincture. It is also remarkably easy to grow in a container garden.
- **Mace** and **nutmeg** are both products of the *Myristica fragrans* tree. Nutmeg is the seed and mace is the weblike coating that protects the seed. The two spices have similar flavors, though nutmeg is more potent and sweeter, and mace is more subtle. The list of flavor compounds found in the spice includes: camphene, pinene, terpineol, geraniol, safrol, and myristicin. Like cloves, nutmeg also contains a fair amount of eugenol, which can numb the palate.
- **Mustard seeds** (*Brassica nigra*, *B. juncea*, and *B. hirta*) are black, brown, or white. The characteristic burn that we associate with mustard is from a set of compounds that are activated only in the presence of water. Used whole, their impact is more earth and less fire. Like many other bitter or sharp spices, mustard used to be a common ingredient in beer, a tradition that survives only in a few beers from Belgium.
- **Pink pepper** isn't really a proper pepper of the *Piper* genus. It is the fruit of the Peruvian peppertree. It has a pepper bite, but not the same heat level as black pepper. Pink pepper has a fruiter flavor as well. Historically it has been used to flavor a few different South American indigenous beery beverages, such as the corn-based Chica.
- **Rose oil** is extraordinarily expensive, because it takes over sixty thousand roses to make just 1 ounce of oil. But homebrewers can either grab a few pounds (1 pound per gallon) of rose petals (from a friendly florist) or hit the nearest Middle Eastern or Jewish market for rose water (add it to taste at packaging).
- **Saffron** is made of the stigmas of the *Crocus sativus*. Saffron is an ancient spice that once was one of the most expensive things you could buy by the ounce. It makes sense when you realize that it takes 1 pound of flowers to get 0.2 ounces of dried saffron. Its intense, sweet hay flavor comes from picrocrocin, while the aroma comes from safranal.

PEPPER PILE PALE ALE

By Denny and Drew

Let's get blazing! Here we'll combine two of our favorite forms of heat, chiles and peppercorns. The trick to avoid blowing your top and get more sweet pepper bite is to use ripe red jalapenos. We're also using Szechuan pepper for its lemony citrus character, which will back up the American hop experience!

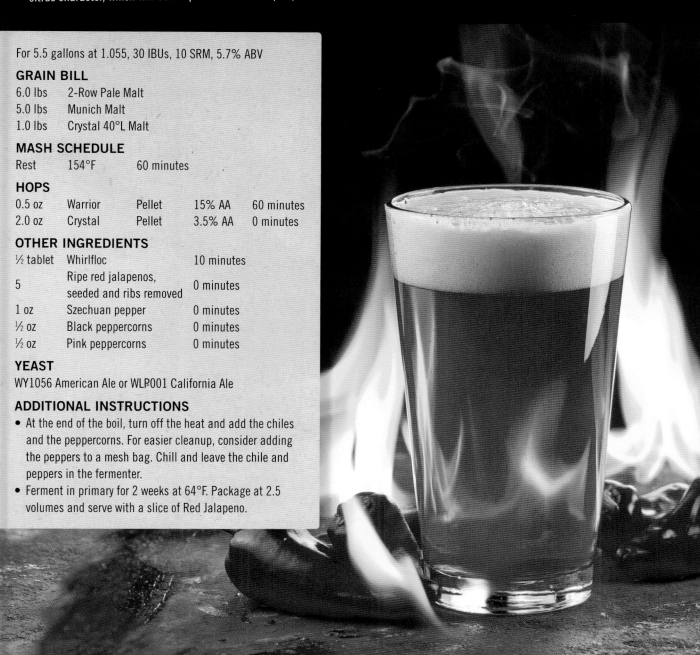

For 5.5 gallons at 1.055, 30 IBUs, 10 SRM, 5.7% ABV

GRAIN BILL

6.0 lbs	2-Row Pale Malt
5.0 lbs	Munich Malt
1.0 lbs	Crystal 40°L Malt

MASH SCHEDULE

Rest	154°F	60 minutes

HOPS

0.5 oz	Warrior	Pellet	15% AA	60 minutes
2.0 oz	Crystal	Pellet	3.5% AA	0 minutes

OTHER INGREDIENTS

½ tablet	Whirlfloc	10 minutes
5	Ripe red jalapenos, seeded and ribs removed	0 minutes
1 oz	Szechuan pepper	0 minutes
½ oz	Black peppercorns	0 minutes
½ oz	Pink peppercorns	0 minutes

YEAST

WY1056 American Ale or WLP001 California Ale

ADDITIONAL INSTRUCTIONS

- At the end of the boil, turn off the heat and add the chiles and the peppercorns. For easier cleanup, consider adding the peppers to a mesh bag. Chill and leave the chile and peppers in the fermenter.
- Ferment in primary for 2 weeks at 64°F. Package at 2.5 volumes and serve with a slice of Red Jalapeno.

HOP GENEVER OAT ALE

By Drew

One of my favorite memories in Belgium was having a beery lunch at t'Hommelhof in the village of Watou. The restaurant is a palace of biere cuisine and in the middle of what remains of Belgium hop farm country. To close off the meal, I threw back a post lunch digestif of an ice cold hop infused Genever (aka Dutch style gin). Bracing, cool, and refreshing!

For 5.5 gallons at 1.056, 17 IBUs, 5.3 SRM, 5.7% ABV

GRAIN BILL

9.0 lbs	Pilsner Malt
2.0 lbs	Flaked oats
1.0 lbs	Caravienne Malt

MASH SCHEDULE

Rest	150°F	60 minutes

HOPS

0.5 oz	Northern Brewer	Pellet	8.5% AA	60 minutes
1.0 oz	Styrian Goldings	Pellet	5.4% AA	0 minutes

OTHER INGREDIENTS

½ tablet	Whirlfloc	10 minutes
0.5 oz	Orange peel	10 minutes
1.0 oz	Juniper berries	10 minutes

YEAST

WY1214 Belgian Abby Ale

ADDITIONAL INSTRUCTIONS

- When 10 minutes remain in the boil, add the juniper and orange peel.
- Ferment in the mid 60°Fs and then package with a high carbonation (~3 volumes) to pop the juniper aroma.

BRATTY BRAT BEER

By Drew

This beer was born of a silly commercial that lampooned homebrewers with one crazy brewer offering his buddies a Bratwurst beer. It was meant as an "ohh, look at this wild crazy thing." Naturally, I took that as a challenge and made this deconstructed bratwurst beer using all the spices of a German brat with hint of bread and grain and spicy rye.

For 5.5 Gallons at 1.057 O.G., 13.8 IBUs, 4.0 SRM, 5.9% ABV

GRAIN BILL

6.0 lbs	Pilsner Malt
5.0 lbs	Wheat Malt
1.0 lbs	Rye Malt

MASH SCHEDULE

Rest	124°F	20 minutes
Rest	150°F	60 minutes (raise via decoction)

HOPS

0.25 oz	Magnum	14% AA	60 minutes

OTHER INGREDIENTS

½ tablet	Whirlfloc	10 minutes
⅛ tsp	Allspice, lightly crushed	5 minutes
⅛ tsp	Black pepper, lightly crushed	5 minutes
⅛ tsp	Caraway seed, lightly crushed	5 minutes
⅛ tsp	Celery seed, lightly crushed	5 minutes
⅛ tsp	Clove, powdered	5 minutes
⅛ tsp	Ginger, powdered	5 minutes
⅛ tsp	Nutmeg, grated	5 minutes

YEAST

WY1010 American Wheat for a neutral profile, WLP380 Hefeweizen IV for a mild German Hefe profile, or WLP410 Belgian Wit II for a spicier finish

ADDITIONAL INSTRUCTIONS

- Take the first quart of runnings and reduce to a cup, allow it to get scary dark to add a bit of smokey complexity to the beer.
- Ferment cool and check spicing. Adjust via tincture.

SAISON GUACAMOLE

By Drew

A huge hit at the National Homebrewer's Convention, this beer was designed to catch people's attention. The spice level on this should be restrained—just enough to let you know it's there, just enough to provide an extra pop, but not enough to keep you away from another glass.

For 5.5 gallons at 1.055, 19.4 SRM, 28 IBUs, 6.2% ABV, 90 minute boil

GRAIN BILL

9.0 lbs	Pilsner Malt
1.5 lbs	Oat Malt
8.0 oz	Pale Chocolate Malt
8.0 oz	Flaked Rye
4.0 oz	Carafa II Special Malt
1.0 lbs	Dark avocado honey (added at flameout)

MASH SCHEDULE

Rest	150°F	60 minutes

HOPS

0.5 oz	Magnum	Pellet	12.9% AA	60 minutes
1.0 oz	Hallertau Saphir	Pellet	4.4% AA	10 minutes

YEAST

WLP568 Saison Blend

OTHER INGREDIENTS

½ tablet	Whirlfloc	10 minutes

Spice Tincture:

1.5 tsp	Black pepper, coarsely crushed
1.5 tsp	Cilantro
1.5 tsp	Coriander, coarsely crushed
1.5 tsp	Dried chile peppers, coarsely crushed
1.5 tsp	Cumin, coarsely crushed
2	Limes, zested
1.5 tsp	Sun dried tomatoes (not the oil-packed variety!)

ADDITIONAL INSTRUCTIONS

Add everything for the spice tincture to ¾ cup of vodka. Soak for one week, shaking frequently. Filter twice through coffee filters and add to the beer at packaging.

- **Sichuan peppercorn** is another not-pepper! (You should have a sense now of how valuable pepper was, because so many things were named pepper.) The Sichuan peppercorn is the seed of the *Zanthoxylum simulans* and *Z. bungeanum*. Oddly, instead of using the seed, we use the seed coat, which imparts a light lemony flavor and an electrical numbing tingle on the lips and tongue. This is thanks to an unusual compound, hydroxy alpha sanshool, that appears to bind with pain receptors in the mouth. Sichuan peppercorn was banned for nearly forty years from the United States due to worries that it could carry citrus canker and threaten U.S. agriculture. It is now required to be heat-treated before importation.

- **Thyme,** or plants of the *Thymus* genus, are a common component in many Western cuisines and were thought by the ancient Greeks and Egyptians to provide courage and good health. Thyme contains our old friend myrcene, linalool, and a new oil, thymol. It is closely related to mint and carries a potent aroma that depends on the variety. When you think of a vague herb aroma, thyme is the hallmark.

- **Common wormwood**, or *Artemisia absinthium*, is infamous in alcohol production circles for being the magic ingredient in the anise-flavored liquor known as absinthe. It contains a compound, thujone, which acts similarly to THC. However, you'd have to add a lot in order to extract enough of the substance to have any effect and would become sick from other causes before achieving a high. Wormwood is an extraordinarily bitter plant that has been used in gruits and other beer bittering concoctions for centuries. You can think of an ounce being the equivalent of 20–30 IBUs when added at 60 minutes.

COFFEE OR BEER? WHY NOT BOTH?

For coffee aroma, you have a couple options. You can do the coffee version of dry hopping (dry beaning?) by adding 4–5 ounces of coarsely cracked coffee beans in a muslin bag to the fermenter after the activity of primary fermentation has subsided. Start tasting after about 4–5 days. Once the beer has the level of aroma you're after, either remove the beans or rack the beer.

You can also add brewed coffee when you package the beer. Brew the coffee stronger than you normally might. Cold brewing is favored by some homebrewers. Pour four 2-ounce samples of the beer (before adding your priming sugar if you're bottling). Add a different, measured dose of the coffee to each sample and taste critically. Maybe even have someone else taste, too, so you can find a consensus amount. Then scale the amount of flavoring in the sample you prefer up to the size of your entire batch.

Drew: If you want to avoid heat altogether, take a page out of my morning breakfast routine. The night before, mix 1 cup of coarsely ground coffee with 2–3 cups of cold filtered water in a French press. In the morning (or 8 hours later), press the coffee and pour off the newly saturated coffee concentrate. For breakfast, that gets poured over ice and diluted with a little water, but for the beer, it goes straight into the carboy. The advantage of the procedure is that cold water extraction avoids all of the harsher, bitter compounds and leaves you with the sweeter, fruity coffee tones.

THE NOT-SO-BORING WORLD OF VANILLA

Vanilla can be used in several different forms. You should always start by obtaining the best vanilla you can find, whether it's vanilla beans or extract. Beans should be moist, pliable, fat, and juicy. We recommend that you buy beans online because they are generally cheaper and of higher quality than anything you'll find in the grocery store. Another bonus: You can usually find Grade B beans, which aren't as pretty as Grade A but work dandy. They're a lot cheaper, too—usually around a third of the price!

For extracts, the way to go is the homemade tincture recipe on page 179 with the best beans you can find. However, if you go store-bought, you need to look for the more expensive varieties made with just vanilla bean. Here are a few warning signs for extracts you should avoid:

- Avoid ingredients other than vanilla, such as fake aromas or flavors.
- Avoid extracts made with wood byproducts. Although some of these may be good, a lot of them are not. Do some research and be prepared to audition different forms from different sources to make your choice.
- Avoid extracts that don't list vanilla bean, or that explicitly list tonka bean. Tonka is a fake vanilla flavor that also contributes coumarin, a powerful liver toxin.

Okay, so you know all about quality. It's time to move on to the exciting world of vanilla varieties. Each of the bean types that follow offers a different flavor profile that you can use to generate a different effect. Even better, you can blend them in different ratios to achieve yet more complexity. Imagine a Belgian tripel spiced with a touch of Ugandan vanilla and a big splash of Tahitian vanilla. With a cool ferment you'd end up with a light vanilla and chocolate cake aroma topped with flowers. If that doesn't say special occasion, what does?

- **Bourbon vanilla**, made from the *Vanilla planifolia* orchid, is the classic when you think vanilla. It's a big potent blast of vanillin, the main active flavorant associated with vanilla. The bold character makes it perfect for anything that you want people to smell, taste, and immediately say, "Vanilla!" Historical note: The Bourbon name has little to do with Bourbon whiskey. Both Bourbon County, Kentucky, and Bourbon Island (Réunion Island off the coast of Madgascar) get their name from the French Royal House of Bourbon.
- **Mexican vanilla** is made from the same *V. planifolia* orchid as the Bourbon vanillas. The Mexican vanilla flavor is lightly smoky and not as buttery as the Bourbon variety.
- **Tahitian vanilla** comes from the *V. tahitiensis* orchid. Tahitian vanilla is softer and more perfumy than Bourbon, with a strong floral note that makes it a favorite of pastry chefs for subtle applications. This is the one you reach for when you want your tasters to be puzzled and pleased.
- **Ugandan vanilla** is also grown from a variety of *V. planifolia*. The Ugandan beans are considered the world's most potent vanilla. They provide an additional tone of chocolate from the dark, leathery bean.

TAHITIAN BLISS TRIPEL

By Drew

One of my favorite commercial beers is Allagash's Curieux, a bourbon barrel aged tripel. This beer is a deconstruction of wood aging, since a chief contributor to wood aging is Vanillin, the compound that smells and tastes like vanilla. By using straight vanilla, we can get that impact without the rest of the flavors, like bourbon. Using the Tahitian vanilla gives you a softer, more floral sensory experience than the bold Bourbon vanillas.

For 5.5 gallons at 1.075, 33 IBUs, 4.7 SRM, 8.2% ABV

GRAIN BILL
13.5 lbs   Belgian Pilsner Malt
1.0 lbs   Sugar
8.0 oz   Biscuit Malt

MASH SCHEDULE
Rest   150°F   60 minutes

HOPS
0.5 oz   Herkules   Pellet   17% AA   60 minutes

YEAST
WY3787 Trappist High Gravity

OTHER INGREDIENTS
½ tablet Whirlfloc   10 minutes
2.0 oz   Homemade Tahitian Vanilla Extract (see page 179)

ADDITIONAL INSTRUCTIONS
- Mash the grains as normal and collect the runnings in the boil kettle. Add the sugar to a nylon sack and suspend in the boil to dissolve. Otherwise boil and chill as normal. Chill the beer to 64°F before pitching and keep the fermentation below 66°F to suppress excessive yeast character.
- When kegging or bottling, add the vanilla extract just before carbonating.

BEER AND THE CHOCOLATE FACTORY

Chocolate can be used in several different forms. You can use cacao nibs, cocoa powder, or chocolate extract. Each has its advantages and disadvantages. Processed chocolates, including baking chocolate, candy bars, and chocolate chips, contain oils. If you really want to use them anyway, a long, vigorous boil is recommended to volatilize as much of the oils as possible.

But why worry about oils? Oils and fats can cause head forming problems—no bubbles and foam. Chocolate has a ton of fat (cocoa butter), and we'll want to do everything we can to avoid it.

- **Cacao nibs** are the crushed seeds from a cacao plant. They can be added to the mash or boil, although adding them to the fermenter may be the best choice. If you use them in the boil or

Cacao Nib Vanilla Bean Defatted Tincture

Drew: I know Denny already expressed his negative opinion about the use of tinctures, but I've had better results using a homemade tincture from cacao nibs and vanilla beans than any commercial preparation. It requires a step or two beyond the previous tincture recipe, though.

Use the tincture recipe on page 75 with 1 vanilla bean cut and scraped and 4 ounces of raw cacao nibs.

Add the vanilla on its own first and soak it for 3 to 4 days. After the initial soak, add the cacao nibs and soak for no longer than 4 days.

After 4 days, strain the tincture into a jar and place it in the freezer for a day.

Remove the jar, and you'll see a cap of fat on top of the liquid tincture. That's the cocoa butter. Just scrape it off and you now have a perfectly stable, non-head-killing flavoring. The vanilla is

QUATTRO CRAZY

By Drew

Since anhydrous caffeine doesn't like dissolving in cold liquid, boil some water and dissolve the powder in it along with the drink mix. Throw the toxic sludge into the malt liquor, hold your nose, and mix incredibly well. Remember that caffeine powder is dangerous!

For 5.5 gallons at 1.112 OG, 30 IBUs, 6.0 SRM, 12.0% ABV

GRAIN BILL
20.0 lbs Domestic Pilsner Malt
5.0 lbs   Flaked Corn

MASH SCHEDULE
Rest   150°F   60 minutes

HOPS
0.75 oz   Magnum   Pellet   11.6% AA   60 minutes

YEAST
WLP833 German Bock Yeast or WLP855 Zurich Lager Yeast if you can ferment lagers (or switch to WLP001 California Ale or WY1056 American Ale for an ale)

OTHER INGREDIENTS
½ tablet   Whirlfloc   10 minutes
                    Yeast nutrient   20 minutes
Drink mix packets in the flavor of your choice, to taste
4.2 g (or less) Anhydrous caffeine powder

mash, make sure to account for the bitterness they add. It may take a couple test batches to find a balance between the hops and the cacao. If you decide to use cacao nibs in the keg or fermenter, start with 4 ounces per 5 gallons of beer. They should stay in the keg or fermenter for at least a couple of weeks, but there are reports of successfully leaving them in for up to eight months. **Drew: For the record, I think anything over 2 weeks is begging to leech the harsh tannins carried in nibs.**

- **Ground cocoa** will add a dark, bitter flavor to the beer with less perception of chocolate flavor than using nibs. Again, you want to account for how it will interact with the hops. Try adding 8 ounces of cocoa powder to the boil. It will likely leave some sludge in the bottom of your kettle, but most of the powder will dissolve in the wort. One of the advantages of using powder is that it is almost always defatted. That means you won't have to deal with the oils in your beer.

- While you might not want to hear it, **chocolate extract** is probably the best way to obtain chocolate flavor and aroma. It's even used by Rogue Ales in their award-winning chocolate stout. Be sure you get a good-quality chocolate extract to avoid strange flavors. The Star Kay White brand is very good and is available online. To determine the amount to put in your bottling bucket or keg, use the technique outlined on page 190 for using liquor.

BUZZ BUZZ GOES THE BEER

Two of our favorite beer ingredients, chocolate and coffee, share a common bond. It's the stuff that makes the world go round: caffeine. Here are some fun facts:

- 57 percent of Americans drink coffee.
- 62 percent of Americans drink alcohol.
- 100 percent of you reading this book like beer!

From these facts, we can infer that you love to get your buzz on. Judging by the continued popularity of Red Bull and Vodka cocktails, a number of club-goers agree. And what would drinking be without some kind of moral panic?

Back in 2010, America found just that when Four Loko suddenly became popular. Four Loko was a 12 percent malt liquor that came in Grape, Fruit Punch, Watermelon, and Blue Lemonade. The kicker was that it also contained the caffeine punch of two cups of coffee. All of this in a 24-ounce tall boy earned it the nickname "Blackout in a Can." The worry, hospitalization, and one death caused various government agencies to ban the product. Finally, the FDA stepped in and forbade the combination of alcohol and caffeine for commercial sale.

Of course, everyone can still go and buy caffeine powder online. If you truly miss the fun of something like Four Loko, then here's your chance to give it a shot. Last caffeine fun fact: Powdered caffeine is quite literally one of the most bitter things you can ingest and is used as the gold-standard bitterness reference.

Warning: Pure caffeine powder is dangerous, and it's a cheap, quick way to cause heart issues, including the ever-popular death due to ventricular fibrillation. Use a really accurate scale, and don't go overboard. Save the macho for the hops. Use 4.2 grams in 5 gallons to mimic the published levels of caffeine in fully leaded Four Loko (156 milligrams in 23.5 ounces). Remember the FDA's recommendation is 200–300 milligrams of caffeine daily for adults.

WEE SHROOMY

By Denny

This beer uses a couple of different experimental techniques. One is the boiling down of a gallon of first runnings to a thick syrup, then adding it back to the main wort to enrich the flavor. The other is the treatment of the mushrooms. While traditionally the way to use adjuncts like this is to soak them in vodka and add a tincture, I found in my trials that the vodka added a harshness that conflicted with the smooth, malty character of the beer. So I just add the mushrooms themselves instead! Between the high alcohol content of the beer, the low pH post-fermentation, and the freezing of the mushrooms, I have never had a problem with the mushrooms infecting the beer. If you're a worry wort (pun intended), you can give the chopped mushrooms a very light spray of Star San, but make sure they aren't wet going into the freezer. So, with thanks to Randy Mosher and Scott Abene, here's Wee Shroomy.

For 5.5 gallons, 26 IBU, 15.9 SRM, 9.6% ABV

GRAIN BILL

20 lbs Simpson's Golden Promise Malt (see Notes)
4 oz Roasted Barley (450°L)

HOPS

1.1 oz	Northern Brewer	Pellet	10% AA	45 minutes

OTHER INGREDIENTS

½ tablet	Whirlfloc	10 minutes
2 lbs	Chanterelle mushrooms (see Notes)	

YEAST

WY1728 Scottish Ale in 3-qt starter

INSTRUCTIONS

- Mash for 90 minutes, vorlauf until free of grain pieces, then run off wort to boil kettle.
- Remove 1 gallon of first runnings to a separate pot for boil-down. (See Notes.)
- Boil for 90 minutes. You can add the wort previously removed for the boil-down at any point during the main wort boil.
- Chill to 55°F–58°F. Pitch decanted yeast starter.
- Aerate well with the method of your choice.

NOTES

- This is a high-gravity beer, and aeration is crucial to a good fermentation. Ferment at 55°F until final gravity is reached. This could take 2–4 weeks. When final gravity is reached, add 2 pounds of prepared chanterelle mushrooms (see note) to a sanitized secondary container and rack the beer onto the mushrooms. Leave the mushrooms in for 2 weeks, then transfer the beer to another container for cold conditioning. Condition at 35°F–40°F for at least a month. Keg or bottle with a moderate carbonation level.

- While this recipe can be made without Simpson's Golden Promise malt (and I've done that several times), the results are so much better using Golden Promise that I urge you to seek it out and use it for this recipe. Between the Golden Promise and the chanterelles, this is not an inexpensive beer to brew, but the results are worth every penny you spend.

- For the boil-down, remove 1 gallon of the first runnings to a separate pot. Boil until the wort is reduced to a quart or less. It should be almost a syrup by the time you get done. Add to the boil kettle during the main boil, before chilling the wort.

- For the mushrooms, thoroughly brush the dirt off 2 pounds of chanterelle mushrooms. Do not wash them, or if you must, use as little water as possible. Roughly chop the mushrooms. At this point, you can give them a *light* spray of Star San if you wish, but make sure the mushrooms are very dry. Put them in a vacuum-sealed bag, seal it, and freeze the mushrooms for at least a week. Remove the mushrooms from the freezer at least a day before adding them to the beer. Put the mushrooms and any liquid in the bag in a sanitized secondary container and rack the beer onto them.

- Depending on what your water chemistry is like, you may need to add some calcium chloride (CaC_{12}) to the mash and/or kettle. Shoot for a total of about 50 ppm each of calcium and chloride.

- If you have access to other varieties of mushrooms, try a porter with candy cap mushrooms. Use the same mushroom procedure I describe for the Wee Shroomy and apply it to your favorite robust porter recipe.

BECAUSE I'M A FUN GUY WITH DENNY

When I was a new homebrewer, I was like a lot of other homebrewers in one respect: I started thinking about brewing beer using any flavor that I found appealing. What I hadn't learned at that point was to think about how that flavor might work in a beer. Consequently, I ended up making things like a porter with molasses and spruce tips in it, among other things. My main recollection of that beer is that it tasted like menthol smells.

But one weird combination I had read about really worked. Randy Mosher had a recipe called Nirvana. It was a wee heavy Scotch ale that had chanterelle mushrooms added to it. Living in the Pacific Northwest, I had already developed a love of chanterelles. They have an aroma with notes of apricot and a rich, sweet flavor. I could almost taste the combination in my mind. And I was right. Well, really, Randy was right. The malty wee heavy and earthy, apricot-y chanterelles seemed like a combination of flavors that was meant to be. I also found that when I mentioned this beer to people, the reactions went from mild amusement to outright disgust. Oh, ye of little faith!

BREWING WITH MEAT

We racked our brains to come up with a joke to start this section. We thought about meat puns, meat double entendres, and meat stories. Then we realized that the joke *is* brewing with meat!

For years Denny has run an *Iron Chef*–type brewing competition for his homebrew club. Teams of brewers show up with equipment and basic ingredients for brewing and are given a secret ingredient to incorporate into their beers (the secret ingredient is often not something they'd normally use in a beer). He had joked for several years about giving the brewers pork chops as a secret ingredient. It was strange enough to amuse people, and it was obvious that no one would ever brew with pork chops. Right?

One club member, Jeremiah Marsden, took the joke seriously and made a batch of beer he called "Pork Soda." Jeremiah is apparently an otherwise sane person, but you can see his recipe and comments on the next page.

PORK SODA

By Jeremiah Marsden

I wanted the essence of pork chop to come through—savory, herbal, and smoky. So I chose what is basically a brown ale with fairly low IBUs as a base. The pork chops were seasoned with black pepper, sage, and rosemary and then grilled. They were added only to the mash. The grain bill included smoked malt to enhance the smoky grilled flavor, some darker crystal, and pale chocolate. Black pepper, seeds of paradise, and sage were added at the end of the boil, and then a sage-vodka tincture was added in the secondary. It was a nice savory beer; the sage came through very well, as did the light smoke. Make sure to mash high to enhance the malt, since the smoke and herbs dry it out a bit.

For 5.5 gallons at 1.055, 27 IBU, 6.3% ABV

GRAIN BILL

8.25 lbs	2 Row Pale Malt
1.65 lbs	Cherrywood Smoked Malt
1.1 lbs	Caramel/Crystal Malt 40°L
4.0 oz	Caramel/Crystal Malt 120°L
4.0 oz	Chocolate Malt (350 SRM)
4.0 oz	Pale Chocolate (170 SRM)
4.0 oz	Special Roast (50 SRM)

MASH SCHEDULE

Rest	154°F	60 minutes

HOPS

2.2 oz	Tettnang	Pellet	2.90% AA	60 minutes
0.75 oz	Saaz	Pellet	2.20% AA	30 minutes
0.75 oz	Saaz	Pellet	2.20% AA	2 minutes

OTHER INGREDIENTS

1.00 lbs	Pork chops	5 minutes
2.00 oz	Grains of paradise	5 minutes
1.00 oz	Ground sage	5 minutes
0.50 tsp	Black peppercorn	5 minutes
2.00 oz	Ground sage	Secondary, 5 days

YEAST

WY1450 Denny's Favorite in 2-qt starter

INSTRUCTIONS

Chill to 62°F–65°F. Pitch decanted yeast starter. Aerate well with the method of your choice. Ferment at 62°F–65°F for approximately 1–2 weeks. Transfer the beer to a sanitized secondary fermenter and add 2 ounces sage. Let the beer sit for 5 days, then bottle or keg. Use sugar or force-carbonate to about 2.5 volumes of CO_2.

BACON HELLES

By Charlie Essers

Sage of the ages, Homer Simpson, when told that ham, pork chops, and bacon all come from the same animal expressed disbelief that such a magical animal could exist. Out of the three, bacon seems to be everyone's favorite ingredient, and that means you have to find a way to get it into a beer. Charlie Essers, aka Push Eject of the Brewing Network, found a clever way of safely adding bacon to his Helles recipe. The bacon itself was baked to ensure even cooking with no charring. (Since the Helles is a delicate beer, any char would translate into an unpleasant, in-your-face burned aroma.) The bacon wasn't added directly to the beer either; it was crumbled and soaked in vodka for a few days first to dissolve the bacony essence. The resulting tincture was then added to a half portion of the helles to allow Charlie to serve both the regular Helles and Schweinchen Helles at the same time.

For 5.5 gallons at 1.050, 18 IBUs, 4 SRM, 5.0% ABV

GRAIN BILL
10.0 lbs   Weyermann Pilsner Malt
12.0 oz   Munich Malt
4.0 oz   Melanoidin Malt

MASH SCHEDULE
Rest   151°F   60 minutes

HOPS
0.3 oz   Magnum   Pellet   14%   60 minutes

YEAST
WLP820 Oktoberfest Lager

OTHER INGREDIENTS
2 Strips of bacon, thick cut (see Additional Instructions)

ADDITIONAL INSTRUCTIONS
- Chill the beer to about 50°F before pitching a large (½ gallon or more) starter. Allow the beer to ferment in primary for 2 weeks at 48°F–50°F. Raise the fermentation temperature to 65°F for 2 days and then slowly lower to 35°F for 4 weeks.
- Create the bacon tincture by cooking the bacon on a rack in the oven at 320°F for 40–50 minutes or until perfectly crispy (but not burnt!). Pat off the grease and allow it to cool. Crumble the bacon and cover with the vodka. Shake every day until packaging the beer.
- On packaging day, filter the bacon tincture through a sieve and coffee filter and add to the keg or bottling bucket. Proceed as normal.

MEAT IN HISTORY

Now before you run away, thinking we're being silly for the sake of being silly, meat in fermented beverages has great historical precedence. If you search online, you'll find recipes for Cock Ale, which was made in Britain around the 1600s and 1700s. The recipe calls for ale to be boiled with an old rooster, fruits like dates and raisins, sack (sherry), and spices like nutmeg and clove. It was considered a fine drink with medicinal qualities. Also, some cider makers used to throw raw pork sides into their ciders when the ferment had gone wrong. Turns out that what these brewers had stumbled on before they understood it was the power of protein and the clarifying impact of collagen and gelatin.

The introduction of the meat also added valuable amino acids that allowed the yeast to rise up and do their thing more effectively. (Remember, this is one hundred to two hundred years before yeast was even recognized as a key cause of beer.) These guys weren't carefully growing up pure cultured yeast starters with ideal cell counts, high viability, proper nutrition, and so on. They were

DIGBY'S COCK-ALE, MODERNIZED

By Drew and Denny

Sir Kenhelm Digby may have invented the modern wine bottle and been a strange enchanting figure of the English religious civil wars, but he didn't have the knowledge to fear raw chicken like we do—so in his honor we present this beer.

For 5.5 gallons at 1.080, 42 IBUs, 12 SRM, 8.3% ABV

GRAIN BILL

14.00 lbs	Maris Otter Malt
1.00 lbs	Crisp Brown Malt
1.00 lbs	Weyermann Rauch Malt

MASH SCHEDULE

Rest	156°F	60 minutes

HOPS

1.0 oz	Target	Pellet	11% AA	60 minutes

YEAST

WY1275 Thames Valley

OTHER INGREDIENTS

5.0 lbs	Bone-in chicken parts
2.5 lbs	Raisins
6.0 oz	Dates
¼	Nutmeg, grated
1	Mace
2 750ml bottles	Sweet sherry

ADDITIONAL INSTRUCTIONS

- After primary fermentation, take the chicken and bring to a gentle boil for 2 hours to make a broth and make everything, including the bones, soft.
- Smash the chicken bones with a cleaver and throw the chicken into a food processor along with the raisins, dates, spice, and ¼ bottle of sherry. Do this in batches according to food processor size. Create a rough mince by pulsing the mix several times. Make it resemble a sticky ground beef.
- Add the mix and the rest of the wine to a bucket and rack the beer onto the mix. Let age for a week before racking off and packaging as usual.

either using the stuff from the air or stuff that lived in the vats or from previously fermenting beer. All of it was less than healthy and needed all the help it could get. Yeast exposed to meat fermented more strongly, producing a drier, clearer ale that would be rated as fine.

As for recreating this fine ale today, you'll have a big problem. Commercial birds aren't allowed to get old. The average age of a factory raised bird is about 6 to 7 weeks. Compared to a hen or rooster of the Cock Ale period, that's insanely young. A rooster destined for the pot would be a few years old. And that age is important! As the bird ages, the meat becomes tougher and laden with connective tissue—the home of collagen. It's this collagen and the gelatin from the bones that aids in the clarification of the beer. If you can find a stewing hen, you'll be much closer but still a little off. Stewing hen breeds are usually birds raised for egg laying, but when their productivity dips (after about 20 months), they consume more feed than their egg output warrants, and off they go, ready for the pot.

PEANUT BUTTER

If you want to approach the fringe, how about a peanut butter beer? Well, beer aficionados, beer judges, and Cicerones will all tell you that the faintest trace of fat in a glass absolutely murders the head of a beer, and hence your glasses need to be "beer clean," which involves secret chants, powerful chemicals, and lots of hot water. (Okay, really just a solid scrub with a nonsoap cleaner and lots of rinsing and air drying.)

For that reason, adding incredibly fat-laden peanut butter is probably not the world's best idea. There are liquid peanut butter flavorings available. However, they lack the classic peanut butter richness. But now there's a dried, defatted peanut butter powder called PB2. Developed for culinary and dietary purposes, it is 98 percent fat-free. It's meant to be rehydrated with water or yogurt to create a thick, peanut-butter-like concoction. Brewers of the Brewing Enthusiasts of the Antelope Valley Region (BEAVR) homebrewing club gained attention a few years back with the Chocolate Covered BEAVR Nuts recipe that used PB2. For that, they dump a few jars of the stuff into the boil kettle and let it boil for a few minutes.

MARY MEET JANE

With the rise of medical marijuana, and even recreational marijuana, in a number of states, apparently homebrewers have decided that the thing to do is combine their herbal medicine with their homebrew. After all, hops and marijuana are biological cousins, both being part of the Cannabaceae family. (Incidentally, so are hackberry trees. Who knew?)

Now, obviously, there are many, many aspects of the government and society that have a rather unhappy view of these sorts of activities, so proceed under that veil of warning. Neither of us have actually done this, but we're sick of answering the question online. So here's our response: Umm, don't. It's a waste of everything and bound to get you in trouble with someone. The results reported back by those foolish enough to do this via dry hopping or tinctures concur that it's not worth the result and the taste is pretty nasty. If you medicate, we recommend enjoying all your meds in their prescribed forms.

PEANUT BUTTER JELLY TIME

By Drew

Okay, let's take that peanut butter idea a step further and turn it into a peanut butter and jelly sandwich. Using a fruity English yeast to ferment out a crispy, toasty brown ale base gets you a jammy, fruity beer. Borrowing a technique from IGOR Donald Boyle, I soak a 12-ounce bag of PB2 in the highest-proof neutral grain spirit I can find, like an Everclear or 151, for a few days. Then it's just a matter of adding the slurry to a keg, racking the beer on top, and shaking it to mix. Let it settle cold for a week and then rack to a clean keg. Pure peanut butter and jelly time!

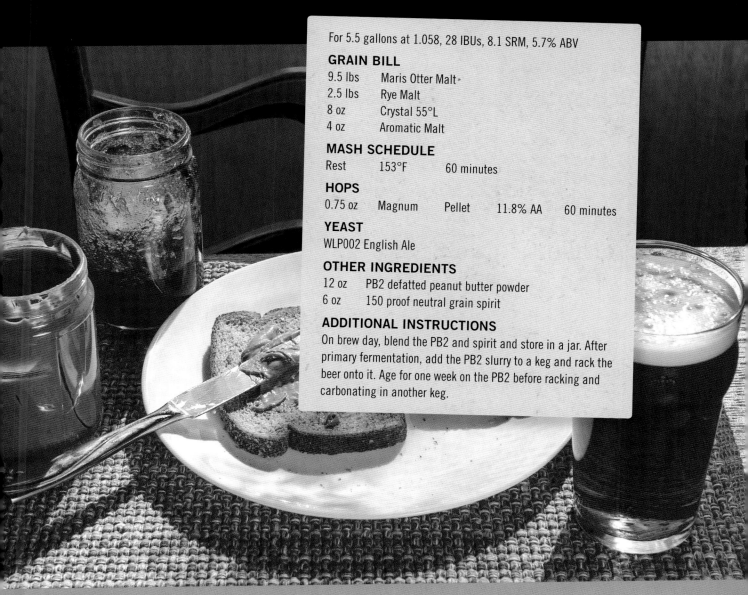

For 5.5 gallons at 1.058, 28 IBUs, 8.1 SRM, 5.7% ABV

GRAIN BILL
9.5 lbs	Maris Otter Malt
2.5 lbs	Rye Malt
8 oz	Crystal 55°L
4 oz	Aromatic Malt

MASH SCHEDULE
Rest	153°F	60 minutes

HOPS
0.75 oz	Magnum	Pellet	11.8% AA	60 minutes

YEAST
WLP002 English Ale

OTHER INGREDIENTS
12 oz	PB2 defatted peanut butter powder
6 oz	150 proof neutral grain spirit

ADDITIONAL INSTRUCTIONS
On brew day, blend the PB2 and spirit and store in a jar. After primary fermentation, add the PB2 slurry to a keg and rack the beer onto it. Age for one week on the PB2 before racking and carbonating in another keg.

CANDY IS DANDY, BUT LIQUOR . . .

Since the discovery of distillation in the ancient Middle East, human kind has discovered a number of different hard alcohol preparations with different flavors, different impacts, etc. There's even a whole industry built around the idea of delivering booze without you realizing you're drinking it (see the five thousand varieties of flavored vodka on the shop of your liquor mart). When it comes to brewing, think about what flavor you really want to promote with a booze addition. Is it a high heat and burnt sugar, like rum? Is it a fruit flavoring like raspberry? Or maybe you want to capture the sweet almond flavor of amaretto? Here are a few rules of thumb:

- Avoid the white spirits. They tend to be easily lost in the mad flavor rush of a beer.
- Don't reach for the top shelf unless there's a very specific flavor you're aiming for. People will be hard pressed to tell the difference between Pappy Van Winkle and Ten High Bourbon when it's put into a brew.
- Add the booze when you'll lose the least from it—meaning in secondary or at packaging.
- Make sure to give any sweet liqueurs a chance to either ferment out or keep the beer cold after introducing the sugar to avoid it fermenting out.

When using liquor as a flavoring, you can figure out the additional alcohol content as follows. Take the amount of liquor you add and multiply by the alcohol content of the liquor. So, if you add 500 ml of 80 proof (40 percent alcohol), you can think of it as 40×0.5 liters = 20 points. If you are adding it to a 5-gallon (19-liter) batch that is 7 percent alcohol, the beer already has $7 \times 19 = 133$ points. Add them together and you have 19.5 liters with 153 points, which works out to $153/19.5 =$ ~7.85 percent alcohol in the final batch. The formula is:

$$ABV_{total} = \frac{(ABV_{beer} \times Volume_{beer}) + (ABV_{liquor} \times Volume_{liquor})}{Volume_{total}} \times 100$$

Breaking the equation into steps:

$$Volume_{ethanol\ addition} = Volume_{liquor\ addition} \times Alcohol\ Percentage_{liquor}$$

$$Volume_{ethanol\ fermentation} = Volume_{beer} \times Alcohol\ Percentage_{beer}$$

$$Volume_{ethanol\ total} = Volume_{ethanol\ addition} + Volume_{ethanol\ fermentation}$$

$$Volume_{liquid\ total} = Volume_{liquor\ addition} + Volume_{beer}$$

$$ABV_{total} = \left(\frac{Volume_{ethanol\ total}}{Volume_{liquid\ total}} \right) \times 100$$

EVALUATING YOUR EXPERIMENTS

DRINKING BEER IS DIFFERENT than evaluating it. Evaluating a beer is how you find out objectively if it meets your expectations, has any flaws, changed as you intended . . . or if it's even a damn good beer. Whether you're evaluating a recipe change, a comparison of ingredients, or just trying a new beer, there are some basic steps you need to follow.

First you'll need to recruit some tasters. Sure, you can do it yourself, but in this chapter we'll show you why you can't always trust your own impressions. You'll also need to know the basics of how to taste and be able explain it to your tasters. You'll need a bit of equipment, such as glasses, paper, and writing tools. And you'll need to decide on your method of analysis. Sure, your tasters will need to think about what they're sensing and how to describe it. But it's a fun job—and we've never had anyone refuse a beer tasting!

HOW TO TASTE A BEER

Your beer is ready. It's a new recipe or a new variation of a classic. It's fermented, packaged, aged properly, and chilled to just the right temperature. It's time to break out the classic beer judge evaluation technique. What follows is based on what we both learned from the Beer Judge Certification Program (BJCP), a process used weekly by many of the 7,500 officially certified beer judges in their blind evaluation of beer.

Before you crack the first bottle, prepare to take notes. A mechanical pencil, pen, or even a computer works well. But trust us, you don't want cedar aroma on your fingers from a wooden pencil. If you want to go a step further, head to the BJCP website (www.bjcp.org) and download the official BJCP score sheet for your notes. Also, it helps if you're in a relatively quiet and odor-free place, so your senses won't wander. And don't go smoking a big ol' cigar when you're trying to evaluate.

Step 1: Pour about 4–6 ounces of beer into a clean, clear glass.

You weren't going to drink it from the bottle, were you? Pour vigorously enough to get a moderate head on the beer, but not so much as to interfere with drinking it.

Step 2: Swirl and smell the beer. Write your notes on the aroma.

Gently swirl the glass to release some CO_2. The carbonation helps carry aromas to your nose. Sit back and relax.

Start with three drive-bys: pass the glass under your nose and take a short, sharp sniff of the aroma. Think about the smell. Do that twice more. Write down your impressions. Did it smell sweet? Fruity? Pungent? Dirty? Whatever it smells like, think of it as a description, not a judgment. Don't try sounding fancy with phrases like *tones of a warm Belgian lawn*. However, if the beer smells like fruit punch with grass in it, then write it down. Your notes are for helping you remember, not for impressing the crowd with your sagacity.

Note: If you're having trouble finding the aroma of the beer, try an old trick to help cleanse your sense of smell. Before you sniff the beer, smell your shirt sleeve. No, not your armpit! It's amazing how plain cotton can neutralize your sense of smell and let the aroma of the beer come through.

Step 3: Examine the visual nature of the beer. Observe the color, clarity, and head.

Take a good look at the beer, paying special attention to its color and clarity. Hold it up to a light or shine a flashlight through it to perform a thorough inspection. Examine the head on the beer. Is it tight or loose? Are there big bubbles or small bubbles? What color is it? Does the head last or does it dissipate quickly? Again, jot down your impressions.

Step 4: Smell the beer again.

Go back and do another couple of drive-bys. As the beer warms and CO_2 escapes from solution, aromas change. You'll want to see if you smell anything that you didn't smell earlier. Sometimes a particularly strong aroma on your first passes dissipates by the time you revisit the beer.

Step 5: Taste the beer.

Okay, now the good part: taste the beer. Take a small sip, maybe an ounce. Swirl the beer around your mouth so that it coats your gums, the roof of your mouth, and all parts of your tongue. Swallow the beer and immediately exhale through your nose. That's called retronasal stimulation (ooh, science!) and will really bring out the aroma and flavors.

Think about what you taste. Is it sweet, malty, sour, bitter, fruity, or alcoholic? What's the mouthfeel like? Is it full-bodied and mouth coating? Is it thin and digestible? Is it highly carbonated and spritzy or is it smooth and mellow? What's the balance like? Is it malty or hoppy? Is the finish dry or sweet?

Drew: You may be asking yourself if this is all a bit too wine snob–like. Yes, yes it is. But the reality is that for just a moment, you need to focus all of your organoleptic sensors on gleaning every last bit of data from the beer. Your experiment's impact can be surprisingly subtle, and you'll never glean the effect if you sit and drink without intention. What you learn based on the tasting can result in changed, corrected, and improved beer.

THE SCIENCE OF TASTING OBJECTIVITY

The most difficult part of evaluating a beer is remaining objective. You brewed the beer, you know what went into it, you know how hard you worked on it and what you expected it to turn out like. But you have to be sure you aren't fooling yourself when you taste it. It's the difference between mounting an investigation and proving a hypothesis. To prove a hypothesis, you assume something is true and try to verify that. When you do an investigation, you're looking for answers without a notion of what you may find. Each approach has its place, but by mounting an investigation, you won't have preconceived ideas getting in the way of objective evaluation. There have been a number of experiments done to show how preconception can influence perception. Let's take a look at a few of them.

One of the most interesting experiments was chronicled in the *Journal of the Institute for Brewing* (Vol 8, No. 1, 2002). Charles Bamforth and J. E. Smythe conducted tastings in three different countries. There were twelve tasters from Ireland, all untrained; twelve from Finland, trained in sensory evaluation; and fourteen from Belgium, rigorously trained and highly tested. In the first test, tasters were told that one beer was produced using traditional techniques and took 15 days to produce, while the other beer used new technology and yeasts that allowed it to be produced in only 10 hours. For the other test, tasters were told that one beer was produced strictly according to the Reinheitsgebot (using only malt, hops, water, and yeast), while the other beer got 30 percent of its fermentables from sugar. What the tasters didn't know was that all of the beers were poured from the same bottle!

The more experienced the tasters were, the fewer preferences they described, but all tasters showed some preference for what they thought were the more traditionally brewed beers. This indicates that just the suggestion of a beer's history can play a large role in the perception of tasters. This is why brewers continue to push romantic stories of farmhand beers or IPAs on ocean journeys. They create a potent predisposition in the drinker's mind.

Another very interesting example, albeit with wine rather than beer, came from Frédéric Brochet in a 2001 experiment at the University of Bordeaux. He assembled a panel of fifty-four experienced wine tasters for evaluation of what they thought were four different wines. In the first test, they were given two glasses of wine, one white and one red. However, the red wine was actually the same white wine as was in the other glass with red food coloring. Nearly every taster described the red wine in terms ordinarily used to describe red wine, including words like jammy and crushed red fruit—terms that are seldom, if ever, used to describe white wines.

But that's wine, right? That could never impact us in the beer world, where the ingredients we use to color the beer carry distinctive qualities! Who would ever confuse pilsner malt and chocolate malt? Well . . .

On a Norwegian beer blog called Larsblog, Lars Marius posted about a blind tasting conducted in 2008 during a judge training class he attended. There were some very experienced tasters involved, including three RateBeer users who had a total of eight thousand ratings, a man educated as a wine sommelier, and two commercial microbrewers.

The participants were given three unidentified black beers and asked to write notes about them before attempting to guess the beer styles. All the tasters notes identified flavors like roasty or caramel. All the tasters were shocked to find out that of the three beers, only one was an actual dark beer. The other two? Ringnes Pils (a super common pils in Norway) and Erdinger Hefeweizen with black coloring added to them! Every one of the ten tasters claimed to taste roastiness in the beers, and not a single taster had any idea that beer might actually be a pilsner or a hefe. It appears that their senses of taste and aroma were completely fooled by the color of the beer.

Looking back to Brochet, in another test he took two bottles of wine, one a *grand cru* and the other an ordinary *vin de table*, poured them out, and filled both bottles with a mid-level Bordeaux. Tasters then described exactly the same wine in almost completely opposite terms. The wine in the grand cru bottle was described as agreeable, woody, complex, balanced, and rounded, while the supposed vin de table was weak, short, light, flat, and faulty. Brochet's conclusion was that the perception of the wine was often more important than what was actually in the glass. Kind of makes you wonder about your own tasting skills and susceptibility to labels, doesn't it?

Finally, in 2008, *Avenue Vine* published an article about how actual physiological changes took place in tasters' brains based on their perception of the price of the wine they were tasting. They found that people who paid more for wine actually enjoyed it more! Brain scans of people who were told they were drinking a more expensive wine confirmed that their pleasure centers were activated much more than people who were told that they were drinking a less expensive wine. They found changes in a part of the brain called the medial orbito-frontal cortex, which plays a main role in many types of pleasure. The cortex became more activated by the supposed expensive wines than the cheap ones.

So, what do we as homebrewers need to do to evaluate our experiments and be reasonably certain they're objectively assessed? First, we must gather our tasters!

FINDING GUINEA PIGS . . . ER . . . TASTING PANELISTS

The problem with trying to evaluate your own beer is that you know how you made it, and you know what you're looking for. That makes it extremely difficult to evaluate your own beer objectively. You need a tasting panel!

Does that mean you need beer experts or supertasters? Not necessarily. If your goal is to find out if a change in process or ingredients produces a beer that people prefer, the tasters only need to like beer and have some idea of what it is they like. However, if you're hoping to compare two beers with different sulfate levels, the tasters need to be experienced and sophisticated enough to pick out and describe qualities of bitterness and dryness as well as potentially elevated mineral levels.

It just so happens there's a place you can find both types of tasters: your homebrew club! Clubs have a wide range of beer lovers, from those who just like beer to BJCP judges. It's not uncommon to find professional brewers in the ranks of club members as well. Keep in mind that even for more serious tastings, it can be valuable to have a range of experience and ability in your panel to give you a balanced impression of the beers. Sometimes a novice taster will pick out something that a more experienced person has overlooked. Here's why we love science: to us someone is a novice taster, but to a scientist that person is a seminaïve assessor.

Additionally, experienced tasters may have built-in biases that may not reflect general taste preferences. For example, in 2006 *Cook's Illustrated* magazine did a taste test of olive oil where they ranked inexpensive Spanish and Greek olive oils over the vaunted and expensive Italian oils. Alexandra Kicenik Devarenne, an olive oil expert, convened a panel of trained tasters to sample the same oils, and their results were almost reversed. Who's right? The panel of cooks and regular Joes or the trained tasters who obsess over oil? The trained group asserted that *Cook's Illustrated* got it wrong, because they were looking for flavors familiar to the American palate that are considered defects by the olive oil community. *Cook's Illustrated* said they're right because the oils tasted better for the applications called for in an American kitchen. In sensory science, this is the battle and difference between "consumer panels" (*Cook's Illustrated*) and "descriptive panels" (Devarenne's group).

Are You a Supertaster?

Roughly 35 percent of women and 15 percent of men are supertasters. These folks have been given a special skill. No, they can't fight crime. Their palates are much more sensitive to a number of flavors, especially bitter. You can test to see if you're one of the lucky ducks with a bit of food coloring, a hole reinforcement label (the things you put on a punched paper to prevent it from ripping out of a binder), and a good camera.

Douse a cotton swab with blue food coloring. Paint the front of your tongue with dye.

Carefully place a reinforcement label on your tongue in the colored section.

Take a photo of your tongue and zoom in on the hole. Count the number of pink dots inside the circle. These are the papillae that house your taste buds.

If you count more than thirty-five, you're probably a supertaster and have a legitimate reason for hating broccoli. Below fifteen? Oh boy, you're a nontaster. If you're in the middle, welcome to being perfectly average!

We see this battle all the time in the beer world. Take a look at a beer-rating site like Beer Advocate. In their top twenty-five beers, they have, as of this writing, only two beers that are below 7 percent alcohol, and one of those is a decidedly nonaverage Cantillon Lambic. Lists like that this, compiled by the insanely passionate, end up dominated by bold styles like Double IPA, Imperial Stout, Belgian Quad, and so on. Now go look at what sells the best. In recent years, amongst the self-selected crowd of craft beer drinkers, the top sellers have been Seasonals, Pale Ales, and IPAs. That's your expert-versus-common-taster dilemma in two lists.

Note: Over time, make sure you learn the biases and perception skills of your judges. If your test centers on Belgian beers, you probably don't want to invite the guy who thinks all Belgian beers taste like shoes soaked in alcohol. Also, be aware if anyone in your group is a supertaster (see above) and watch closely for their evaluations.

ONE IS THE LONELIEST NUMBER: THE BLIND SIDE

If, for some reason, you're unable to find people to evaluate beer for free, your course of action is a little less clear. First, you clearly need better friends and acquaintances. Second, if you have a spouse, a minister, a helpful bartender, anyone other than you, you can have them serve as your blind.

The blind is how scientists ensure objectivity. Everything you as a tester can remove to avoid bias, you remove. That means: Use the same cups, the same level of cleanliness, the same lighting, the same aromas in the setting, and so on. Ideally, your evaluators have no differences except the key one, under test, to add potential bias their evaluation. You can thank the French for this concept, which, shockingly, was first recorded in 1784.

Since you'll be the one with all the knowledge about what's being tested, you'll be acting as the blind in your panel tastings. Think of the classic soda wars style taste-off. The guy pouring the soda knows which is Coca-Cola and which is Pepsi, but none of the tasters do. In the case of our tasting panels, you'll usually want to run two sets of tastings. The first tasting is where the tasters are blind to what the difference is (for example, whether a certain process creates more hop aroma). After seeing if there's a perceivable difference, the second pass can have the tasters focus on questions like "what do you notice about the hop aroma?"

So, if it's to be a tasting panel of one (you), make sure that you have someone else pouring your samples. Not having someone else pour the unmarked sample means your awareness of the samples makes your evaluations subject to all the biases you bring.

To be truly hardcore, you can take it a step further. Since it turns out that the guy running that cola taste-off could be subconsciously giving signals to the tasters as to which cola is his preferred taste, it can be a good idea to go double blind. Beyond signaling, in observational tests, an observer with knowledge may let that knowledge about the samples affect what's recorded. (For example: "Aha! I think Denny winced a little when he tried sample B, which is the doctored version, so that's a positive hit," when in reality Denny was wincing because Drew put on the Grateful Dead in the background.)

A double blind study moves the chain of knowledge—which sample is which, what part of a group someone is in, and so on—back away from the folks running the experiment and to the ultimate researchers. You'll be hard pressed to double-blind a tasting of one, but for your regular panels, double-blinding is as easy as turning the sample pouring and observation recording over to someone who doesn't know what you're testing.

TYPES OF TESTING

TRIANGLE TASTING: THE GATEWAY TO VALIDITY

The best way to evaluate a beer objectively is to use what's known as blind triangle tasting. In a nutshell, have someone else pour two samples of one of the beers you want to evaluate and one sample of another. The objective is to pick out the sample that's different. If you can't do that, then you know that whatever you're testing for doesn't really matter. If you can pick out the different sample, then you can go ahead and use the techniques discussed on page 200 to evaluate it.

Triangle testing is a cornerstone of beer evaluation. In the world of sensory science it is considered a difference test. The taster is given no guidance about what's different. He or she is just handed three samples and asked which two are the same.

A triangle test can help determine if a difference exists at all. Think about the major debates like: Does decoction mashing make a difference in the flavor of the beer? If it does, the tasters will detect it. If not, then the test tentatively indicates that your uncontrolled variable (decoction mashing versus infusion) makes no perceptual difference.

It can also serve as a test of panelist quality. (For example, a better, more trustworthy panelist will spot the difference.) You can use this during your panels to select judges for further tastings ("Great! Now tell us about the character differences you perceive and evaluate sample B fully") or to weight their feedback above those who missed the difference.

Keep in mind that this technique doesn't work for vastly different beers, like a pilsner and a stout. The beers need to be the same beer with a slight difference. Look at the sample process above. The two beers are pilsners with the only difference being the mashing method. It could as easily be two

Basic Triangle Test Procedure

Beer 1: A Pilsner made with a decoction mash

Beer 2: A Pilsner made with a standard infusion mash

Question: Does decoction mashing have a perceivable impact on the beer flavor/aroma?

Needs: 1 coin, 3 numbered slips of paper, 3 frosted cups per taster numbered 1, 2, and 3

PROCESS

Flip a coin. Heads means beer 1, tails means beer 2.

Put three numbered slips of paper in a hat. Pull the numbers. The first two pulled are for the beer selected by the coin flip. The last is for the other beer.

Pour the beer selected by the coin flip into the two cups selected by the slip pull.

Pour the beer not selected into the remaining glass.

Serve the beer to the panelists. Give no direction beyond, "Choose the two samples that are the same." If the test isn't about the visual quality of the beer, ask the panelists not to evaluate the beer's appearance. If the panelists choose the correct two samples overwhelmingly, congratulations! You have a determinable difference. Now you need to determine if it's actually from your process change or because one sample got infected, was colder, and so on.

Scottish ales with concentrated kettle runnings in one and the other just plain. Maybe the same wort with two difference yeast strains, and so on.

If you want to get all super science-y when you're using a tasting panel, you may want to use weighting to determine how many panelists are likely to choose the odd beer simply by chance. There are resources available online to help you with weighting.

Cathy Haddock is a sensory specialist at Sierra Nevada Brewing Company in Chico, California. Part of her job is to conduct blind triangle tastings of the beers produced by Sierra Nevada. Sometimes it's to evaluate new recipes being considered for production, and sometimes it's for quality assurance, in order to make certain a batch of beer meets Sierra Nevada's high standards and is consistent with previous batches. Cathy has a few tips for homebrewers who want to conduct a blind triangle tasting:

Proper protocol needs to be followed in order to trust your results. Proper protocol includes following procedures in which a taster's response is not biased or influenced due to any psychological factors or environmental conditions. Those psychological/environmental factors that can influences a taster's response when doing a triangle test are numerous, but I will sound off on a few that I feel are most important:

1. We will not tell the tasters anything about the samples they are tasting in a triangle test other than the brand so that they do not have any information to bias their response.
2. We serve the samples in a frosted glass to help eliminate visual cues biasing a taster's response.
3. All samples are poured the same amount of beer, with careful attention as to not have one beer more foamy than the others.

If that is not enough, I also ask that they not even look at the samples, just simply grab the glass, noting its three-digit code, and evaluate the sample. This way, we can have confidence the tasters are not biased by any visual cues.

We also run the triangle tests in a random balance order to help eliminate First Order effect, which is where the first sample evaluated is perceived stronger—whether negatively or positively—and therefore may be chosen as the odd sample out. This type of presentation format employs that the odd sample out is evenly tasted in the first, second, and third position in a three-sample triangle set. I also allow tasters to retaste if necessary.

Other external controls we employ to help offset bias is that other tasters in the tasting area do not verbalize, whether through speech or body language, any opinions on the samples they are tasting in triangle test.

Consider This

When you're planning your experiments, here are some things you need to think about.

*   *Questioning: Sometimes the trickiest part about designing an experiment is telling your panel what to look for without triggering bias. Even something like "Is there a difference in the hop character?" can result in biased evaluations. In general, your tests should strive to conceal the targeted characteristics for as long as possible.*
*   *That's so random: Another important aspect of good testing that you may want to give consideration to is randomness. In a real-deal Holyfield evaluation, you'll find that researchers will randomly assign options to different sets of panels. Panel 1 will get Beer A and then Beer B, but Panel 2 will get Beer B and then Beer A. The idea is to avoid positional bias. You've no doubt seen it at a tasting or judging before: The first beer is either the best because it's the first or, more likely in our experience, gets downgraded to leave room for the other beers to be scored higher. If you run your beer through multiple groups, it's a good idea to do this just to be sure.*
*   *Stacking the deck: Since you've gone through all the trouble of assembling your tasters, there's no sense in letting them going to waste. For instance, take an experiment comparing the effect of whirlpool hops to dry hops. You can run multiple evaluations at the same time. Do a duo-trio test to determine who can match the reference sample. Ask the testers to give a descriptive analysis of the samples. Then run a paired comparison test: Which beer presents more hop aroma? Follow it with a hedonistic ranking: Which beer do you prefer? That's four tests for the cost of one panel! When you do this sort of stacking, you should track results by taster and their ability to correctly answer the triangle or duo-trio tests. Regardless of those first question results, you should continue to collect additional information from all of your panelists.*

An alternate version of the classic triangle test is a duo-trio test. In this type of test, you still work with three samples, but one sample is designated to the tasters as the reference. The tasters then must choose which of the remaining two beers matches the reference sample. The primary effect is allowing a different set of tasters on to the second level of evaluation.

QUALITATIVE DIFFERENCE TESTING

With the question of "Can we notice a difference?" out of the way thanks to the triangle test, there are other things that you're probably concerned about including the all-important: What is the difference between these beers? Since there's no right or wrong answer, the important part is to watch and observe the reactions of your tasters. Try to keep the participants from talking to each other, though, since you don't want a lot of chatter influencing their opinions.

Hedonistic Testing

All things pleasurable are good is the core of hedonism as a philosophy. In evaluation, hedonism is simply the measurement of your enjoyment of a sample. A taster is given a set of samples, with or without information about differences, and asked to rate the samples on a scale of 1 to 10.

The evaluators can rank the sample anywhere they want; there's no need for unique scores. If an evaluator feels that all of their samples are worth a 10 rating, then that's their call. These ratings can show you the general preference of tasters. Whereas a number of these other tests focus on discerning single changes, a hedonistic test shows how a person actually trying the beer feels about it in general.

Rating Difference Testing

A rating difference test is like the hedonistic test in that it allows evaluators to rate a beer and assign a score. Unlike the hedonistic test, it focuses on a particular characteristic. Instead of asking, "Do you like this beer?" you ask evaluators something like, "Rate this beer's hoppiness." Tasters then assign a score according to the characteristic you ask about on a scale of 1 to 10. Using a rating difference test allows you to hone a taster's responses and detect patterns that might otherwise be obscured.

RANK TESTING

Sometimes you're faced with a set of samples that need to be sorted into discrete positions. For instance, maybe you have five samples of different levels of dry hopping. You then ask your evaluators to rank the five samples in terms of absolute dry hopping character. No two samples can have the same ordinal value.

You can test other characteristics here as well. For example, by asking evaluators to do things like put two beers in order of color from light to dark, you can determine any color difference contributed by a process like wort reduction or late extract additions. If the evaluators don't show consistent rankings, you can safely ascribe no discernable difference to the processes involved.

PAIRED COMPARISON TESTING

Sometimes you'll want a focused response from your tasters. With a simple question like "Which of these two beers is hoppier?" you can use your evaluators to determine if there's a pointed directional difference between two samples. If enough evaluators choose the same sample, you know that difference is significant. However, if there isn't a clear tendency toward one of the samples, then you know the change between the two versions isn't overt and can be considered a wash.

The samples don't always have to be different, either. Some panels use a comparison test to weed out evaluators. They do this by presenting the same sample twice to a taster. An accurate taster should note that there's no difference.

TESTING IN ACTION

You've run your testers through the gauntlet. Data has been recorded. The results are in. But do they mean anything? There are whole courses of statistical analysis to determine the meaning of your results.

To start with, math is good but can be scary—so we'll try and keep this simple. For tests like the ranking tests and hedonistic tests, you can glean a lot of information from the simple average of each beer sample. When you lay out the scores, you'll see clear preferences.

One of the classic statistical tests was invented at the Guinness Brewery and is called the "Student's T-test." William Sealy Gosset, a Guinness chemist, created the test in 1908 when he wanted to figure out how to verify statistical significance when you only have a small number of evaluators. His pseudonym was "Student," hence Student's T-test. He used a pen name because Guinness didn't want their competitors to catch on that they were making better beer using math! Is there anything beer math can't do?

Here's what Student's T-test looks like for an equal set of evaluations like what we're running.

$$t = \frac{\overline{X}_1 - \overline{X}_2}{\sqrt{\frac{1}{2}(s_{x_1}^2 + s_{x_2}^2)} \times \sqrt{\frac{2}{n}}}$$

In the stats world this is a simple equation. What it basically says is this: Take the difference of the average scores of the two evaluations (beer1 and beer2) and divide it by the standard deviations (the s variables) and the sample size (n). This t value is then used to calculate the probability (p) that the Null hypothesis (your change didn't matter) is true. This p value ranges between 0–1 and is compared to a standard value (usually, 0.10, 0.05, or 0.01). If the p value is less than the chosen value, your difference is significant.

In the modern world of computers, don't fret the equation. There are plenty of websites and spreadsheets that will do the calculation for you. Excel, for instance, has a function called "T.TEST" that you feed two groups of cells (with your score data), the number of tails (2), and a type (2 for normal). It returns back the final p value.

STUDENT'S T-TEST EXAMPLE 1: TWO BEERS SCORED

Beer 1 Scores	Beer 2 Scores
35	20
34	21
38	22
23	33
42	28

In example 1 we have two beers that have been scored in a BJCP-like fashion. Beer 1 scored much higher with the tasting panel than Beer 2. Running the scores through a simple two-tailed Student's T-test, we get a returned p value of 0.044, which is under the 0.10 and 0.05 thresholds. This means that whatever change this test was checking is significant. Given how most judges use the BJCP scoring system (almost all scores fall in the 20–40 range), it seems fairly standard to assume anything below 0.1 is significant when tested this way.

STUDENT'S T-TEST EXAMPLE 2: TWO CLOSER BEERS SCORED

Beer 1 Scores	Beer 2 Scores
34	22
33	23
37	24
22	35
41	30

This second test shows a minor change in scoring; the tasters liked Beer 1 exactly one point less than before and like Beer 2 two points more than before. The resulting p-value? 0.14—above the threshold of the null hypothesis, indicating that our change isn't as significant as we thought.

EXAMPLE EVALUATION WITH DENNY

Here's an example of an experiment I performed a few years ago with a blind triangle test evaluation. The objective was to compare the effects of a beer that received first wort hops only to a beer that received an equal amount of hops as a single 60-minute addition. I told the tasters nothing about the beers or the purpose of the tasting. I served each of them two glasses of one of the beers and one glass of the other. The samples arrived in identical glasses for all the beers. I didn't hide the color of the beers since they were two 5-gallon batches made from the same batch of wort. We told the participants nothing about the beers they were tasting. They were given three glasses labeled A, B, and C. Two of the beers were the same, and the tasters were asked to answer a set of questions about which beers were the same. Unlike the standard procedure where if a taster was able to identify the different beer, they were given a second set of questions to answer asking them to describe the beers, I let all tasters answer the second set of questions, even if they were incorrect in identifying the different beer. That's because I was interested in what their perceptions were, and I knew I could filter the wrong answers if I desired that. The tasters received questionnaires with the following questions.

Part 1 (Triangle Test)

1) These three samples are:
   • The same
   • One is different from the other two.
   • All three are different from each other.

2) If two or more beers are the same, list which they are.

3) If you detected a difference, describe what was detected for each sample.

4) Did you prefer one of the samples?

   A   B   C   no preference

5) If you had a preference, what was it about the sample that you preferred?

PART 2 (Qualitative Testing)

At this point, identify the two different samples and relabel them as 1 and 2.

1) Thinking of bitterness, did one sample seem more bitter? (Rank Testing)

   1   2   no preference

2) Subjectively describe your impression of the bitterness of each sample. (Hedonistic Testing)

3) Thinking of hop flavor, did one sample seem to have more hop flavor? (Rank Testing)

   1   2   no preference

4) Subjectively describe your impression of the hop flavor of each sample. (Hedonistic Testing)

I also sent the beers to two different laboratories to have the bitterness analyzed. (Thanks to Scott Bruslind at Analysis Laboratory and to Bob Smith at S. S. Steiner.) The result surprised me, but it was educational to see that even though the FWH beers had a slightly higher analyzed bitterness, a number of tasters (including myself) actually found them to taste less bitter.

GAS CHROMATOGRAPHY RESULTS

Beer	IBU
A (FWH)	31
B (60)	28.7

HPLC (HIGH PRESSURE LIQUID CHROMATOGRPAHY) RESULTS

Beer	Iso-alpha-acids	Alpha-acids	Humulinones
A (FWH)	24.8	3.5	1.9
B (60)	21.8	4.7	1.8

The alpha-acids are not bitter though they contribute to bitterness units value.
The humulinones are oxidized alpha-acids and are slightly bitter.

Interpreting the Results

The results of the tasting are summarized in the graph that follows. Quickly summarized, you can see there were eighteen total tasters. Thirteen said they found a difference, but only seven correctly identified which beer was different. Of those seven, five preferred beer B, which was the FWH beer. As you can see, there was no clear consensus. So, what do you do in a case like that? Trust yourself! Even though the experiment didn't point in any one direction, I feel that I can taste the difference that FWH makes, and I continue to use the procedure extensively to this day. Sure, it may be counterintuitive, but it's my beer, and I like it!

FWH TESTING RESULTS

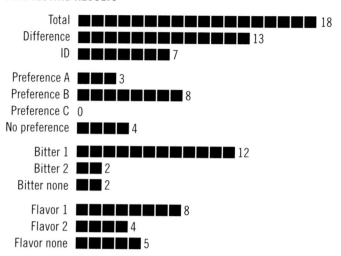

Total	18
Difference	13
ID	7
Preference A	3
Preference B	8
Preference C	0
No preference	4
Bitter 1	12
Bitter 2	2
Bitter none	2
Flavor 1	8
Flavor 2	4
Flavor none	5

CONCLUSION

In the end, after all the science and objective tasting, there's a final criteria to consider: Do you like the beer? Would you have another pint? That's what determines if a beer is "moreish." Do you want another one? Or two?

Both of us will readily admit that there are times we've gone in favor of blind, stupid decision making in spite of all the experimental evidence in front of us. It happens. We're human and assume you are, too. Just be sure that if you do that you are aware of the ramifications of your decision. It might mean you spend extra time and effort doing a decoction mash because you love the process even if you don't think it really makes a better beer. Or it may mean that you make an ingredient choice that you love but that everyone else who tries your beer hates. Wait a minute . . . maybe that's not a bad thing!

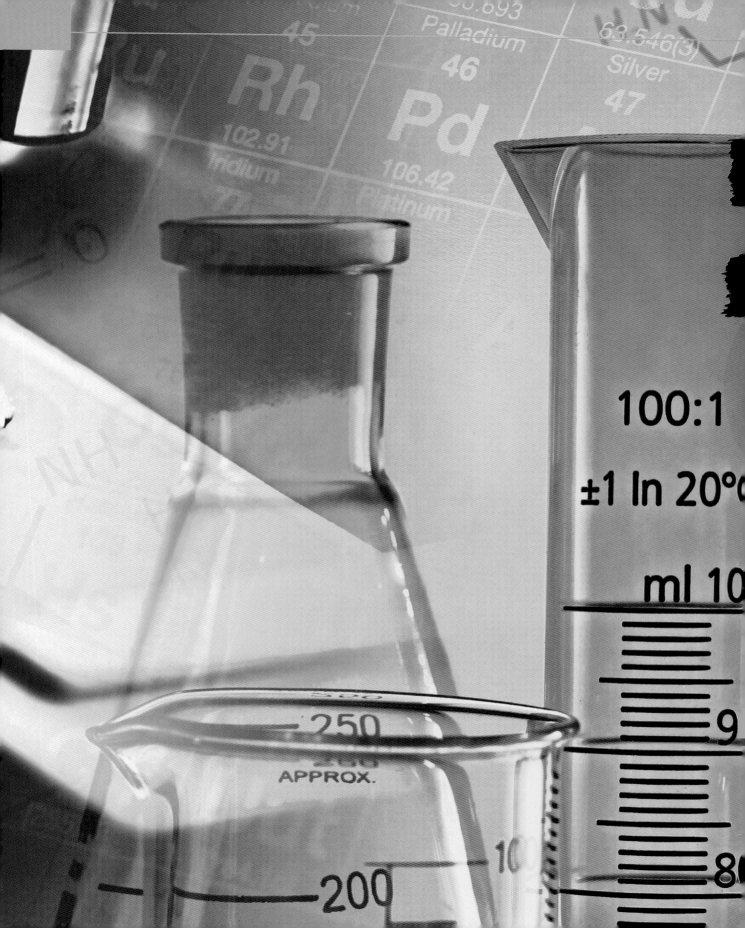

CHAPTER 10

THE EXPERIMENTS

BEFORE WE DIVE INTO our experiments, we need a word on control. It is crucial. A lack of control means unwanted variables. Without that control, suddenly the question you're asking is not "Are the beers different due to factor X?" but "Are the beers different due to factor X or because this other thing changed?"

In short, here's what you have to watch out for when you do these tests: changes in ingredients, particularly the age and lot numbers of your malts and hops; temperature control, both for your mash and your ferment; consistent boil strength and boil-off rate; consistent yeast pitches (rates and health); consistent fermentation profiles; and consistent packaging techniques.

Get comfortable with making repeatable batches or making two batches at once in two different kettles or mash tuns. For some of these experiments, it helps to have multiple mash tuns. This is what friends are for! Or go solo and build the Cheap 'n' Easy Mash Tun from page 60. You'll also want to get comfortable with the triangle testing and ranking testing methods in Chapter 9 (page 199 and page 203).

Remember that what you see here in the book is a just a fraction of the experiments we can do. That's why you'll see a code for each experiment. Those numbers are there to help you find the experiment on www.ExperimentalBrew.com so you can report your results and discuss them with other homebrewers. Join us!

EXPERIMENTS FOR THE MASH

For all grain brewers, this is where we start. The maltster has delivered a high-quality product to our doorstep. Now is our time to either make something fantastic or screw it up royally. Naturally, there are lots of arguments over techniques!

STEP MASH IMPACT ON BODY AND FLAVOR

Step mashing proponents claim that with multiple temperature rests, their beers have improvements to body and mouthfeel without sacrificing a fully fermentable wort. However, most agree that including a protein rest (120°F–127°F) with today's highly modified malts isn't necessary. If step mashing makes better beer, then we want to make the effort—but remember the mantra: The best beer possible with the least effort possible while having the best time possible!

Denny: Step mashing is one of the things I have tested many times. Name a step, and I've tried it! My conclusion: None of these make enough difference in my beer to be worth the time and effort. I think a protein rest might be useful for beers with a high percentage of wheat, though I'm not totally convinced. The same holds for decoction. I asked five brewers from around the world to brew two identical batches, one decocted and one with an infusion mash. The brewers were given flexibility in their brew, recipe, brew step, and so on. The brewers each did a blind tasting at their own locations using a set of questions that I had devised and, unfortunately, the decoction didn't stand out. If you want to see the whole experiment and results, log on to www.ExperimentalBrew.com.

Experiment

Code: E-M-1

Question: Does step mashing affect our beer flavor in a perceivable manner?

Hypothesis: Step mashing better controls the body and flavor of a beer compared to a single infusion mash.

Brewing Sessions Needed: 2

Protocol:

1. Mash one batch of beer with a stepped mash, with rests of 145°F for 30 minutes and 158°F for 30 minutes.
2. Mash a second batch at 152°F for 60 minutes.
3. Ferment both batches the same way: Yeast strain, temperature, and fermenter geometry must be consistent.

Evaluation: Perform the triangle and ranking tests, asking the tasters rank the samples in order of most to least body, head formation, and head retention. Ask them which they prefer and why.

Further Exploration:

- Do different rest temperatures make a difference?
- Do different malts react differently to each mash schedule?

IMPACT OF WATER CHEMISTRY ON FLAVOR

Water chemistry is supposedly a big factor in the world's beer styles. But what is the exact impact? Find out! Pick a style of beer you enjoy. Get your water analysis. Look at the water you've been using to brew the beer and at the exemplar water profiles for the style. Adjust your water to the archetype you choose. Brew and evaluate. Be aware, though, that many modern brewing centers neutralize their waters.

Experiment

Code: E-M-2

Question: Does adjusting your water chemistry for style produce a more enjoyable beer than the same recipe using unadjusted water?

Hypothesis: Using the correct water profile for a particular style of beer will produce a better tasting beer. Additionally, getting the proper mash pH will increase the efficiency of your mash.

Brewing Sessions Needed: 2

Protocol:

1. Choose a recipe that you enjoy and are familiar with.
2. Brew one batch with your normal water.
3. Get a water analysis and plug the values in the water calculator of your choice.
4. Choose a target water profile. Find them listed in your water calculator, a book, or on the Internet. Calculate your adjustments in the program.
5. Brew a second batch with your new water adjustments.
6. Ferment both batches the same: same yeast strain, temperature, and fermenter geometry.

Evaluation: Perform the triangle and ranking tests, asking your tasters which sample most closely tastes like the style it's supposed to be, as well as asking about body and sweetness. Ask them which they prefer.

Further Exploration:

- Does a too high (>5.6) or too low (<5.2) mash pH change the flavor? Does it affect your mash efficiency?
- Are mineral additions that improve one style detrimental to another style?
- For a hoppy beer, how much sulfate do you prefer?
- For a malty beer, how much calcium chloride do you prefer?

THREE WAYS TO USE DARK MALTS

There are a few different ways to add dark malts to your mash:

- Chuck 'em in with everything else and adjust your water to compensate for a pH drop (or don't).
- Add the dark malts on top of the mash during the sparge. The advantages: much less effect on mash pH and great extraction of malt color. The disadvantage: not as much flavor extraction.
- Cold steep (see page 212) and add the liquid to the kettle. This method gives you lots of color and a clean, nonacrid roast flavor. You avoid potential pH issues entirely and it works smoothly. The downside: It very inefficiently extracts flavor and color. (You use 2–3 times the malt.)

Experiment

Code: E-M-3

Question: How does changing the method of adding dark malts to the mash affect the flavor?

Hypothesis: Adding dark malts into the mash early yields more acrid aromas and flavors than when they're added late to the mash. Both produce more aromas than the same amount of malt cold steeped and added to the boil.

Brewing Sessions Needed: 2 or 3

The Cold Steep

In the late 1990s, the late Dr. George Fix wrote about cold steeping in the Homebrew Digest *newsletter:*

The cold steeping procedure was designed to maximize the extraction of desirable melanoidins, and at the same time minimize the extraction of undesirable ones. The former are simple compounds which yield a fine malt taste. The undesirable ones come from more complicated structures. Polymers with sulfur compounds tend to have malt/vegetable tones. Others yield cloying tones, which to my palate have an under fermented character. . . . The cold steeping procedure was developed by Mary Ann Gruber of Briess. My version goes as follows.

- *One gallon of water per 3–4 lbs of grains to be steeped is brought to a boil and held there for 5 minutes.*
- *The water is cooled down to ambient, and the cracked grains are added.*
- *This mixture is left for 12–16 hours at ambient temperatures, and then added to the brew kettle for the last 15–20 minutes of the boil.*

The upside of cold steeping is that it works. The downside is that it is very inefficient both with respect to extract and color. In my setup I am using 2–3 times the malt that would normally be used. As a consequence I have been using it for "adjunct malts" such as black and crystal. I also am very happy with the use of Munich malts with this process when they are used as secondary malts.

Note: Feeling pressed for time on a brew week? Steep your color malts well ahead of time, strain, and store cold in the fridge until brew day. Congratulations, you've made something like Sinamar (Weyermann's Rheinheitsgehbot-compliant beer coloring). For additional stability, boil the strained mixture and store cold in sanitized jars.

Protocol:

1. Choose your favorite stout or porter recipe.
2. Brew one batch with the dark malts (180°L or darker) mixed into the main mash.
3. Brew again with the dark malt added to the mash just before lautering.
4. Brew again with cold-steeped dark malt extract added to the boil for 10 minutes.
5. Ferment and package identically.

Evaluation: Do the triangle and ranking tests, asking your tasters about harshness and dark malt character.

Further Exploration:

- Does the amount of roasted malt affect the perception of harshness or smoothness?
- Are different varieties of dark malts affected differently?

ADDITIONAL MASH EXPERIMENTS

Here are a few more ideas for experimenting with the mash. Follow the format we've outlined in the other experiments by defining your question, hypothesis, and experimental technique. Don't forget to register your experiment at www.ExperimentalBrew.com and share your results with the world.

- Mash temperatures: How much do you have to change the mash temperature to notice the effect? What are the effects of a very low mash temperature (140°F) or a very high one (165°F)? Note: for very low mash temps, lengthen the mash to 90 minutes to ensure complete conversion.

- Mash times: In theory, conversion takes 15–20 minutes. If so, why mash longer? Try batches with mash lengths of 15, 30, 45, 60, and 90 minutes. Compare original and final gravities, mash efficiencies, and the flavor and body of the resulting beers.

- Batch versus fly sparging: Make the same beer but sparge differently. What are the impacts, if any, on the beer? Make sure to use a mash tun designed for fly sparging.

- No or low sparge: Can you skip the sparge step altogether? Or sparge less? Some brewers swear by no sparging to make beautifully smooth beers for a few dollars more malt.

- Concentrated runnings versus using crystal malt: Some brewers boil down a gallon of wort to a thick syrup to simulate the use of crystal malt, but does it really simulate it? Using a recipe that includes crystal malt, make a batch that leaves out the crystal. Take a gallon of first runnings; boil down to a pint. Add to the kettle with the remaining wort. Make another batch using crystal malt, but no boil-down.

- Antioxidants to prevent staling: Does cinnamon prevent beer oxidation and extend shelf life? Charlie Papazian has been using cinnamon for years. He adds a teaspoon of cinnamon to every mash to keep the beer in prime condition for a longer time. Also, the March 2002 issue of *The Brewer International* states that dark malts have a profound effect on preventing staling. Some use a small amount of roast barley (approximately ½ ounce per 5 gallons) to slow the staling process in their beer. Some claim the same benefit from a half-pound of medium crystal (30°L–80°L).

EXPERIMENTS FOR THE BOIL

Just as with mash experiments, there are two ways to approach the experiments for the boil. To keep the tightest control over the variables, the best way to do these experiments is to split a batch of wort between two kettles. Alternatively, you can brew two batches back-to-back, but you need to make sure you keep everything the same between them, other than the variable that you're testing.

FIRST WORT HOPPING

If there's one subject that will elicit radically different opinions, it's the first wort hops (FWH) technique. Adding FWH is a traditional German technique where you throw hops to the kettle as the wort runs off the mash, preboil. Traditionally, one third of the total hops were used for FWH. Low alpha acid noble hops were used to add a more pleasant aroma and bitterness.

Dr. George Fix introduced the process to American homebrewers for the first time in 1995. Homebrewers used the technique in ways never considered. They substituted potent American hops for the low alpha noble hops for more punch. The common consensus: FWH gives great flavor but little in aroma. Homebrewers also appreciated FWH's mellower bittering characteristics.

All of this comes from a single German study with a single panel's judgment. Regardless of the cause (protein binding?), one thing is certain: FWH has given American brewers another place to jam some hops into the process! Should it be used as a replacement for the aroma or bittering hops? Some felt that FWH was a substitute for the flavor hop addition and provided bitterness on par with a 20-minute hop addition. Others simply moved the standard bittering addition to FWH. Obviously, this is an experiment waiting to happen!

Denny: Several years ago, I did this experiment myself. See page 204 for the experiment and results.

Experiment

Code: E-B-1

Question: How does the bittering from FWH compare to the bittering from a 60-minute addition?

Hypothesis: Some studies have shown that FWH actually produces about 10 percent more measureable IBUs than a 60-minute addition, but it tastes less bitter.

Brewing Sessions Needed: 1 (split with two kettles)

Protocol:

1. Evenly split your wort into two kettles. Add your nominal 60-minute addition in one kettle as FWH before adding the wort. Note: We recommend Cascade hops for testing due to their noticeable but nondominating character.
2. Steep the hops in the kettle while you sparge. Evenly split the sparge runoff between the 2 kettles.
3. Bring both kettles to a boil.
4. Add the same amount of the same hops as a 60-minute bittering charge to the other kettle after it comes to a boil. Boil both kettles for 60 minutes with no other hop additions.
5. Cool, pitch, ferment, and package.

Evaluation: Perform the triangle and ranking tests, asking tasters about the quality of bitterness (harsh, neutral, smooth) and hop flavor.

Further Exploration:

- Do different hop varieties change the result?
- Do higher or lower amounts of hops change the result?
- Compare the bitterness and flavor from FWH to the bitterness you get from a 20-minute addition. These should be the only hop additions in the beer.
- Does the amount of FWH steeping time make a difference in the bitterness or flavor you get?

HOT SIDE AERATION

Hot side aeration (HSA) has been a hotly (yeah, we said that) debated topic for years. Can you ruin a beer by incorporating oxygen into it when it's hot? The theory is that wort splashed or shaken while over 85°F will make the beer oxidize and thus taste like wet cardboard, metal, or even caramel.

For years, homebrewers lived in fear of HSA and treated their wort gently all the way through the chilling phase. But a few years ago, people began asking why. Yeast consumes oxygen during fermentation, including any oxygen that had gotten into the wort while hot. Luminaries like Bamforth declared that HSA is a minor concern for homebrewers. Our personal opinions are that HSA is not a myth, but it's not a major problem waiting to bite you.

Experiment

Code: E-B-2

Question: Does HSA negatively impact beer flavor?

Hypothesis: Incorporating oxygen into your wort when it's over 85°F will oxidize your beer.

Brewing Sessions Needed: 1

Protocol:

1. Brew the California Magnum Blonde (page 27). At the end of the boil, before chilling, transfer half of the wort to a bucket fermenter. Be as rough and incorporate as much oxygen as possible. Pour it from a height and splash it. Chill the other half of the wort as you usually do and transfer it to the same type of fermenter. **Warning:** Do not put hot wort into a glass carboy! You run the risk of breaking the carboy and possibly sustaining a serious injury. Cool the wort before putting it in glass!

2. Cool, pitch, ferment, and package.

Evaluation: Perform the triangle and ranking tests, asking tasters about flavors like wet cardboard, metal, sherry, and exaggerated caramel flavors.

Further Exploration: Oxidation becomes more evident as a beer ages. Store some of the beer and taste it at one-month intervals. Take good notes so you can compare from month to month.

IMPACT OF SUGAR ADDED TO THE BOIL

In Chapter 7, we established that sugar is a useful ingredient for affecting both body and flavor in a beer. If you use the sugar for flavor, you want to add it late in fermentation to maintain the flavor. But what if you're using cane sugar to lighten the body of a beer? Does it matter if it's added to the kettle rather than the fermenter? Many brewers add the sugar to the fermenter, believing that the beer will have a healthier fermentation and a higher attenuation if the yeast is introduced to the sugar later. On the other hand, we both make tripels and always add the sugar to the kettle, early in the boil. We see great attenuation, no off flavors, and there's no chance of forgetting to add it later.

So, does it matter when you add the sugar? Here's an experiment to help you decide.

Experiment

Code: E-B-3

Question: Will adding sugar to the kettle negatively impact beer flavor or attenuation?

Hypothesis: Adding simple sugar to the boil will cause yeast health and attenuation problems.

Brewing Sessions Needed: 1

Protocol:

1. Brew the Westcoastmalle Tripel (page 112). Split the wort evenly into 2 kettles. Add the sugar to one kettle at the beginning of the boil.

2. Treat the beers the same through to the middle of fermentation.

3. After 4–5 days, add sugar to the batch that didn't receive it in the kettle. Let both batches ferment for another 1–2 weeks. Be sure to take a final gravity reading for each batch.

4. Package each batch the same way.

Evaluation: Perform the triangle and ranking tests, asking the tasters about sweetness and dryness as well as off flavors that could be attributed to poor fermentation, such as sourness, phenolics, and diacetyl.

FERMENTER EXPERIMENTS

Before we get to the action, keep in mind that many of these experiments depend on pitching the same amount of yeast into different batches of wort. That can be a real challenge. One way to get there is to make a large starter with liquid yeast, decant almost all the spent wort after the starter ferments out, swirl up the remaining wort and yeast slurry, and carefully weigh it into two portions before pitching. Remember to use an accurate scale and a steady hand. Keep the edges of your yeast container sanitized if you need to pour back and forth to achieve equal weights. But the easiest way is to use dry yeast. You'll just have to acquire two packages with the same date code and buy them at the same time from the same shop to make sure they were shipped and stored under the same conditions.

PLASTIC VERSUS GLASS FERMENTERS

Ask a few brewers if it's better to ferment in plastic buckets or bottles or glass carboys. Stand back and watch the sparks fly! Each side has arguments to support its point of view. Proponents of glass say that plastic buckets or bottles get scratched and harbor germs that will infect your beer. They say buckets retain colors and odors, which carry over to your next batch. They'll talk about the oxygen permeability of plastic and claim that can lead to premature beer staling. They'll usually tell you how much they enjoy watching the yeast move about during fermentation inside a glass carboy.

On the other side, homebrewers who prefer plastic talk about the fragility of glass and the danger of injury should a glass carboy break. They'll also tell you how much less room it takes to store buckets, since you can stack them, and how much less they cost to buy. Buckets are easier to clean because they have a larger opening than carboys. And although they may be more permeable to oxygen, generally your beer won't spend enough time in the fermenter for that to be a consideration.

Experiment

Code: E-F-1
Question: Does the oxygen permeability of plastic buckets negatively affect beer left in contact with the plastic for a month in comparison to glass or steel fermenters?
Hypothesis: For beers that have been actively fermenting and are still in contact with the yeast for a brief period (less than 4 weeks), the impact is negligible.
Brewing Sessions Needed: 1
Protocol:
1. Split a batch of wort between a plastic fermenter and a glass or steel fermenter.
2. Pitch equal amounts of yeast. They should have the same fermentation temperatures throughout fermentation.
3. When fermentation is complete, keg or bottle both batches using the same techniques.

Evaluation: Perform the triangle and ranking tests, asking tasters about off flavors and any differences between the beers.

Further Exploration:
- Does the age of the plastic fermenter affect the flavor of the beer? Do the experiment using a bucket that's been used at least ten times and a new bucket.
- Do lighter-flavored beers pick up leftover fermenter flavors or aromas?

STEEL AND FERMENTER GEOMETRY

Buckets and carboys aren't the only way to ferment your beer. Stainless steel is a great option, but a lot of homebrewers don't have the space or financial resources to use a stainless conical fermenter. One way to use stainless steel is to ferment in your boil kettle. Veteran homebrewer Jeff Renner has done this for years with excellent results.

But a lot of homebrewers have kegs for serving their finished beer. What about fermenting in a corny keg? If you use a 5-gallon keg, you'll have to limit yourself to 4-gallon batches. Not too bad, huh? But one big complaint about fermenting in cornies is that the geometry isn't optimal for yeast circulation. Does it matter to you as a homebrewer?

Experiment

Code: E-F-2

Question: Does fermenter geometry affect fermentation quality?

Hypothesis: Because increased height restricts optimum circulation of the yeast in the wort, we'll see increased off flavors and reduced attenuation levels in the beer fermented in the 5-gallon keg.

Brewing Sessions Needed: 1

Protocol:
1. Split a batch of wort between a bucket or glass carboy and a 5-gallon keg. Make sure that each fermenter is thoroughly cleaned and sanitized. Fill the keg with 4 gallons of wort. Fill the bucket with the usual 5 gallons. Take close notes on volumes, temperatures, and times.
2. Treat the batches the same throughout fermentation and packaging.

Evaluation: Perform the triangle and ranking tests, asking about off flavors or signs of poor fermentation.

Further Exploration: Would there be a difference if you filled the corny keg to the top and allowed the fermenting beer to blow off the yeast?

YEAST EXPERIMENTS

In the world of actual biological science—you know, the one where they actually know what they're doing with statistics and beakers—our friend *S. cerevesiae* is a major player in experimentation because of its docility. For our purposes, we'll start with the most basic experiment you can perform, and then we'll move onto a few questions and techniques that can change how you look at your beer.

STRAIN COMPARISON

Each yeast strain has its own characteristics and quirks. No amount of textual description will tell you the things you need to know. It takes time and experience playing with them. There's no better way to know your different options than by making the same beer with different strains.

Drew: Look at the segment on saison (page 123). Much of that knowledge comes from years of brewing, but it was really cemented by pulling off this experiment. I did it with 65 gallons of wort, but you can do it in a smaller fashion with 1-gallon batches.

Experiment

Code: E-F-3

Question: Do the three main American ale yeast strains (Safale US-05, WY1056 American Ale, and WLP001 California Ale have different impacts on flavor, attenuation, aroma, mouthfeel, or other aspects of your beer?

Hypothesis: Because the three strains have been isolated at different times and may have undergone minor genetic drift, they do create slightly different fermentation profiles.

Brewing Sessions Needed: 1

Protocol:

1. Split a batch of wort among three fermenters.
2. In each fermenter pitch one of the three yeasts in equal cell count volumes. (Target 6 million cells per milliliter based on viability.)
3. Ferment each beer to completion. Record the final gravity per strain. Package the beer and carbonate to the same level. Chill and serve to your evaluators.

Evaluation: Perform the triangle and ranking tests, asking your tasters to describe any difference in the beers in terms of body, sweetness, and bitterness.

Further Exploration: How does the result vary based on temperature, oxygen levels, and so on?

USING MULTIPLE YEASTS

Using more than one yeast strain in your beer can develop interesting flavor profiles. Using more than one strain in a batch, you can blend characteristics to achieve flavors not possible any other way. Let's take a closer look.

One way to approach using multiple yeasts is to pitch them all at the same time (simultaneous pitching). Wyeast and White Labs have created packs of yeast blends that do this for you. Or you can pick any strains you'd like to mix. Pitching the yeasts simultaneously, you skip any timing issues associated with pitching additional yeast into your fermenting beer before all the sugars are gone. This makes things easy—just the way we like it. The drawback is that you have little to no control over which strain dominates. One may take over to the extent that there's little to no contribution from any other(s). Efforts to control dominance by changing starting populations or manipulating temperatures is fraught with issues for homebrewers.

Sequential pitching offers more control of each yeast strain. Start by pitching one strain. Later, during fermentation, you pitch another one. You can optimize the conditions for each strain, giving each its optimal environment. This method is often used for sour beers, with a starting pitch of a neutral yeast strain to handle primary fermentation followed by later pitching of *Brettanomyces* (or bacteria) to achieve the desired flavor profile. Don't wait too long to pitch the other yeasts, or the fermentable sugars will be used up. Bacteria are easy and will eat through sugars that the yeast has left behind and ferment them.

Interview with Greg Doss

Greg Doss is a microbiologist and quality control manager at Wyeast Laboratories, one of the world's largest producers of brewing yeast. We asked him some questions about using multiple yeast strains in a batch of beer.

Drew and Denny (D&D): When you guys put out a blend of yeast, how do you decide on the proper proportions?

Greg Doss (GD): Our blends and proportions are based on test fermentations in the lab.

D&D: Do you worry about one strain dominating the blend?

GD: Yes. We take the growth rates, sugar/nutrient utilization, flavor contribution, and fermentation kinetics into consideration when designing a blend. This is not as much of a concern when working with multiple Saccharomyces cultures, but definitely something we think about when involving Brettanomyces or bacteria cultures. Culture domination is also a problem if the brewer wants to harvest and reuse the yeast. Inevitably, some strains will dominate the fermentation, causing subsequent culture populations (proportions) to be skewed from the original blend. Although this is not necessarily a bad thing if the resulting cultures make a nice beer, consistency, and replicating the beer may be difficult.

D&D: Is there any way to control which strain does or doesn't dominate?

GD: Proportions of the blend is probably the best way to control the process, though sugar/nutrient utilization and fermentation temperature can also be used.

D&D: What is the meaning of life?

GD: Rye IPA is a good start.

D&D: Love it! Science and humor!

Blending differently fermented batches is the easiest way to control the flavor profile from using multiple yeast strains. Just split your wort into individual fermenters and pitch one strain into each portion. When the fermentations are finished, blend the various beers to get the flavors from each strain into one batch of beer. A drawback is the extra equipment and sanitation worry.

Experiment

Code: E-F-4

Question: Does the way you use multiple yeasts change the flavor?

Hypothesis: Pitching more than one yeast at a time yields unpredictable results. Pitching strains sequentially gives each a chance to develop flavors independently and improves repeatability for future brews.

Brewing Sessions Needed: 1

Protocol:

1. Split a batch of wort between two fermenters.
2. In one fermenter, pitch two different yeast strains. In the other, pitch only one of the two strains used in the first fermenter. Be sure to pitch the same amount of yeast into each. That means that the total of the two yeast batches will equal the amount in the one yeast batch.

3. After three days to a week, pitch the other strain into the second fermenter (the fermenter that originally got only one strain). Pitch the same amount of this yeast as the original strain so that one will have less chance of overwhelming the other.

4. Let the ferments finish and package.

Evaluation: Perform the triangle and ranking tests, asking tasters to describe any differences in flavor, aroma, or mouthfeel. Does the flavor of one beer show more or less of a yeast flavor characteristic than the other?

Further Exploration:

- Does the timing of adding the second yeast to the sequential batch make a difference?
- Does the order of the yeast additions on the sequential beer make a difference?
- Harvest some of the combined yeast and repitch it. Do you get the same results?

PITCHING RATE

Received wisdom of the ages: Underpitching a beer will increase ester production. The technique has been used for styles from British bitters to German hefeweizen. However, in the last few years a debate has sprung up about whether pitching less yeast really increases ester production, or if the result is exactly the opposite.

Proponents of the opposing viewpoint say that the same enzyme, acetyl coenzyme A (acetyl-coA), is responsible for both yeast growth and ester production. When it is busy growing yeast cells, it's not available for ester production. Increasing biomass (cell growth) through methods like aeration or stirring will decrease ester production. The more biomass produced, the more acetyl-coA is used and not available for ester production. Conversely, low nutrient levels or low oxygen levels slow cell growth and cause an increase in ester production. Dr. Clayton Cone of Lallemand notes that a drop in available O_2 from 8 ppm to 3 ppm can cause a fourfold increase in ester production.

Tomme Arthur, mad monk of Lost Abbey Brewing, has said that at Port/Lost Abbey they overpitch their beers but inject less oxygen into the wort. The belief is the combination creates additional esters without other negative side effects like underattenuation. Also, to keep the yeast in check, they follow the same Belgian-esque procedure we recommend: Start low (64°F) and let the yeast free rise. If you've not had any of the Lost Abbey beers, trust us, they develop plenty of esters despite the high pitching levels. So, who's right? Well, all that really matters is that you know what works for you. Here's where the experiment comes into play.

Experiment

Code: E-F-5

Question: What is the effect of yeast pitch rate on ester production?

Hypothesis: Pitching less yeast will result in fewer esters due to lack of acetyl-coA to create esters while it builds yeast cells.

Brewing Sessions Needed: 1 (split batch)

Protocol:

1. Save the yeast slurry from a 5-gallon batch of beer in two sanitized containers. The easiest way to do this is to weigh the slurry so you have about ⅔ of the total in one container and ⅓ in the other.

2. Produce a batch of wort and split it evenly between two fermenters. Pitch one container of slurry into each fermenter.

3 Ferment, package, and serve. Take periodic specific gravity readings to compare the fermentation profiles.

Evaluation: Perform the triangle and ranking tests, asking the tasters about their perception of fruity esters.

WORT PREPARATION EXPERIMENTS

With the fermenters chosen and the yeast ready to go, we get to how your wort preparation affects the final product. Here we'll look at the steps that we take to get the wort ready for the addition of yeast. We'll focus on aeration and making strong yeast in the wort, including the popular and controversial olive oil experiment.

AERATION

Brewers have used everything from a vigorous splash, a venturi tube, a healthy shake, a whisk, a mix-stir wine degasser (Denny's favorite) all the way to inline oxygenation systems (Drew). Just as many brewers simply let the beer go into the fermenter without oxygen. Who's right?

Experiment

Code: E-F-6

Question: Is aeration necessary to produce good beer?

Hypothesis: Using aeration provides the necessary ingredients to produce healthier yeast. Aerated worts will have lower terminal gravities and more complete fermentation characteristics, including reduced levels of diacetyl, in shorter periods of time.

Brewing Sessions Needed: 1 (two-way split batch)

Protocol:

1. Using the California Magnum Blonde recipe (page 27), produce enough wort to split into two fermenters.
2. Rack an equal amount of wort to each fermenter. In one fermenter, aerate via your favorite method. In the other, do nothing.
3. Ferment and package.

Evaluation: Perform the triangle and ranking tests, asking the tasters about their perception of fruity esters.

Further Exploration:
- Is there a detectable difference between beer produced with aeration versus oxygenation?
- Can we produce beer that tastes the same as oxygenated beer, just by using more yeast?

Note: Be sure to take into account the type of yeast you use. Some may need more aeration than others. It's generally true that dry yeast doesn't have as much need for aeration as liquid, so liquid yeast might be a better choice for this experiment.

OLIVE OIL INSTEAD OF AERATION

Yeast cells need oxygen to synthesize sterols to keep cell walls flexible for reproductive budding. Homebrewers are constantly looking to generate the best yeast health for the least amount of fuss and expense, and some saw the Holy Grail in olive oil.

In September 2005, Grady Hull came up with a completely new method of aeration when he published his master's thesis. He used a small dose of olive oil during yeast storage to remove the need to oxygenate the wort prior to pitching. Here's a bit of the introduction of the paper:

> This paper reports the findings of a series of full-scale production tests that were conducted in an operating brewery to evaluate the effects of another type of yeast treatment. By mixing olive oil into the yeast, during storage, instead of aerating the wort, fermentations can be achieved with only a minor increase in fermentation time. The beers produced from these fermentations were comparable in flavor and foam retention to beers produced by traditional wort aeration. The ester profile of the beers produced using olive oil addition was significantly higher than the controls and the flavor stability of these beers was significantly improved.

Homebrewers seized on adding olive oil as a way to get around other aeration methods. A liter of cheap olive oil is many times less expensive and lasts longer than the available cans of O_2. What most overlook: The technique was used on yeast in storage. It had nothing to do with adding olive oil to the fermenter. Yet folks were adding it to the fermenter and reporting, "Well, it didn't hurt," or, "It seemed to work." (Remember, there are plenty of homebrewers out there who do no aeration whatsoever and report that their beers are fantastic.)

There was little accounting for the infinitesimally small amount of olive oil needed for a five-gallon batch of homebrew. Reducing Grady's numbers to our brew lengths brings the dose to less than 0.05 milliliters of oil per 5-gallon batch. The closest we can get without using lab equipment is to use a drop on the end of a pin or needle. Brewers attempting to use this technique usually also missed out on dissolving the oil in a solution of ethanol first to ensure that it would blend into the wort and not float in the watery wort. We specifically asked Grady about how homebrewers were taking his research and using it in their own ways. Grady replied:

> We never tried using olive oil in propagations. Our tests were centered around using it as a nutrient in yeast storage vessels to eliminate the need for aeration at knockout. Also, we never tried adding the oil to the wort after pitching. The oil was always added to the yeast in the storage vessel and given plenty of time to mix and be absorbed into the cells prior to pitching. We found a slight increase in esters and a slight improvement in shelf life by using olive oil and not aerating. We do not currently use olive oil in our yeast storage vessels. The results did not bear out the shelf life improvements we were hoping for and did not justify installing an olive oil dosing and handling system.

Experiment

Code: E-F-7

Try experiment E-F-6 (on page 221) using a drop of olive oil the size of a pinhead rather than no aeration. Compare to a batch aerated with your usual method. Ask the tasters the same questions as in E-F-6.

FERMENTATION EXPERIMENTS

With the fermenters chosen, the yeasts chosen, and the wort made ready, it's time to look at the fermentation itself. In this segment, we'll take a quick look at what it means to perform an open or closed fermentation, just how lazy you can be when it comes to temperature control, and how we end our fermentations.

OPEN FERMENTATION

From the first time homebrewers brew, the need to keep the fermenter sealed to prevent infection is drilled into us. What kind of yahoo ignores these warnings and ferments beer unprotected? The wackos at Sierra Nevada, for one! Their Kellerwiess ferments in open tubs. Ommegang, Anchor, Jolly Pumpkin, and plenty of other American, English, Belgian, and even German breweries do it as well. For the thousands of years beer has existed, it was mostly fermented in the open.

Open fermentation also makes it easy to harvest yeast. Commercial brewers claim that the harvested yeast is healthier due to less CO_2 toxicity and less pressure damage. Additionally, open fermentation supposedly creates more complex, nuanced ester profiles.

It's no surprise, but sanitation is even more important in open fermentation. Also, open fermentation doesn't mean fully uncovered. Just place your fermenter in an area (perhaps a closet) that doesn't get much use. Completely cover the fermenter until you see krausen.

And remember, as long as your bucket lid is loose, it's still open. Are the benefits of open fermentation worth the potential infection problems? Is it more benefit to commercial brewers? It's up to us to try it.

Drew: I do all of my ferments quasi-open. Instead of fiddling with airlocks and blow-off tubes, I sanitize aluminum foil and slap it over the carboy mouth or open keg lid. It's not on tight; it's just enough to keep dust out. When the krausen falls down, I close the fermentation.

Experiment

Code: E-F-8

Question: What is the impact on beer flavor between using closed or open fermenters?

Hypothesis: Open fermentation will produce a more complex ester profile and healthier yeast.

Brewing Sessions Needed: 1 (two-way split batch)

Protocol:

1. Brew the California Magnum Blonde (page 27) and split it evenly into two sanitized fermenters of the same shape, be they buckets, pots, or tubs. Pitch equal yeast amounts.
2. Start with both fermenters covered. At full krausen, uncover one of the fermenters. You can loosen the covering or remove it completely.
3. Ferment, recording gravities as you go, and package as normal.

Evaluation: Perform the triangle and ranking tests, asking about the level of fruity esters the tasters perceive in each beer.

Further Exploration:

- Is open-fermented yeast healthier? Harvest yeast from each batch. Repitch it into two new batches of wort. Evaluate the performance of each.
- To prove your geekitude, try staining and counting cells from each batch. (See page 91.)

EARLY FERMENTATION TEMPERATURE CONTROL

We hope nobody debates that temperature control plays a large role in beer quality. How tightly to maintain fermentation temperature control is hotly debated, though. Yeast produce flavors and aromas mostly during the lag and reproductive phases while not actively fermenting. Is tightly controlling temperature only during the first 48–72 hours of fermentation sufficient?

On the other end of the spectrum, Bamforth states that for every 18°F increase in beer temperature, you double the rate at which your beer stales. But for quickly fermenting ales, if the experiment holds out, you may free your chilled fermentation space faster by letting beer finish warmer (70°F–80°F).

Drew: I aggressively maintain my fermentation ice baths for 3–4 days. After that, mostly out of laziness, it's occassional checkups only. The results have been great, but admittedly the beers with continous temperature control have tasted more polished to me.

Denny: I do pretty much the same thing, except that after 4–7 days I remove the fermenter from its water bath completely and let the temperature rise to whatever the ambient temperature is—seldom above the mid 70'sF. And my beers are better than Drew's. (Okay, maybe not!)

Experiment

Code: E-F-9

Question: Is controlling the fermentation temperature for the first 72 hours post-pitch sufficient for producing a clean beer free of excessive esters, phenols, and fusels?

Hypothesis: Because the majority of flavors produced by the yeast are created early, temperature control during that critical period is sufficient for creating clean fermentations.

Brewing Sessions Needed: 1

Protocol:

1. Split a batch of wort between two identical fermenters with equal pitches of yeast. Begin fermentation at the same temperature.

The Pros' Thoughts on Open Fermentation

In the January–February 2008 issue of Brew Your Own, *editor Betsy Parks interviewed open fermentation–loving brewers. Here are a few of their comments:*

RON JEFFRIES, brewmaster at Jolly Pumpkin Artisan Ales (Dexter, Michigan):

Our open fermenters have a shallower height-to-diameter ratio, which is 1:1. This shape tends to create different flavor esters because of the way the yeast behaves. I think that this type of fermentation makes for superior beers.

The benefit of open fermentation is the flavors you can create. There are ester profiles that are more complex. . . . Also, beer from an open fermenter is less likely to absorb sulfur aromas, as you can't off gas as easily as you can in a cylindroconical. Top cropping yeast is also superior in open fermentation, and you can harvest a much healthier yeast crop.

Find a spot that can be as free of dust as possible and definitely away from any pet hair. You really don't want to worry about stuff falling into the beer. Use a stainless steel pot or plastic bucket that has a loose-fitting lid to let gas escape, but otherwise the normal fermenting procedure is exactly the same as if you were brewing in a closed fermenter.

STEVE DRESSLER, brewmaster at Sierra Nevada Brewing (Chico, California), home to several Yorkshire-square open fermenters:

I do feel that the ester notes from open fermentation are exceptional, and there is very little stress put on the yeast by CO_2 saturation and hydrostatic pressures that you get in larger cylindroconical fermenters. We still have four 100-barrel (3,400-gallon) fermenters at the brewery and use them all the time.

The pitfalls are, of course, that you need to have a very clean fermentation environment (you should anyway) and watch your micro closely. . . . After primary fermentation, the beer needs to be moved into the secondary tank. This should be done when there is still a small amount of extract left in the beer, so that at the end of fermentation, the yeast can take up any oxygen that the beer comes in contact with during the transfer.

Our takeaways: Good healthy yeast, a clean and draft-free fermentation area, and the right fermenter geometry are very important. A flatter fermenter contributes better ester production and yeast health. Buckets or stainless-steel kettles will work fine for experimentation, but you might want to find a more traditionally shaped fermenter. Use shallow containers like restaurant bus tubs. Loosely covered, these perfectly mimic traditional open fermenters

2. After 72 hours, move one fermenter and allow the temperature to rise 5°F–15°F.

3. When fermentation is complete, package the beer.

Evaluation: Perform the triangle and ranking tests, asking the tasters about off flavors and fruity esters.

Further Exploration:

- Does the yeast strain affect the results?
- Does the choice of beer style matter?

PRE-PACKAGING EXPERIMENTS

Before we can get to the bottle, glass, or cellar, we do have a few remaining processes that can impact our beer.

WOOD AGING

For most homebrewers, filling a 50–60 gallon barrel is an impossible chore. Instead, most turn to oak alternatives developed by the wine industry to rejuvanate old barrels. What is the character difference between a barrel and an oak alternative? Barrel wranglers argue that a key component of barrel aging is micro-oxidation. The semiporous wood allows just enough oxidative characters to soften the tanninc nature of oak. Alternatives users argue that we primarily desire the vanillin and trehalose found in abundance in the freshly toasted oak products.

How do you properly prepare alternatives for use? Some steam them for 10–15 minutes, ensuring fresh oak flavor. Others prefer to soak them in spirits for at least 2 weeks.

Experiment

Code: E-P-1

Question: What is the impact on beer flavor between aging in a barrel versus aging with oak alternatives?

Hypothesis: Aging in a barrel will yield softer wood flavors due to micro-oxygenation.

Brewing Sessions Needed: 1 15-gallon batch (two-way split)

Protocol:

1. You'll need one 5–8 gallon whiskey barrel and 2 ounces American oak cubes. This is a great project to work with a brewery. The brewery can ferment one batch and provide consistent finished unaged beer for testing.

2. Using the Base Imperial Porter recipe (page 122), produce enough to fill your barrel and oak cube fermenter.

3. Bulk-ferment the beer in one vessel or uniformly mix before aging.

4. Rack and fill the barrel. Add barrel alternative to a secondary container and fill with the other portion of the beer.

5. Age the beers for 2 weeks and check the flavor. Due to the higher surface to volume ratio, you'll be done quickly. When they're done aging, rack to a keg and carbonate.

Evaluation: Perform the triangle and ranking tests, asking tasters about any perceived differences in the beer. Ask which they prefer.

Further Exploration: With a small barrel, there's less time for exposure to oxygen. Is the effect different if the beer is aged in a full-size 50–60 gallon barrel for 6 months?

HOP TO THE SCHEDULE

Brewers have long debated the best temperature for dry hopping. New studies at the Barth-Haas Group, the world's largest supplier of hops, show that best results are obtained at temperatures below 50°F. However, many commercial brewers report that their best results come from dry hopping at temperatures in the 70°sF. What's a homebrewer to do? Yeah, you've got it!

Experiment

Code: E-P-2

Question: At what temperature is the hop aroma best extracted from dry hops with the fewest off flavors?

Hypothesis: Dry hopping at cold temperatures (under 60°F) will produce grassy, vegetal flavors and aromas.

Brewing Sessions Needed: 1

Protocol:

1. Brew the Basic IPA recipe on page 108 or the hoppy beer of your choice.
2. After fermentation is complete, split the beer into two containers. Add an equal amount of the same dry hops to each. Age one container around 70°F and the other one in a 50°F fridge for one week.
3. Package and serve.

Evaluation: Perform the triangle and ranking tests, asking which has the most hop aroma and flavor. See if the tasters detect harshness, grassiness, or vegetal aromas.

PACKAGING EXPERIMENTS

The moment that you finish packaging your beer is the moment that you surrender active control over it. The fate of your beer in the package is now in the hands of capricious fates of infection and oxidation. The question is always how to best to keep them at bay. (Spoiler alert: Keep your beer clean and cold with scant oxygen for best longevity.)

EFFECT OF PRIMING SUGAR CHOICE

Most homebrewers prime their bottles with corn sugar, but others use dry malt extract (DME) or table sugar. DME supposedly produces finer bubbles with improved head. Our experience: Any difference is perceptively minimal. Here's an experiment to help you decide. A quick science note: Although both sugar and DME have the same potential (about 45 ppg), sugar is 100 percent fermentable, while DME is not. It makes DME priming a little tricky. We follow the standard practice of using more DME than corn sugar, but your DME may be more or less fermentable.

Experiment

Code: E-P-3

Question: Does using different priming material affect the final characteristics of a bottled beer?

Hypothesis: Priming a beer with DME will produce a finer bubble structure with improved head retention.

Brewing Sessions Needed: 1

Priming with Gyle

Brewers have used unfermented wort, referred to as gyle, to prime their beers for ages. It's a way to use the sugar in wort instead of other sugar. It's essentially a purer version of priming with DME. Unlike DME, the specific gravity of the gyle varies, so you need to calculate how much to use. To gyle-prime, refrigerate wort from the batch in a clean, sanitized container. Set aside the gyle before you pitch your yeast. When the beer has finished fermenting, add the gyle to prime and package.

Of course, the big question is how much to save. The formula is:

$$Gyle_{quarts} = \frac{12 \times Wort_{gallons}}{Wort_{original\ gravity\ points}}$$

For example, for 5 gallons of wort that has a specific gravity of 1.050:

$$Gyle_{quarts} = \frac{12 \times 5}{50} \quad \bigg| \quad Gyle_{quarts} = \frac{60}{50} \quad \bigg| \quad Gyle_{quarts} = 1.2\ quarts$$

Protocol:
1. Brew and ferment the California Magnum Blonde (page 27).
2. To one bottling bucket add 2.2 ounces of dextrose, boiled for 5 minutes in ½ cup of water. To the other bottling bucket add the 3.1 ounces of DME, boiled for 5 minutes with ½ cup of water.
3. Fill each bucket with 2.5 gallons of wort, alternating the fill.
4. Bottle into standard 12-ounce bottles.
5. Age for at least 2 weeks at room temperature. Every 2 weeks thereafter, chill and open a bottle of each and evaluate.

Evaluation: Perform the triangle and ranking tests, asking your tasters which beer has finer bubbles, better head retention, and smoother mouthfeel.

Further Exploration: Do other flavor or aroma characteristics change?

Effect of Keg Carbonation Methods: There are a couple of main ways to carbonate a keg. You can force-carbonate or you can treat the keg like a giant bottle and add the priming of your choice. Then let it sit at room temperature until carbonated. What's the difference?

Experiment

Code: E-P-4

Question: Does beer kegged and primed (keg conditioning) taste and age differently than force-carbonated beer?

Hypothesis: Yeast in a primed keg has a long-term impact on the flavor and aging characters by suppressing oxidation reactions.

Brewing Sessions Needed: 1

Protocol:

1. Brew the California Magnum Blonde (page 27).
2. To one keg, add 1.25 ounces of dextrose boiled for 5 minutes in ½ cup of water. Rack 2.5 gallons onto the syrup. Seal the keg with 10 psi of CO_2 added to the keg. Set the keg aside at 60°F–66°F for 2 weeks.
3. Fill the second keg with the other half of the batch. Carbonate using Drew's Quick Force-Carbonation Method (next page).
4. Allow both kegs to settle for 1 week at serving temperature (45°F–50°F)
5. Every two weeks, perform an evaluation and record the observations. Keep the kegs chilled and still to avoid disturbing the sediment in the primed keg.

Evaluation: Perform the triangle and ranking tests, asking your tasters to rank which beer has the best head and which is most carbonated. Ask them if the carbonation has a coarse or smooth mouthfeel.

Experiment

Code: E-P-5

Question: When force-carbonating a keg, does the method affect bubble size or foam stability?

Hypothesis: For non-adjunct heavy beers, sufficient foam positive compounds exist to counteract the foam negative effect of agitation.

Brewing Sessions Needed: 1

Protocol:

1. Brew a batch of the recipe of your choice.
2. Split the beer evenly between the two kegs. Seal both kegs with 10 psi of CO_2 and chill to 35°F overnight.
3. Carbonate one keg using Drew's Quick Force-Carbonation Method (next page).
4. Connect the second keg at 10.75 psi and leave it cold for 10 days.
5. Let the carbonated kegs settle overnight at serving temperature (45°F–50°F) before serving.

Evaluation: Perform the triangle and ranking tests, asking your tasters evaluate the samples for head size and retention, aroma, and overall carbonation level. Ask them if they have a preference. Test the beers again at 1-week intervals. Do they seem to be more the same or more different as they age?

AGING EXPERIMENTS

Now that the beer is safely packaged, we have to wonder how it will fare as lone sedentary package full of beer. One problem that we may have to examine is our own attitude toward beers and age. In comparison to some periods, when preservation was a beloved and respected art (see the canning of produce), we live in a modern time that fetishizes freshness. Freshness is good, but it is also an abnormal thing that accompanies a world of continuous plenty. This is all to say that we fervently believe that well-packaged and well-stored beer can survive for a lot longer than we give it credit for.

Drew: For instance, I brewed a Belgian Session Beer that survived a few outside trips (a round trip of over 2,000 miles in a pickup truck) and yet even after 2 years, the beer was intact and drinkable. I credit this to a few things: sanitation of the keg, cold storage, and a lack of excess O_2 thanks to purging.

Drew's Quick Force-Carbonation Method

We both use the slammed carbonation method. Our experience has shown us that it works well, and the beer is ready to drink sooner! Others hook the gas up to the keg and walk away for a week. Proponents of this slower method claim that the quality of carbonation is better. They claim a smaller bubble structure, increased head retention, and better mouthfeel.

You can decide that for yourself. But there will undoubtedly be times you're going to want your beer carbonated fast. Here's the method we recommend:

1. *Chill the beer to 35°F overnight.*
2. *Lookup the psi setting to achieve desired carbonation volumes at 35°F (for example, 10.75 for 2.6 volumes). Set your regulator for 1 over that number (for example, 11.75).*
3. *Hook up the gas to the gas port, lay the keg on its side, and rock for 10 minutes.*
4. *Disconnect the gas and allow the keg to settle for 1 hour before serving.*

EFFECT OF STORAGE TEMPERATURE ON STALING

There's been a lot of information and misinformation about the effect of storage temperature on beer. One that amuses us is that repeated warming and cooling of beer will skunk it. In truth, that comes from the effects of exposure to UV light. Repeated heating and cooling will do little damage to the beer as long as the high temperatures aren't too high for too long. But how high *is* too high? How long does the beer have to be at that high temperature in order to sustain damage? How does it compare to beer stored at a cooler temperature?

Experiment

Code: E-A-1

Question: Does storing bottle-conditioned beer at warmer temperatures shorten the lifespan of the beer?

Hypothesis: Since oxidative reactions run faster at higher temperatures, storing a beer at higher temperatures will shorten the lifespan of a beer despite the presence of oxygen scavenging yeast.

Brewing Sessions Needed: 1

Protocol:

1. Brew the California Magnum Blonde (page 27) or other mild-flavored ale.
2. Bulk prime 5 gallons of beer with 4.4 ounces dextrose. (The dextrose should be boiled for 5 minutes in 1 cup of water first.)
3. Bottle the beer into standard 12-ounce bottles.
4. Store your bottles for at least 2 weeks at cellar temperatures and verify the carbonation of the beer.

5. Separate the beer and place 12 bottles in a fridge and another 12 bottles in a warm, but not hot, environment (70°F–80°F). Place another 12 bottles in a hot environment, like a garage in the summer. Protect all the bottles from direct sunlight exposure.

6. Every 2 weeks, chill a sample of each and compare.

Evaluation: Perform the triangle and ranking tests, asking the tasters about flaws like wet cardboard or metallic aromas and having them rank the beers by the level of flaws.

KEG DRY HOPPING EFFECTS

One of the things we really like about kegs is that you can put dry hops right into the keg to keep that fresh hop aroma until the very last drop of beer. Some people put the dry hops in for a set amount of time and then pull them out, hoping to avoid grassy or vegetal flavors from leaving the hops in the beer for too long. Others, like us, leave the hops in the keg until the beer is gone—which could be as long as 2–3 months. What's the right approach for you?

Experiment

Code: E-A-2

Question: When dry hopping, is there a maximum contact time with the hops before the flavor is negatively impacted?

Hypothesis: Traditional dry hop practices call for no more than 2 weeks of contact between the hops and the beer at fermentation temperature. Colder storage temperatures obviate this need to avoid extracting more chlorophyll and tannin flavors.

Brewing Sessions Needed: 1

Protocol:

1. Brew a batch of a recipe of your choice that would benefit from dry hopping.

2. Split the beer evenly between the two kegs. You'll need 4 ounces of your favorite dry hop; 2 nylon mesh hop bags; 2 sets of nonreactive weights (glass marbles, stainless-steel nuts); and 2–3 3-gallon or 5-gallon kegs. Split the hops between the hop bags and weights (both sanitized). Either tie the hop bags to the keg lid or allow them to sink to the keg bottom. Seal both kegs with 10 psi of CO_2. Carbonate both kegs using Drew's Quick Force-Carbonation Method (opposite page).

3. Store the carbonated kegs for 1 week at room temperature. With one keg, either remove the hop bag or gently transfer via jump line to a new keg.

4. Allow both kegs to settle for one additional week at serving temperature (45°F–50°F) before evaluating.

Evaluation: Perform the triangle and ranking tests, asking your tasters to evaluate the beers for hop flavor and aroma. Note the mention of grassy or chlorophyll aromas or flavors, as well as overall preference.

Further Exploration:

- Does one beer have more head than the other?
- Store the beers for month or two and taste weekly. Do your impressions change?
- Do different hop varieties age differently?

HOP AROMA SURVIVAL OVER TIME

To our minds, one of the best things is the aroma and flavor of hops. Oh sure, nice malty beers are great, too, but in our houses hops reign supreme.

Denny: In fact, my wife will drink wine if all the beer is under 70 IBU!

But how do you keep that great, fresh hop aroma and flavor vibrant as the beer ages? How do you keep your IPA from turning into an ESB?

Experiment

Code: E-A-3

Question: Can storage temperature affect the amount of time hop aroma and flavor remain in a beer?

Hypothesis: Heat is known to increase the staling process in beer. Does storing beer cold keep the hop aroma and flavor on the beer longer than storing it at room temperatures?

Brewing Sessions Needed: 1

Protocol:

1. Brew the Basic IPA recipe (page 108) or a dry hop–friendly recipe of your choice.
2. After fermentation is complete, dry hop the beer. Make sure to use at least 1 ounce of dry hops.
3. Package the beer in bottles or split it between two kegs. Store half the beer at room temperature. Store the other half in the refrigerator.
4. Let the beer age for at least 2 weeks before sampling and evaluating.

Evaluation: Perform the triangle and ranking tests, asking your tasters to evaluate the hop flavor and aroma from each beer. Ask them which one has the most aroma, hop flavor, and which they prefer.

SERVING EXPERIMENTS

And now, at last we are at final days with our temperamental children that we've created, coaxed, and cajoled into being. Even now, at this last stage, there are questions about what we can and can't do and how it will affect all our effort.

THE IMPACT OF GLASSWARE

The treatment of glassware in the beer world is one of a few things, depending upon on your perspective: important, a needless aping of the wine world, an exercise in marketing, or a blend of all three. A focus on glassware also provides many handy collectable items that make our partners roll their eyes at our silliness as we bring home yet another glass. It's a sickness, but what is the real impact of a pretty glass on your experience as a beer lover?

Let's start with the impact of the shape and size of the glass on your beer experience. Big companies like Boston Beer (Sam Adams) spend a chunk of change working with Riedel glassware to develop specialty glassware. They talk of concentration and aiming the beer at the appropriate spot on the palate via the lip shape. The experiment is going to require a bit of subterfuge on your part. You don't want your tasters to know what you're testing, as that will bias them. So, put on your best acting hat and apologize that you didn't have time to buy the right sample glasses.

Experiment

Code: E-S-1

Question: With all the glassware on the market and different styles available to consumers, does the glass actually affect a drinker's perception of the beer being drunk?

Hypothesis: Since we're serving the same beer and asking for differences, we expect our panelists will detect differences, but that they won't consistently point to major character impacts for glass style.

Brewing Sessions Needed: 1

Protocol:

1. Brew the California Magnum Blonde (page 27) or a similar lightweight nonhoppy recipe.
2. Keg the beer and carbonate to 2.5 volumes.
3. Apologize to the tasters for the lack of appropriate glassware and serve the beer in two different glasses (using a set of the same glasses for each taster).

Evaluation: Perform the triangle and ranking tests, asking your tasters which beer has better flavor and aroma. Ask them if there are any substantive differences between the samples, as well as which beer they prefer and why.

Further Exploration: Repeat the experiment but with an IPA. Do the tasters' reactions change? Pay particular attention to their comments about hop flavor or aroma.

CLARITY AND FOAM

Since we taste with our eyes first, we need to consider how the appearance of our beer affects a taster's enjoyment. Can a muddy beer taste like a beautifully polished beer but not be enjoyable? Does the flat dull lifeless appearance of a headless beer make it less enjoyable?

Experiment

Code: E-S-2

Question: Will tasters prefer a clear beer over a hazy one when all else is the same?

Hypothesis: Tasters are susceptible to suggestion. Haze will negatively impact their enjoyment of a beer.

Brewing Sessions Needed: 1

Protocol:

1. Brew the California Magnum Blonde (page 27) or a similar lightweight recipe. Focus on making exceedingly clear beer with a course of cold crashing at 35°F for 10 days and gelatin or SuperKleer finings if needed.
2. Keg the beer and carbonate using Drew's Quick Force-Carbonation Method (page 230).
3. Prior to service, dispense the beer into two pitchers. In a small glass, add ⅛ teaspoon of cornstarch for every 36 ounces of beer you plan to serve cloudy. Add a little beer to the glass and stir well to dissolve the cornstarch. Stir the sample into one of the pitchers. Be very gentle, to avoid degassing the sample too much. With a clean implement, gently stir the nonstarched beer for the same amount of time.

Evaluation: Perform the triangle and ranking tests, asking your tasters which beer has better flavor and aroma. Are there any substantive differences between the samples? Which beer do they prefer and why?

Further Exploration: Repeat the experiment with an IPA. Do the tasters' reactions change? Pay particular attention to their comments about clarity and hop flavor or aroma.

Experiment

Code: E-S-3

Question: A raging debate has occurred for years—head or no head on your beer. Proponents argue that a head helps release aromatics and provides a better experience. Will tasters register a difference?

Hypothesis: We believe that for a beer like an IPA, the lack of a head will impact the taster's overall experience of hop aroma and flavor.

Brewing Sessions Needed: 1

Protocol:

1. Brew an aromatic IPA, like the Basic IPA (page 108) or a similar aromatic IPA recipe.
2. Keg the beer and carbonate to 2.5 volumes.
3. Prepare your opaque glasses lightly oiling one or two of the glasses with neutral vegetable oil. (Place a little on a paper towel and rub it into the side of the glasses.) Alternatively, use a drop of foam control in each glass. Vigorously pour the beer to agitate it, but without leaving a head.
4. Pour the glasses remaining as usual so that there is some head.

Evaluation: Perform the triangle and ranking tests, asking your tasters which beer has better flavor and aroma. Ask them if there are any substantive differences between the samples, as well as which beer they prefer and why.

Further Exploration: Repeat the experiment, but this time, instead of doctoring the glasses, pour one beer to generate a frothy head and pour the other gently down the glass to avoid agitation. What changes for the tasters without the agitation necessary to create a head?

Acknowledgments

DREW

Any writer, except the preternaturally talented ones, knows that writing requires acts of willful isolation. I would like to thank my wife for putting up with the shambling space cadet of a partner that she finds whenever I'm writing. Without her patience, there would be no book.
With that said, Honey, do you want a beer?

Thanks to the crew at Voyageur Press for allowing Denny and me the opportunity to explore what experimental homebrewing is all about. Thanks to Thom for taking a jumbled heap of words and finding a book inside of them.

Thanks to the Maltose Falcons, America's oldest homebrew club, who gave me a home, taught me everything I know, and gave me an opportunity to teach them, too. (That and they put up with all the blowback from my crazy ideas.) That goes double for the Brewgyver himself, Kent Fletcher, without whom most of my good ideas would still be scribbles on a desk.

Thanks to everyone who asks questions, from the clubs to the forums and the Reddits of the world. You force me to confront the number of things I don't know and continue to astonish me with the wide breadth of things you're doing.

Thanks to all our IGORs who've helped us with guidance and all the IGORs to come at www.ExperimentalBrew.com.

And of course, thanks to Denny, the man with two red shoes (Converse, natch). He's been the Ben to my Jerry, the Statler to my Waldorf, the Laverene to my Shirley. He's always maintained a sense of fun and play, and that's just what this book needed, man!

DENNY

My contribution to this book could never have happened without the love and support of my wife. She bought me my first homebrewing kit and stood by me while I got caught in the whirlwind. (I like to think that she would still have bought me that kit even if she had known what would happen.)

Thanks to Thom, our editor for this book and the fifth Beatle in the band.

Thanks to my homebrew club, the Cascade Brewers Society, for their support and for allowing me to practice my wackiness all these years.

Thanks to homebrewers all over the world. Remember, you learn from those before you, so pay it forward to those coming after you.

Finally, huge thanks to Drew, who invited me to coauthor this book. Not only is he a great brewer, he's a great friend. I value that above all else, and I appreciate all your work and help on this book, buddy!

Resources

Find the website for this book at www.ExperimentalBrew.com. All the experiments in the book—and more—have a home here. You can post your own results, discuss them with other homebrewers, and post about new experiments you've done.

Denny's website is www.DennyBrew.com. It is the original home of the Cheap 'n' Easy Mash Tun, as well as one of the first sources for batch sparging information.

Drew's website is www.BrewWriter.com. It's where he stores his past and current thoughts about brewing. On www.MaltoseFalcons.com, the website of Drew's homebrew club, you can find more of Drew's writings and projects.

The American Homebrewers Association website, www.HomebrewersAssociation.org, and discussion forum, www.HomebrewersAssociation.org/forum, are the two premier homebrewing sites on the Internet. You can find both Denny and Drew on the forums.

Kai Troester's website, www.BrauKaiser.com, is a beer science geek's idea of heaven. Kai has done many experiments of interest to homebrewers and published his results there.

Martin Brungard's website for water software is called Bru'nwater (sites.google.com/site/brunwater). It's a repository of water knowledge. Not only can you download a free copy of the program, Martin's site will help you understand what you doing and why you're doing it.

To calculate the size of yeast starter you need for your beers, go to www.MrMalty.com or Brewers Friend (www.brewersfriend.com/yeast-pitch-rate-and-starter-calculator).

Drew's previous books, *The Everything Homebrewing Book* and *The Everything Hard Cider Book*, are invaluable resources to have on hand, of course.

How to Brew by John Palmer is the quintessential homebrewing instructional book.

Brew Like a Monk by Stan Hieronymous is an incredible resource for brewing Belgian-style beers. It's also loaded with general brewing information that we find useful no matter what style we're brewing.

An Analysis of Brewing Techniques and *Principles of Brewing Science: A Study of Serious Brewing Issues*, both by Dr. George Fix, will satisfy your craving for geeky brewing science.

Works Cited

Bamforth, Charles, and J. E. Smythe. *Journal of the Institute for Brewing (Vol. 108, No. 1, 2002)*. "A Study of the Effect of Perceived Beer History on Reported Preferences by Sensory Panels with Different Levels of Training."

Brew Your Own. "Open Fermentation Tips from the Pros." January–February 2008 (byo.com/stories/item/1211-open-fermentation-tips-from-the-pros).

Buhner, Stephen H. *Sacred and Herbal Healing Beers.* Boulder, CO, Brewer's Publications, 1998.

Cook's Illustrated. "Premium (High-End) Extra-Virgin Olive Oils." 1 November 2006.

Cone, Clayton. "Yeast Growth." (www.danstaryeast.com/articles/yeast-growth).

Conn, Denny. "Recipe Formulation: A Road Map to a Tasty Beer." *Zymurgy*, May–June 2012.

Doss, Greg. Interview by Denny Conn. 5 December 2013.

Fix, George. *Homebrew Digest.* 1995, 2000.

Garshol, Lars Marius. "Experiments in Blind Tasting." (www.garshol.priv.no/blog/187.htm). 20 November 2008.

Haddock, Cathy. Interview by Denny Conn. 22 July 2013.

Hull, Grady. Interview with Denny Conn. 16 December 2013.

———. "Olive Oil Addition to Yeast as an Alternative to Wort Aeration." September 2005.

Kuske, Dave. "Brewing with Briess." (www.brewingwithbriess.com/Homebrewing/FAQs.htm#a).

Lehrer, Jonah. "Does All Wine Taste the Same?" (www.newyorker.com/online/blogs/frontal-cortex/2012/06/wine-taste.html). 13 June 2012.

The Brewer International. (www.igb.org.uk). "The Role of Oxygen in Brewing." March 2002.

Troester, Kai. "Microscope Use in Brewing." (braukaiser.com/wiki/index.php?title=Microscope_use_in_brewing). 6 October 2012.

About the Authors

Drew Beechum has been brewing and writing about brewing since he first picked up a kettle in 1999. He is the author of *The Everything Homebrewing Book*, *The Everything Hard Cider Book*, and *The Homebrewer's Journal*. Beechum has also written for *Zymurgy*, the journal of the American Homebrewers Association, and he writes a regular column for *Beer Advocate* and *Beer & Brewer*. He lives in Pasadena, California, with his lovely wife, a dedicated brewery, and his loyal army of dogs and cats.

Denny Conn brewed his first batch of homebrew in 1998 and has since brewed 500-plus more. He is a BJCP national-ranked beer judge and has been a member of the governing committee of the American Homebrewers Association for nine years. His recipes have been brewed by several commercial breweries in both the United States and Europe, and he currently consults for several breweries. He was a contributing author to *Craft Beer for the Homebrewer*. He lives in the foothills of the Coast Range in Oregon with his wife, five cats, and two dogs.

Index